Working through the Crisis

.

DIRECTIONS IN DEVELOPMENT
Human Development

Working through the Crisis

Jobs and Policies in Developing Countries during the Great Recession

Arup Banerji, David Newhouse, Pierella Paci, and David Robalino, Editors

THE WORLD BANK
Washington, D.C.

Contents

Acknowledgments   *xiii*
Abbreviations   *xv*

Chapter 1   Overview   1
             Introduction   1
             Impacts   3
             Policies   5
             Recovery   7
             Looking Forward   9
             Annex 1A   10
             Notes   14
             References   14

Chapter 2   Fewer Jobs or Smaller Paychecks? Aggregate Crisis
             Impacts in Selected Middle-Income Countries   17
             Gaurav Khanna, David Newhouse, and Pierella Paci

             The Disconnect between the Impact of the Crisis and
                 the Policy Responses   17
             Data and Methodology   18
             The Extent and Nature of the Labor Market Adjustment   20
             In Which Countries Were Adjustments Unexpectedly Large?   24
             How Accurate Were Projections of Employment Changes?   27
             From Evidence to Policy Responses   29
             Annex 2A   30
             Notes   33
             References   35

Chapter 3   How Did the Great Recession Affect Different Types of
             Workers? Evidence from 17 Middle-Income Countries   37
             Yoonyoung Cho and David Newhouse

             About This Study   37
             What Explains Differential Impacts across Groups?   39
             Data and Methodology   45
             Aggregate Labor Market Adjustments   52

Group Differences in Labor Market Adjustments   56
Group Differences among Active Workers   61
Conclusion   68
Annex 3A   73
Technical Note   73
Notes   78
References   81

Chapter 4   Labor and Social Protection Policies during the Crisis
             and the Recovery   85
             David A. Robalino, David Newhouse, and Friederike Rother

             The Role of Labor and Social Protection Policies during a
                Downturn   87
             Social Protection and Labor Policies and Their Link to
                the Type of Shock and Labor Market Adjustment   93
             What Can Be Done to Be Better Prepared in the Future? 113
             Annex 4A: Description of the Policy Inventory   120
             Notes   126
             References   130

Chapter 5   The Labor Market Impact of the 2009 Financial Crisis
             in Indonesia   135
             Neil McCulloch, Amit Grover, and Asep Suryahadi

             Indonesian Macroeconomic Context   136
             The Response of the Indonesian Government to the Crisis 138
             Data   140
             Results   142
             Summary and Conclusions   157
             Notes   158
             References   159

Chapter 6   Weathering a Storm: Survey-Based Perspectives on
             Employment in China in the Aftermath of the Global
             Financial Crisis   163
             John Giles, Albert Park, Fang Cai, and Yang Du

             Analyzing the Effects of the Crisis   163
             The Trajectory of China's Economic Growth and the
                Global Financial Crisis   164
             The Financial Crisis and Shocks to Employment   167
             Government Policies, the Recovery, and the Labor Market 175
             Wage Income in the Wake of the Financial Crisis   178
             Conclusions   179
             Notes   180
             References   181

Chapter 7   Effects of the 2008–09 Economic Crisis on Labor Markets
             in Mexico   183
             Samuel Freije, Gladys López-Acevedo, and Eduardo
             Rodríguez-Oreggia

             The Nature of the Crisis   184
             Labor Market Adjustments during the Crisis and Recovery   186
             Impacts on Sectors and Types of Workers   190
             Labor Market Transitions during the Crisis   201
             Policies for Coping with the Crisis   210
             Conclusions   217
             Notes   220
             References   221

Figures

1.1   Transmission Channels between Initial Shocks and Micro and
       Macro Outcomes   2
1.2   Changes in GDP Growth and Employment in Selected
       Developing Countries   5
1A.1   Median GDP Growth and Labor Market Indicators in Selected
       Developing Countries   10
1A.2   Share of Population Reporting Good Time to Find a Job, by Year
       and Income Group   11
1A.3   Employment to Population Ratio, by Year, Income Group, and
       Gender   11
1A.4   Unemployment Rate, by Year, Income Group, and Gender   11
1A.5   Share of Employment in Full-Time Wage Work, by Year, Income
       Group, and Gender   12
2.1   Growth of GDP, Real Earnings, Employment, and the Wage Bill,
       March 2007–September 2009   20
2.2   Growth in Hours Worked, the Consumer Price Index, Real
       Earnings, and Nominal Earnings in Selected Middle-Income
       Countries, March 2007–September 2009   21
2.3   Change in the Growth of Hours Worked in 14 Developing
       Economies, Postcrisis Period vs. Precrisis Period   22
2.4   Decomposition of the Change in the Growth of the Wage Bill,
       Earnings, and Wage Rates in 14 Developing Countries,
       Postcrisis Period vs. Precrisis Period   22
2.5   Breakdown in the Causes of the Slowdown in the Growth of
       GDP per Adult in 33 Developing Countries, Postcrisis Period vs.
       Precrisis Period   23
2.6   Change in Employment Growth in Nine Developing Countries,
       Postcrisis Period vs. Precrisis Period   23
2.7   Change in Earnings and Employment Growth by GDP Growth,
       Postcrisis Period vs. Precrisis Period   24

2.8   Change in Unemployment and Participation by GDP Growth, Postcrisis Period vs. Precrisis Period   25

2.9   Correlations between Country Characteristics and Employment Loss and Earnings in 35 Developing Countries, Postcrisis Period vs. Precrisis Period   26

2.10   Correlations between Country Characteristics and Change in Unemployment and Participation in 36 Developing Countries, Postcrisis vs. Precrisis Period   28

3.1   Sectoral Employment Shares by Gender, 2007   41

3.2   Sectoral Employment Shares by Age Group, 2007   42

3.3   Aggregate Adjustment among Labor Force in Unemployment Rate and Employment Sector, 2006–09   53

3.4   Aggregate Adjustments among Workers in Earnings, Hours, and Wage Rates, 2006–09   54

3.5   Group Comparisons: Employment-to-Population Ratio, 2006–09   57

3.6   Group Comparisons: Wage Employee–to-Population Ratio, 2006–09   58

3.7   Group Comparisons: Nonparticipation-to-Population Ratio, 2006–09   59

3.8   Age and Gender Comparisons with Three Groups: Employment Ratio, 2006–09   60

3.9   Group Comparisons: Share of Wage Employment among Labor Force, 2006–09   62

3A.1   Gender Comparisons by Education: Employment Ratio, Unemployment Ratio, and Nonparticipation Ratio   76

4.1   Typology of Policies to Mitigate the Impact of the Financial Crisis   90

4.2   Risk of Unemployment of Formal and Informal Sector Workers in Brazil, March 2002–September 2009   92

4.3   Percentage of Countries Adopting Labor or Social Protection Policies, 2008–09   94

4.4   Percentage of Labor or Social Protection Interventions That Were New, 2008–09   95

4.5   Average Total Country Expenditure as a Share of GDP, by Year and Program Type, 2008–09   95

4.6   Median Number of Total Program Beneficiaries as a Share of the Labor Force, 2008–09   96

4.7   Policy Responses and Slowdowns in Output and Employment Growth   97

4.8   Programs Targeting Youth and Women and Women in Selected Countries, 2008–09   98

4.9   Share of Policies That Support Income Protection, Labor Demand, and Labor Market Adjustment in Selected Developing Countries, 2009   100

4.10   The Percentage of Chilean Workers Covered by Unemployment Benefits and the Unemployment Rate, 2000–10   112

4.11   Changes in Fiscal Balance and GDP Growth during the Financial
        Crisis in Selected Countries, 2007–10   116
4A.1   Number of Countries in the Policy Inventory and Number of
        Unique Programs, 2008–09   122
6.1   Annual and Quarterly GDP Percentage Growth Rates for China
        and Other Major Economies, 2000–09   165
6.2   Monthly Changes in the Total Value of Imports and Exports,
        January 2006–November 2009   166
6.3   China's Quarterly Growth Rates by Sector, 2004–09   167
6.4   Quarterly Ratio of Vacancies to Job Seekers in China, 2001–09   168
6.5   Quarterly Ratio of Vacancies to Job Seekers in China,
        by Gender, 2001–09   169
6.6   Monthly Share of Rural Labor Force with Off-Farm Employment:
        Actual and Under a Business-as-Usual Counterfactual,
        May 2007–April 2009   174
6.7   Composition of China's 4 Trillion Yuan Stimulus Package in 2009   175
6.8   Real Wages of Employed Migrants according to Three Data
        Sources, 2001–09   178
7.1   Changes in Annual Inflation and the Exchange Rate in Mexico,
        2007–10   185
7.2   GDP and Components of Aggregate Demand in Mexico
        during the Financial Crisis, Second Quarter of 2008–Second
        Quarter of 2010   185
7.3   Total Employment in Mexico, 2008–10   186
7.4   Total Unemployment in Mexico, 2008–10   187
7.5   Quarterly Percentage of Workers by Occupation and Access to
        Social Security Benefits in Mexico, 2007–10   190
7.6   Real Hourly Wage Growth for Formal and Informal Workers in
        Mexico, 2008–10   191
7.7   Quarterly Variation in Numbers of Workers Employed in Various
        Types of Economic Activity in Mexico, 2008–10   192
7.8   Monthly Wage Indexes for Workers in Selected Industries in
        Mexico, January 2007–January 2011   195
7.9   Changes in Employment and Wages Due to the Economic
        Crisis in Mexico, 2009 and 2010   202
7.10   Unemployment Withdrawals from Pension Accounts and the
        Unemployment Rate in Mexico, January 2008–January 2011   216

Map
4.1   Years of Available Data on Country Labor Markets, 2000–08   118

Tables
1A.1   Labor Market Indicators for Selected Developing Countries   12
1A.2   Annual GDP Growth and Labor Market Outcomes in
        Developing Countries   13

2.1   Employment Growth and GDP Growth in 37 Developing
        Countries, Precrisis Period vs. Postcrisis Period   29
2A.1   Summary of Labor Market Trends and Data Sources, by
        Economy, Precrisis Period vs. Postcrisis Period   30
2A.2   Characteristics of Data Sources   32
2A.3   Average Annual Changes in Labor Market Indicators, Precrisis
        Period vs. Postcrisis Period   32
2A.4   Estimates of Elasticity of Employment with Respect to Growth,
        by Period   32
3.1   Data Used for the Analysis   46
3.2   Changes in Employment Trends from Pre- to Postcrisis in Mexico 50
3.3   Decomposition of Employment Ratio between Changes Due to
        Employment Rate and Those Due to Labor Force Participation 64
3.4   Decomposition of Gender Disparities in Employment Ratio
        Changes by Sector and Status   66
3.5   Decomposition of Age and Education Disparities in Employment
        Ratio Changes by Status   69
3A.1   GDP Growth Rates and Their Slowdown, 2007–09   73
3A.2   Labor Market Adjustments by Gender, 2006–09   74
4.1   Budgets for Employment Services as a Percentage of GDP in
        Selected Countries in Europe and Central Asia, 2008 and 2009 105
4.2   Adjusting Labor and Social Protection Policies as Countries
        Move from an Economic Downturn to Recovery   120
4A.1   Classification Scheme for Policies   123
4A.2   Construction of the Policy Inventory   126
5.1   Selected Macroeconomic Variables for Indonesia before, during,
        and after the Crisis, 2008 and 2009   138
5.2   Participation, Unemployment, and Hours of Work by Age and
        Gender in Indonesia, February 2008–August 2009   143
5.3   Hours of Work and Share of Employment by Sector in
        Indonesia, February 2008–August 2009   146
5.4   Share of Employment by Category of Work in Indonesia,
        February 2008–August 2009   147
5.5   Real and Nominal Wages by Age Category and Gender,
        Indonesia, February 2008–August 2009   148
5.6   Real and Nominal Wages by Sector, Indonesia, February
        2008–August 2009   149
5.7   Real Income and Real Wages by Category of Worker, Indonesia,
        February 2008–August 2009   150
5.8   Real Income for Single-Person Businesses and Casual
        Nonagricultural Workers Disaggregated by Sector, Indonesia,
        February 2008–August 2009   150
5.9   Nominal and Real Wages by Category of Work Controlling
        for Compositional Change, Indonesia, February 2008–
        August 2009   152

5.10   Total Share of Workers Ending Employment or Changing Jobs
        by Age and Gender, Indonesia, August 2008–August 2009   153
5.11   Share of Workers Ending Employment or Changing Jobs,
        Indonesia, August 2008–August 2009   153
5.12   Share of Workers Who Ended Employment Either because
        They Were Laid Off or Their Business Collapsed Due to
        Falling Demand by Previous Employment Sector, Indonesia,
        August 2008–August 2009   154
5.13   Share of People Who Worked Before but Stopped Working and
        Share of New Entrants as a Percentage of Those Currently
        Employed, by Age and Gender, Indonesia, August 2008–
        August 2009   154
5.14   Share of Workers Joining and Leaving a Sector as a Percentage
        of the Total Number of People Employed in That Sector,
        by Age and Gender, Indonesia, August 2008–August 2009   155
5.15   Average Number of Months Spent Looking for Work by Age
        and Gender, Indonesia, February 2008–August 2009   156
6.1   Annual Percentage Changes in Employment in China, 2008–09   171
6.2   Changes in Employment of Migrants vs. Changes in
        Employment of Local Residents in China, June 2008,
        December 2008, and June 2009   171
6.3   Share of Migrants in Selected Employment Sectors in China,
        2008–09   176
6.4   Working Hours and Earnings in China, September 2008–
        February 2010   179
7.1   Annual Changes in Main Components of the Mexican Labor
        Force, 2007–10   188
7.2   Annual Changes in Job Losses and Gains by Economic Activity
        and Firm Size, 2008–10   193
7.3   Change in Real Wages in Mexico by Sector and Firm Size,
        2007–10   196
7.4   Decomposition of Year-on-Year Gains and Losses in Employment
        in Mexico by Sex, Education, Age, and Geographic Location,
        2008–10   197
7.5   Decomposition of Annual Gains and Losses in Employment in
        Mexico by Position, Health Insurance Status, and Wage
        Category, 2008–10   199
7.6   Decomposition of Annual Changes in Unemployment by Sex,
        Educational Level, Age, and Geographic Location, 2008–10   200
7.7   Change in Real Wages in Mexico by Sex, Educational Level,
        Age, and Geographic Location, 2007–10   201
7.8   Change in Employment Status of Mexican Workers between
        2007 and 2008   204
7.9   Change in Employment Status of Workers in Mexico between
        2008 and 2009   204

7.10   Change in Employment Status of Workers in Mexico between
        2009 and 2010   205
7.11   Marginal Probabilities of Losing a Job in Mexico by Sex,
        Education, Geographic Location, Age, and Household Position,
        2007–10   207
7.12   Marginal Probabilities of Finding a Job in Mexico by Sex,
        Education, Geographic Location, Age, and Household
        Position, 2007–10   209
7.13   Mexico's Temporary Employment Program, 2001–10   212
7.14   Services Provided by Mexico's National Employment System,
        2005–10   214

Acknowledgments

This report is a product of efforts undertaken jointly by the Social Protection and Labor team of the Human Development Network and the Poverty team in the Poverty Reduction and Economic Management Network of the World Bank. The report surveys how the Great Recession affected workers in developing countries and how governments responded. It aims to draw lessons from this crisis that can help policy makers address macroeconomic shocks in the future. The book was edited by Arup Banerji (Social Protection and Labor), David Newhouse (Social Protection and Labor), Pierella Paci (Poverty), and David Robalino (Social Protection and Labor). Chapter authors include Gaurav Khanna, David Newhouse, and Pierella Paci (chapter 2 on aggregate crisis impacts); Yoonyoung Cho and David Newhouse (chapter 3 on different types of workers); David A. Robalino, David Newhouse, and Friederike Rother (chapter 4 on the policy response); Neil McCulloch, Amit Grover, and Asep Suryahadi (chapter 5 on Indonesia); John Giles, Albert Park, Fang Cai, and Yang Du (chapter 6 on China); and Samuel Freije-Rodríguez, Gladys López-Acévedo, and Eduardo Rodríguez-Orregia (chapter 7 on Mexico).

Detailed and insightful comments were provided during the review stage by Gordon Betcherman (University of Ottawa), Gary S. Fields (Cornell University), Jesko Hentschel (Europe and Central Asia Department, World Bank), and David McKenzie (Development Economics Research Group, World Bank). The work also benefited from insightful comments by participants in a conference organized by the World Bank and the International Labour Organization (ILO) in Geneva in February 2010, including Jose Manual Salazar, Moazam Mahmood, and Catherine Saget from the ILO's employment sector. Our ILO colleagues also contributed greatly to a joint effort to collect information on policies undertaken in response to the crisis. We gratefully acknowledge funding from the governments of Austria, Germany, the Republic of Korea, Norway, and Switzerland under the Multidonor Trust Fund for Labor Markets, Job Creation, and Economic Growth. Finally, we are indebted to Ariel Fiszbein (Chief Economist, Human Development Network, World Bank) and Tamar Manuelyan Atinc (former Vice President, Human Development Network, World Bank) for their encouragement and support during the process of preparing this book.

Abbreviations

ALMP   active labor market program
ANFEFE National Agreement to Support the Household Economy and Employment
BPS   Bureau Pusat Statistik (Indonesian Central Bureau of Statistics)
CCT   conditional cash transfer
CNRS   China National Rural Survey
ECA   Europe and Central Asia (region)
ENOE   Encuesta Nacional de Ocupación y Empleo (Mexican Occupation and Employment Survey)
EU   European Union
FSP   fiscal stimulus program
GDP   gross domestic product
ILO   International Labour Organization
IMSS   Instituto Mexicano del Seguro Social
LAC   Latin America and the Caribbean (region)
NBS   National Bureau of Statistics
OECD   Organisation for Economic Co-operation and Development
PES   public employment services
PET   Programa de Empleo Temporal (Temporary Employment Program)
PICE   Program to Encourage Growth and Employment
PME   Brazilian Pesquisa Mensal de Emprego
RCRE   Research Center for the Rural Economy
SMEs   small and medium enterprises
SNE   Servicio Nacional de Empleo (National System of Employment)
TVET   technical and vocational education and training
UISA   unemployment individual savings account
VAT   value-added tax
WEPP   Wage Earner Protection Program

CHAPTER 1

Overview

Introduction

Labor markets across the world were hit hard by the "Great Recession" that began with the collapse of housing markets in the United States and Europe in late 2008. Employment outcomes worsened sharply as economies shrank. Advanced economies and countries in Central and Eastern Europe suffered most, with gross domestic product (GDP) contracting by 3.9 and 5.9 percent, respectively, in 2009. In Latin America and the Caribbean, output fell by 1.7 percent. And although the economies of Asia, Africa, and the Middle East did not contract, their trend growth rates of GDP decelerated significantly—in East Asia slowing down from double digits in 2007 to 7 percent in 2009. The level of contagion of seemingly idiosyncratic shocks, and particularly the rapid transmission to middle- and low-income countries, was a potent reminder of the interconnected nature of the global economy and the increasing pervasiveness of systemic risks.

Globally, it is estimated that about 30 million jobs were lost over a period of two years. Where employment did not fall, accommodating the contraction of aggregate demand entailed a sharp drop in total earnings. The gravity of the situation led to an unprecedented degree of government intervention—sometimes through coordinated efforts—to counteract the effects of the recession. Most affected countries introduced large fiscal stimulus packages and developed complex active and passive labor market programs to protect jobs, stimulate hiring, and help the unemployed and the poor.

This book examines both how the Great Recession affected labor markets in developing countries and how governments responded. The six chapters that follow discuss how the crisis affected output across countries, how labor markets adjusted, which workers were more likely to be affected, and which types of policies were implemented. In doing so, the chapters bring together a unique compilation of data and analysis from very different sources, including an inventory of policies implemented during the crisis among countries in Latin America, Eastern Europe, Asia, and Africa.

Despite claims, based on casual empiricism, that the crisis had a large and definite adverse effect on employment for all groups, the analysis in this book paints

Figure 1.1 Transmission Channels between Initial Shocks and Micro and Macro Outcomes

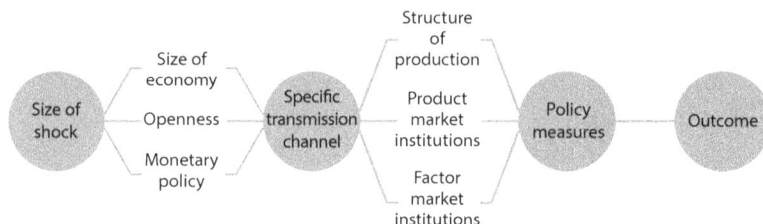

a different picture. In fact, the overall story is that the impacts of the crisis varied considerably. The effect depended on an interaction of five factors (figure 1.1):

- The *size of the original shock* (that is, the extent of the slowdown in output growth).
- The *channels through which the shock was manifested* in each country (for instance, were the primary materializations reductions in domestic credit, a slowdown of export demand, or a fall in remittances?).
- The *structure of production and employment* in the economy (for instance, was it export-oriented, or was there a large domestic market? Was employment mostly in manufacturing, construction, or agriculture?).
- The *structure of institutions in the country, especially labor institutions*. These, however, seem to have played a secondary role in explaining how labor markets reacted.
- The *specific policies* implemented by countries in response to the shock—both aggregate stimulus and specific sectoral policies—and whether these policy decisions promptly and adequately responded to the particularities of the transmitted shock.

As a result of these interactions, countries experienced very different patterns of shock and recovery. Despite these differences, however, several patterns emerged.

In terms of *impact*, the studies in this book generally find:

- Overall adjustments involved reductions in earnings growth rather than employment growth, although the quality of employment was also affected.
- Youth were doubly affected, being more likely to experience both an increase in unemployment and a reduction in wages.
- Contrary to initial expectations, men seemed to have been more strongly affected than women.
- In most countries where data are available, there were no major differences between skilled and unskilled workers or between those living in urban or rural areas.

In terms of *policy responses*, this crisis was characterized by a high prevalence of active interventions in the labor market and the expansion of income protection systems, as well as countercyclical stimulus measures. The book finds that generally:

- Countercyclical stimulus measures in a number of countries, when timed well and of sufficient size to ameliorate the size of the shock, were effective in reducing adverse employment effects.
- Specific sectoral stimulus policies—aimed at financial sectors in industrialized countries and at major loci of employment in developing countries—also had positive effects when they were well targeted.
- But social protection and labor market policy responses were often ad hoc and not in line with the types of adjustments that were taking place.
- Social protection and labor market policy responses were largely based on the types of programs and institutions already in place, and were rarely devised to meet the specific shock. As a result, these policies and programs did not necessarily reach those who needed them the most and, if anything, were biased toward formal sector workers.

In retrospect, there is a sense that developing countries were not well prepared to deal with the effects of the Great Recession, suggesting room for important reforms to social protection and labor policies (Paci, Revenga, and Rijkers 2012).

This book contains seven chapters. The remainder of this overview chapter summarizes the main findings on the impacts of the crisis and policy responses, discusses how the recovery is progressing, and how countries can better respond to future economic downturns. Chapter 2 uses aggregate quarterly labor market statistics from 45 middle-income countries to assess labor market adjustments at the macro level and their potential causes. Chapter 3 looks at the effects of the crisis on specific groups of workers based on a set of detailed cross-sectional household data for 16 countries. Chapter 4 reviews country policy responses during the crisis based on a specially commissioned survey jointly undertaken by the World Bank and the International Labour Organization. The last three chapters present case studies of the crisis, its effects, and government policies in China, Indonesia, and Mexico.

Impacts

Labor markets adjust to a contraction in aggregate demand through a combination of declines in earnings growth and adjustments in the level and composition of employment. In turn, these changes also influence decisions to participate in the labor force and ultimately affect unemployment rates. As discussed earlier, the nature of these adjustments depends on the magnitude of the initial shock, the way in which the shock spreads to different economic sectors and regions, and the nature of the labor institutions. Regulations limiting dismissals, for instance, can attenuate the effects of a downturn on employment, but at the same time force adjustments in wages. Conversely, wage rigidities can exacerbate contractions in employment. But given the complexity of these adjustments, few clear patterns emerge across countries and regions.

An examination of the data shows that the major effects of the crisis in developing countries were felt mainly through reduced demand for exports. Therefore, impacts were mostly concentrated in export-dependent countries in Eastern Europe and Central Asia (where the impacts on growth and employment were comparable in most dimensions to past crises), and to a lesser extent, in Latin America. Elsewhere, effects were much milder. Countries in East Asia like Indonesia, the Philippines, and Vietnam escaped the brunt of the crisis; and East Asian countries that were affected, like China, recovered quickly. In 50 countries in Africa, the Middle East, and South Asia, average GDP growth declined by only 2 percentage points, compared to the average over the previous two years, and the average unemployment rate actually fell. In Latin America, shocks to unemployment and earnings were substantial, but much smaller than in past crises such as the Mexican Tequila crisis, and the twin Argentinian crises of 1995 and 2002. The downturn in Latin America was also short-lived, as average unemployment returned to pre-crisis levels in 2010.

The crisis affected workers primarily through earnings reductions. Employment losses were significant, on the order of 2 to 3 percentage points in Latin America and Eastern Europe. In contrast, average employment effects in most of Africa, the Middle East, and South Asia were likely much weaker.[1] Meanwhile, real wage growth declined substantially, falling by about 7 percent in Eastern Europe and Central Asia and some countries in Latin America, on par with previous crises. While earnings slowdowns were less severe in countries in other regions, they were consistently larger than employment losses.

In general, there is mixed evidence about the extent to which labor regulations drive adjustments in labor markets. Previous studies of structural adjustment episodes in 12 countries during the 1980s had found that, following a devaluation, labor institutions were not a strong barrier to labor reallocation toward tradable goods (see Horton, Kanbur, and Mazumdar 1994). There is also some evidence showing that in Organisation for Economic Co-operation and Development (OECD) countries, there was no statistically significant relationship between the stringency of employment protection legislation and the size of the employment adjustment from 2007 to 2010 (Cazes, Verick, and Al Hussami 2012). The analysis in chapter 2, on the other hand, suggests that countries' labor regulations did play a role. For a given fall in GDP growth, for instance, earnings dropped more, and employment dropped less, for countries with more stringent regulations. These estimates, nonetheless, remain imprecise and sensitive to the mix of countries considered.

The experiences of six large countries—China, Indonesia, Mexico, Russia, South Africa, and Turkey—also fail to show a consistent pattern, demonstrating the importance of local conditions (see figure 1.2). Turkey and Mexico, for instance, experienced a similar slowdown in GDP growth between 2007 and 2009. Yet in Mexico, where separation costs are higher, the contraction in employment was much more severe. Russia, with lower separation costs and experiencing an even more significant slowdown in GDP growth, also saw a smaller reduction in employment levels. This is similar to the reduction observed in China, where

Figure 1.2 Changes in GDP Growth and Employment in Selected Developing Countries

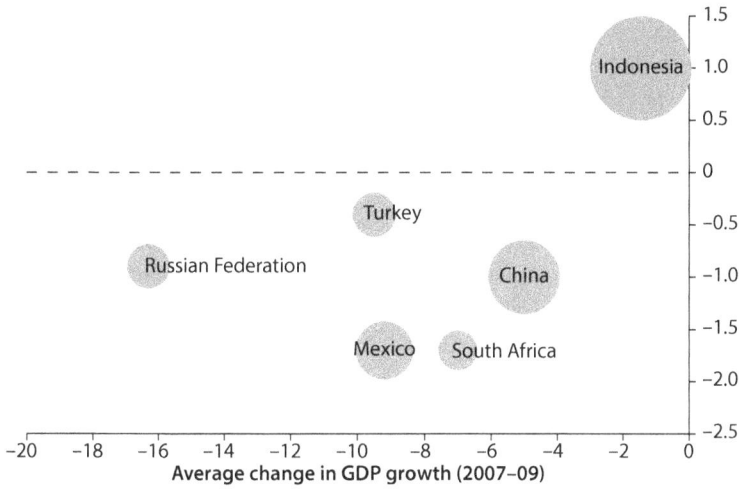

Sources: World Economic Outlook, CEIC.
Note: GDP = gross domestic product.

separation costs are higher and the economic slowdown was less severe. At the other extreme, in Indonesia, the one with the highest separation costs among the six countries, the slowdown in GDP was not accompanied by a contraction in employment. Adjustments in employment in South Africa, however, were more in line with the premise of labor regulations affecting employment outcomes. Separation costs are lower there, and the contraction in employment was as large as that observed in Mexico, even if the slowdown in GDP was less pronounced.

This variation in impacts is, ultimately, not surprising. How labor regulations affect labor market adjustments should depend on the extent of their coverage and how well they are enforced. In middle- and low-income countries where informal jobs—even within firms—are prevalent and enforcement capacity is weak, labor regulations are less likely to affect aggregate employment levels. They could, however, affect the composition of employment. In the case of Mexico, for instance, there is evidence that job losses in the informal sector did not increase during the crisis—this is consistent with observed high dismissal costs. Hiring rates, however, declined considerably, leading to an expansion of informal employment.

Policies

Many governments in both rich and poor countries intervened to mitigate the impact of the crisis through fiscal stimulus packages and sectoral policies aiming to revive aggregate demand. For the first time, countries also implemented policies to protect incomes, support labor demand, and connect individuals to jobs. Although high-income countries were more active and more likely to implement comprehensive packages than developing countries, the extent of government intervention in the latter remains remarkable.

Working through the Crisis • http://dx.doi.org/10.1596/978-0-8213-8967-6

Approximately 85 percent of the countries included in the International Labour Organization–World Bank policy inventory, which is the basis for the policy analysis in this book, adopted expansionary fiscal policies, regardless of income level. In high-income countries, this occurred mainly through reductions in taxes. In developing countries, in contrast, expenditures tended to increase. Countries also intervened in particular sectors. In high-income countries, these measures mainly aimed to stabilize the financial sector; in developing countries, they aimed to support the construction, transport, commerce, and, to some extent, agricultural sectors.

There is little consensus on the effectiveness of expansionary fiscal policy, in large part because it is virtually impossible to isolate the economic effects of fiscal policy in a convincing way (Alesina 2012). However, evidence from the Euro area suggests that expansionary policies helped mitigate the impact of the crisis, and to some extent, facilitate the recovery (Coenen 2012). In developing countries, prior macroeconomic policy reforms helped lay the groundwork for aggressive fiscal policy responses that contributed to a strong short-term recovery (Montiel 2011). This is consistent with the case studies of China, Mexico, and Indonesia presented in this book, which suggest that countercyclical fiscal policy may have played an important role in preventing lasting damage to workers. As detailed in chapter 6, China undertook a particularly large expansion in government spending in early 2009, and also enjoyed a remarkably rapid employment recovery. Indonesia also averted the worst effects of the crisis, in part by implementing a significant fiscal stimulus package. Mexico, on the other hand, pursued a less aggressive fiscal response, and the recovery in labor markets lagged in comparison.

Looking across regions, expansionary fiscal policy in Latin America and East Asia likely contributed to their relatively strong recovery. Besides Europe and Central Asia, the two regions most affected by the crisis were Latin America and the Caribbean, and East Asia and the Pacific, in large part due to their greater reliance on exports to OECD countries. As a response, countries in these regions increased their 2009 fiscal deficits as a share of GDP by about 4 percentage points. In both cases, the fiscal expansion came largely from increased expenditure rather than reduced revenue. Both regions recovered rapidly, however, as growth picked up in 2010.

Social protection and labor policies, on the other hand, likely had modest effects. Crisis measures typically built on programs that were already in place and had weak links with macroeconomic and labor market adjustments. For example, the prevalence of most types of interventions was not systematically related to countries' growth in output or employment. As a result, many of the policies adopted in response to the crisis did not directly address important labor market challenges or the needs of the most vulnerable groups. Most important, the limited data on cost and beneficiaries suggest that most policy responses were too small to have significant effects.

Many of the policies that were implemented focused on addressing employment losses, even though labor markets often adjusted through reductions in earnings. Indeed, with the exception of cash transfers for the poor, the bulk of policies adopted focused on protecting jobs and the unemployed. Outside the OECD, over half of all countries in the inventory implemented policy interventions designed to support labor demand (excluding public works), job search assistance and training, and, in a few countries, the extension of unemployment benefits. Essentially, these policies aimed to prevent dismissals in the formal sector or to protect those who lost formal sector jobs. Savings schemes, which could be a more appropriate response to declining earnings, are largely underdeveloped in middle- and lower-income countries.

Countries' heavy reliance on employment services and training programs can also be questioned, given design problems and the potential for low impact during a downturn. Nearly 40 percent of all middle- and low-income countries implemented at least one of these policies, compared to about 50 percent of the OECD countries. Even though expenditures on these programs were generally limited, efforts to implement them may have diverted precious administrative resources from programs with wider coverage. International experiences show that both employment services and training programs can be effective in helping workers obtain jobs, but only if the programs are designed and implemented well. In the developing world, with a few exceptions, employment services are underdeveloped and suffer from low institutional capacity, while training programs are supply driven and have low external efficiency (see Almeida, Behrman, and Robalino 2011). While intermediation services have an important role to play during the recovery when job vacancies start to grow, their role during a downturn appears to be limited.

In most cases, the policies implemented may have benefited adults more than youth, although the latter were more affected by the crisis. This is, in part, because youth are more likely to be employed in the informal sector, and even those who have formal jobs are less likely to be eligible for benefits, given lower contribution densities. Most policies favored formal sector workers, while many in the informal sector, possibly facing higher risks during a downturn, relied on self-insurance. Indeed, with the exception of cash transfers and public works, most interventions exclusively benefited formal sector workers. For example, wage subsidies or credit to enterprises are tailored to formal sector firms. Unemployment insurance or severance pay is available only to formal sector workers; and insurance arrangements, in general, cover approximately 30 to 40 percent of the labor force in middle-income countries. Even employment services and training programs are more likely to benefit formal sector workers, since the links of the programs are with formal sector firms. The self-employed, a large share of the informal workforce, are unlikely to have benefited from any kind of support.

Recovery

Employment rates have generally improved among the developing countries that were affected by the crisis. Official statistics from a sample of 24 middle-income countries show that since 2010, employment has been growing and median unemployment has fallen from 7.1 percent in the third quarter of 2010 to 5.3 percent in the second quarter of 2012. (see annex figure 1A.1 and table 1A.1) China has had the fastest expansion in employment—over 10 percent during 2012. But even among the countries in Eastern Europe that were hit hard by the crisis, unemployment rates fell sharply and employment expanded between both 2010 and 2011 and between 2011 and 2012.

Data from the Gallup World Poll, however, suggest that labor market outcomes have not improved across the board.[2] Conditions are generally perceived to have improved, as people in middle- and high-income countries were more optimistic about labor market opportunities in 2011 than in 2009. But the story is less clear when looking at labor market outcomes. For instance, the share of those employed among the interviewed fell slightly from 2009 to 2011. In fact, in middle- and high-income countries, employment among those interviewed fell between 2010 and 2011. Similarly, the unemployment rate among those interviewed was higher in 2011 than in 2009, and among upper-middle-income and low-income countries the unemployment rate continued to increase between 2010 and 2011. The indicator that improved consistently, except in the case of low-income countries, is the share of those working in full-time wage employment.

There are also concerns about the future. In several countries, including China, Indonesia, Thailand, Romania, Russia, Turkey, Brazil, Colombia, and Mexico, GDP growth has slowed, in part due to weak demand in the United States and Europe. The effects on employment are still to be felt—but it is likely that growth rates in 2013 will be lower than in 2012. In addition, earnings have become more erratic over time and across countries, and there has been no consistent pattern of wage growth. In both Brazil and Mexico, the share of formal employment increased slightly between 2011 and 2012, but if the economies continue to slowdown, this trend could be quickly reversed. Hence, there is still a downside risk that the labor market situation will deteriorate.

Although developing countries are becoming less closely linked to economic conditions in the OECD, efforts to create good jobs depend, in part, on the recovery in the United States and in Europe. In high-income countries, the recovery has been slow, and there are several risks, both in the United States and in Europe, that can compromise future economic and employment growth. In the United States, things have been improving consistently—although slowly—since the end of 2010. After peaking at 10 percent in October 2009, the unemployment rate finally fell below 8 percent in September of 2012. At that time, however, there were also fewer people participating in the labor force—about 2.3 million—compared to the same month in 2011. For some groups, like workers with less than a high school diploma, the unemployment rate has not changed much.[3]

What will happen next will depend on how the government deals with expected cuts in expenditures, the debt ceiling, and fiscal consolidation. For now, the consensus forecast is that growth in 2013 will be slower than in 2012.[4]

In the European Union and the Euro area, the unemployment rate has not fallen since the crisis; instead, it has continued to increase—reaching 10.5 percent and 11.5 percent, respectively, by the end of 2012. Although most countries affected by the crisis resumed growth at the beginning of 2010, and the region began to grow at about 2 percent each quarter (year on year), the debt crisis and recession in countries like Greece, Italy, Portugal, and Spain brought down economic growth below 1 percent in 2011 and caused negative growth during the last three quarters of 2012. At the beginning of 2013, growth and jobs prospects remain uncertain, particularly for youth who have unemployment rates twice as high as the national average, including in France and the United Kingdom. Future prospects will depend on how the European Commission and the European Central Bank deal with countries in the periphery. It is very likely, however, that both employment and economic growth in Europe will continue to be sluggish.

Looking Forward

There are two main lessons for managing future crises. The first is the need to improve statistical systems to better understand the nature of economic slow-downs, how they spread across sectors and regions, and their effects on labor markets. In middle- and, particularly, low-income countries a major problem is the lack of updated data on labor markets.

Without these data, policy makers are "flying blind" and will be unable to respond with timely and appropriate interventions. Standard employment and unemployment figures for developing countries rely heavily on projections and assumptions based on historical relationships between GDP growth and labor market outcomes. But as shown in chapter 2, estimates based on pre-crisis employment elasticities tend to significantly underestimate the extent of employment loss, because these elasticities change during the crisis. Even in most middle-income countries, reliable and updated labor force surveys are either unavailable or limited to urban areas. China's labor force survey only covers urban areas, and in India, nationally representative labor statistics are published only every five years.[5] It is critical that countries upgrade their statistical systems and institutions and make publicly available household, labor force, and firm surveys.

The second lesson is to improve the design and expand the coverage of social protection and labor systems so that these can be effectively deployed to protect workers during times of economic slowdowns. Few countries, for instance, have unemployment benefit programs beyond severance pay, and these may not be enforced; even existing unemployment insurance systems are able to reach only a small fraction of the unemployed. For countries with the capacity to do so, implementing and expanding the coverage of these programs—and social insurance programs in general—is a necessity. However, because a large proportion of workers are self-employed or informal wage employees, expanding coverage might require moving beyond traditional payroll tax–based systems. In addition, given that labor market adjustments often involve income losses, as opposed to job losses, these systems would also need to incorporate mechanisms to replace income when either the number of hours of work or wages decline.

Programs such as training for the unemployed and employment services will also likely play an important role in future crises. There is a need, however, to improve the design of these programs and to make them accessible to vulnerable populations, including workers in the informal sector. Beyond investments in institutional capacity, this will require changes in governance, administration, and financing arrangements to align the incentives of program managers with those of job seekers and employers.

Finally, the crisis demonstrated the importance of having safety nets that target the poor and that can expand and contract in response to the business cycle. Countries with well-functioning safety nets in place prior to the crisis were able to use them to protect low-income households. Those without these programs were unable to implement new ones in time.

Economic crises are certain to be a recurring feature in both industrialized and developing countries alike. The analyses in this book aim to underline some of the lessons of the most recent crises for jobs so that in more buoyant times countries can equip themselves with better-designed policy responses to safeguard employment outcomes.

Annex 1A

Figure 1A.1 Median GDP Growth and Labor Market Indicators in Selected Developing Countries

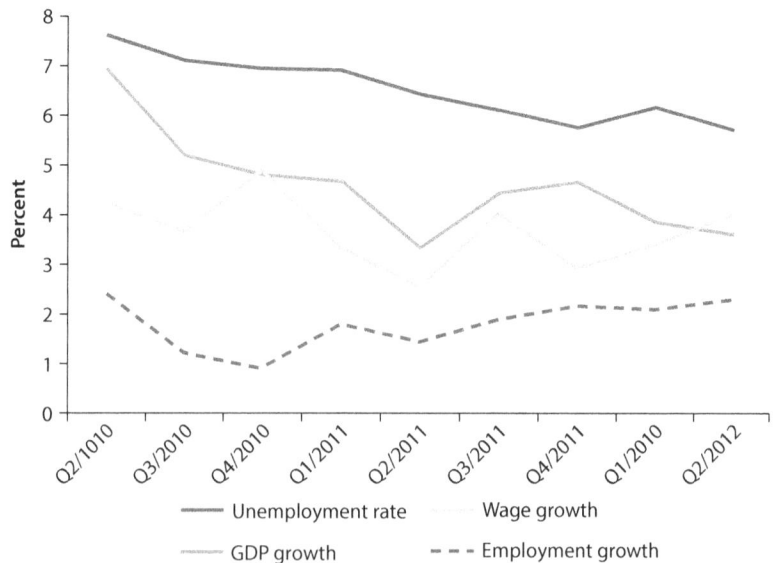

Sources: CEIC Data Company, National Statistical Offices, and the International Monetary Fund.
Note: The series are median values for a subsample of 12 countries with complete series up to Q2 2012 (except GDP for Colombia and Venezuela, employment growth for Romania, and wage growth for South Africa). The countries included in this figure are Belarus, Brazil, Chile, China, Colombia, Mexico, Romania, Russia, South Africa, Thailand, Turkey, and Venezuela.

Figure 1A.2 Share of Population Reporting Good Time to Find a Job, by Year and Income Group

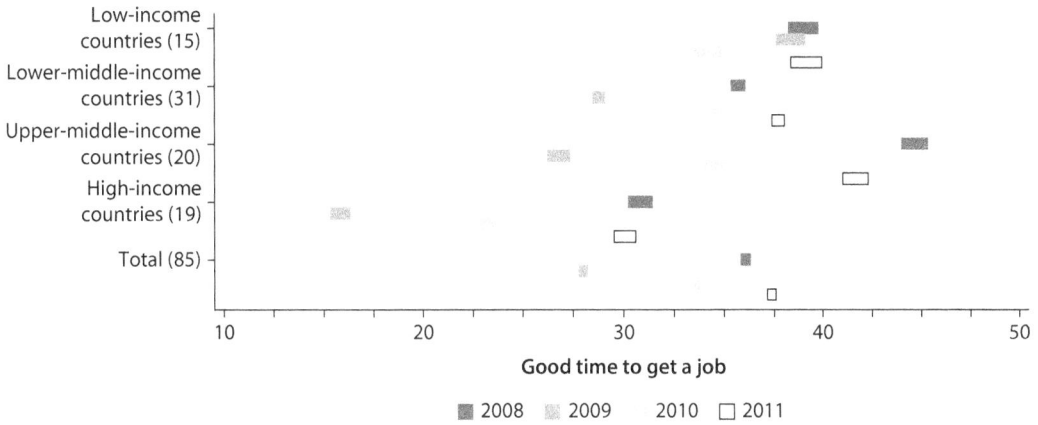

Good time to get a job

■ 2008 ▨ 2009 2010 ☐ 2011

Source: Gallup World Poll.
Note: Width of rectangles represent 95 percent confidence intervals. Averages across countries are weighted by countries' estimated population of adults aged 15 and older.

Figure 1A.3 Employment to Population Ratio, by Year, Income Group, and Gender

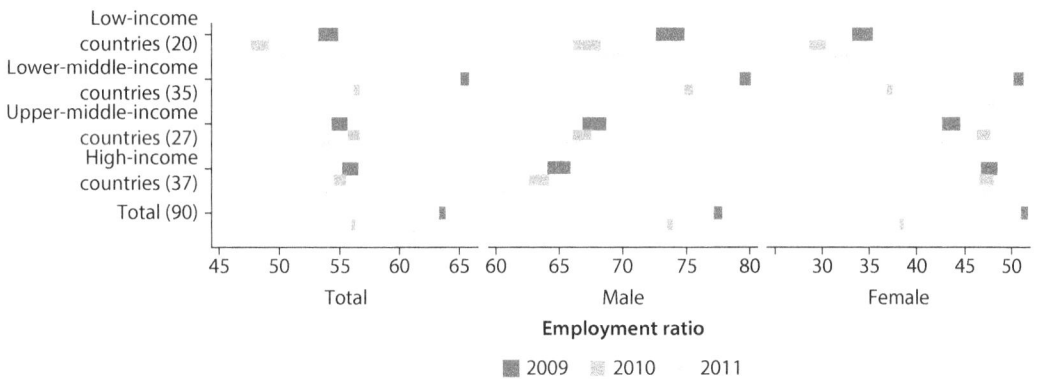

Employment ratio

■ 2009 ▨ 2010 2011

Source: Gallup World Poll. See note to figure 1A.2.

Figure 1A.4 Unemployment Rate, by Year, Income Group, and Gender

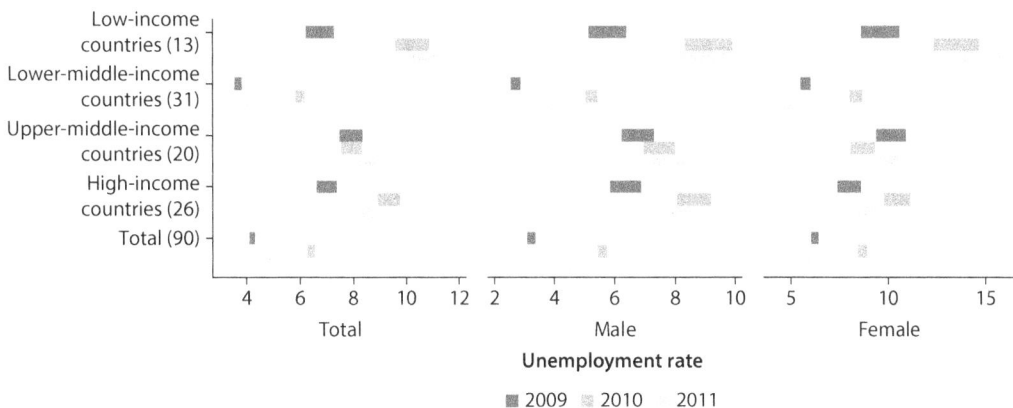

Unemployment rate

■ 2009 ▨ 2010 2011

Source: Gallup World Poll. See note to figure 1A.2.

Figure 1A.5 Share of Employment in Full-Time Wage Work, by Year, Income Group, and Gender

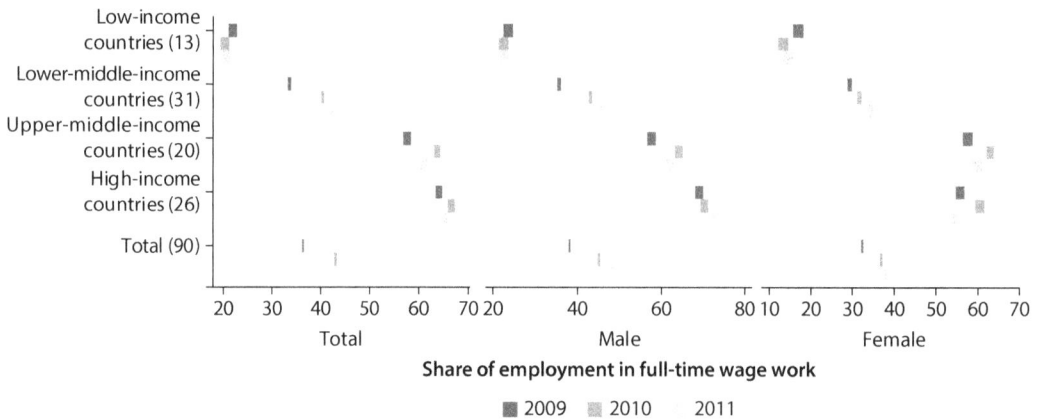

Source: Gallup World Poll. See note to figure 1A.2.

Table 1A.1 Labor Market Indicators for Selected Developing Countries

		GDP growth		Employment growth		Unemployment rate		Wage growth	
Region	Countries	Q2/11	Q2/12	Q2/11	Q2/12	Q2/11	Q2/12	Q2/11	Q2/12
EAP	China	9.5	7.6	4.1	10.3	4.1	4.1	12.1	15.5
EAP	Indonesia	6.5	6.4	3.6	1.4	6.8	6.3	n.a.	n.a.
EAP	Philippines	3.1	5.9	0.8	3.0	7.4	7.2	3.2	1.0
EAP	Thailand	2.7	4.2	1.5	1.6	0.6	0.9	1.0	14.5
ECA	Armenia	1.9	4.7	−0.7	−8.1	17.8	16.5	−2.0	3.8
ECA	Azerbaijan	0.8	0.5	0.5	1.2	n.a.	n.a.	−0.7	7.4
ECA	Belarus	12.0	3.0	0.0	−2.0	0.7	0.7	8.6	15.7
ECA	Kazakhstan	6.8	5.6	1.1	3.9	5.5	5.4	2.1	12.4
ECA	Kyrgyz Republic	3.9	−6.6	0.4	2.7	2.6	2.6	5.4	21.7
ECA	Lithuania	6.5	2.2	0.9	1.9	17.2	14.5	2.4	2.8
ECA	Moldova	8.4	1.0	0.8	−0.6	9.4	7.2	7.9	4.2
ECA	Romania	0.3	1.7	1.5	−0.5	5.1	4.6	−4.6	2.6
ECA	Russian Federation	3.4	4.0	1.0	1.4	6.6	5.5	2.8	11.2
ECA	Tajikistan	6.5	7.2	n.a.	n.a.	2.5	2.6	8.7	15.6
ECA	Turkey	9.1	3.2	6.3	3.0	9.5	8.6	8.1	6.4
ECA	Ukraine	3.9	3.0	0.1	−0.3	8.7	8.4	5.7	16.5
LAC	Brazil	3.3	0.5	2.4	2.1	6.3	5.9	4.4	3.2
LAC	Chile	6.3	5.5	6.7	2.0	7.1	6.6	2.3	3.0
LAC	Colombia	5.0	4.7	3.3	5.3	11.0	11.1	0.4	0.7
LAC	Ecuador	8.8	4.8	−0.1	3.7	6.1	5.1	5.6	5.2
LAC	Mexico	3.2	4.1	0.6	4.5	5.2	4.8	−0.6	1.7
LAC	Peru	6.9	6.1	1.0	1.0	9.1	8.6	5.8	12.1
LAC	Venezuela, RB	4.8	5.6	1.3	2.3	8.4	8.0	5.4	5.6

table continues next page

Table 1A.1 Labor Market Indicators for Selected Developing Countries (continued)

Region	Countries	GDP growth		Employment growth		Unemployment rate		Wage growth	
		Q2/11	Q2/12	Q2/11	Q2/12	Q2/11	Q2/12	Q2/11	Q2/12
SSA	South Africa	3.3	3.0	0.5	2.5	25.7	24.9	5.4	0.5
EAP	Region average	5.5	6.0	2.5	4.1	4.7	4.6	5.5	10.3
ECA	Region average	5.3	2.5	1.1	0.2	7.8	7.0	3.7	10.0
LAC	Region average	5.5	4.5	2.2	3.0	7.6	7.2	3.3	4.5

Sources: CEIC database, National Statistical Offices, and the International Monetary Fund.
Note: EAP = East Asia and Pacific, ECA= Europe and Central Asia; GDP = gross domestic product; LAC = Latin America and the Caribbean; SSA = Sub-Saharan Africa. Region averages refer to the countries in this table. For some variables, the period of reference is Q1-2012 and Q1-2011. Employment: Armenia, Ecuador, Kyrgyz Republic, Lithuania, Moldova, Philippines, Romania, and Ukraine; Unemployment rate: Armenia, Ecuador, Kazakhstan, Lithuania, Moldova, Ukraine, and Venezuela; Wage growth: Lithuania and South Africa; GDP growth: Armenia, Colombia, Ecuador, Kazakhstan, Moldova, and Tajikistan. For South Africa, earnings come from a firm survey and represent only the formal sector; for China, earnings are representative of only urban regions. For the LAC region, labor market indicators, except from Mexico, refer to urban areas only.

Table 1A.2 Annual GDP Growth and Labor Market Outcomes in Developing Countries

	2007	2008	2009	2010	2011
GDP growth					
China	14.2	9.6	9.2	10.4	9.2
Indonesia	6.3	6.0	4.6	6.2	6.5
Mexico	3.2	1.2	−6.0	5.6	3.9
Russian Federation	8.5	5.2	−7.8	4.3	4.3
South Africa	5.5	3.6	−1.5	2.9	3.1*
Turkey	4.7	0.7	−4.8	9.2	8.5*
Employment to adult population ratio					
China	70.7	70.2	69.7	68.1	—
Indonesia	60.9	61.5	61.9	62.9	63.9
Mexico	61.1	61.3	59.4	60.3	59.8
Russian Federation[a]	63.0	64.3	62.1	62.7	63.8
South Africa[b]	44.4	44.8	42.7	40.8	40.9
Turkey	41.6	41.7	41.2	43.0	44.9
Unemployment rate					
China	—	—	—	—	—
Indonesia	9.4	8.4	8.0	7.3	6.7
Mexico	3.6	3.7	4.0	5.5	5.3
Russian Federation	6.1	6.3	8.5	7.5	6.6
South Africa	22.3	22.8	23.9	24.9	24.7
Turkey	10.2	10.9	14.0	11.9	9.8
Percentage of workers in wage employment					
China	—	—	—	—	—
Indonesia	28.1	27.5	27.8	30.1	34.4
Mexico	65.6	66.5	65.9	66.4	66.2
Russian Federation	92.7	92.7	92.5	93.1	92.8

table continues next page

Table 1A.2 Annual GDP Growth and Labor Market Outcomes in Developing Countries *(continued)*

	2007	*2008*	*2009*	*2010*	*2011*
South Africa	—	84.0	84.6	84.4	84.5
Turkey	60.4	61.0	60.1	60.8	61.7
Percentage of workers in agriculture					
China[c]	40.8	39.6	38.1	36.7	—
Indonesia	41.2	40.3	39.7	38.3	35.9
Mexico	14.1	13.3	13	12.9	13.1
Russian Federation	9.0	8.6	8.4	7.9	7.9
South Africa	5.5	5.7	5.1	4.9	4.6
Turkey	23.6	23.6	24.6	25.3	25.4

Sources: World Economic Outlook, CEIC and National Statistics Offices.
Note: — = not available; GDP = gross domestic product.
a. Age 15–72.
b. Age 15–64.
c. Percentage of workers in primary industry.

Notes

1. The employment data reported in table 1A.2 in the annex are only representative of five countries in these regions. The broader set of countries in table 1A.1 reported only a minor slowdown in growth, combined with a decline in average unemployment rates, suggesting that, in general, employment effects were weaker.

2. The Gallup World Poll is an annual survey of at least 1,000 adults from each of approximately 90 countries between 2009 and 2011. It represents roughly 85 percent of the world's adults, and 70 percent of adults in low- and middle-income countries. In most developing countries, it is a face-to-face survey. More details on the data can be found in Clifton (2011).

3. See U.S. Department of Labor 2013.

4. See IMF 2012.

5. There is also an Indian Quarterly Employment Survey of firms, but it is too narrow to provide an accurate picture of national or even urban outcomes as it is only representative of firms in eight economic sectors in 20 cities, covering 11 of the 35 states.

References

Alesina, A. 2012. "Fiscal Policy after the Great Recession." *Atlanta Economic Journal* 40: 429–35.

Almeida, R., J. Behrman, and D. Robalino, eds. 2011. *The Right Skills for the Job? Rethinking Training Policies for Workers.* Human Development Perspectives. Washington, DC: World Bank.

Cazes, S., S. Verick, and F. Al Hussami. 2012. "Diverging Trends in Unemployment in the United States and Europe: Evidence from Okun's Law and the Global Financial Crisis." Employment Working Paper 106, International Labour Organization, Geneva, Switzerland.

Clifton, J. 2011. *The Coming Jobs War.* New York: Gallup Press.

Coenen, G. 2012. "Fiscal Policy and the Great Recession in the Euro Area." *The American Economic Review* 102 (3): 71–76.

Horton, S., R. Kanbur, and D. Mazumdar, eds. 1994. *Labor Markets in an Era of Adjustment*. Washington, DC: World Bank, Economic Development Institute Development Studies.

IMF (International Monetary Fund). 2012. *World Economic Outlook—Growth Resuming, Dangers Remain*. Washington, DC: IMF.

Montiel, P. J. 2011. "On Macroeconomic Reforms and Macroeconomic Resiliency: Lessons from the Great Recession." *Modern Economy* 2: 528–37.

Paci, P., A. Revenga, and B. Rijkers. 2012. "Coping with Crises: Policies to Protect Employment and Earnings." *World Bank Research Observer* 27 (1): 106–41.

U.S. Department of Labor. 2013. "The Employment Situation—February 2013." Bureau of Labor Statistics, Washington, DC.

CHAPTER 2

Fewer Jobs or Smaller Paychecks? Aggregate Crisis Impacts in Selected Middle-Income Countries

Gaurav Khanna, David Newhouse, and Pierella Paci

While policy responses to economic downturns tend to focus on protecting employment, evidence from the developing world shows that employment reduction is not the only, or even the most significant, effect. Although economic crises are difficult to predict, their recurrence is a salient feature of emerging market economies. Nevertheless, many developing countries continue to lack an effective policy infrastructure for mitigating the impacts of economic downturns on employment opportunities. Moreover, when this infrastructure exists, it focuses mostly on maintaining existing jobs, providing alterative employment, or replacing income with unemployment benefits for workers that lose formal sector jobs. However, job losses are only one of the possible ways in which labor markets adjust to economic downturns, and the prevailing adjustment mechanism depends on the nature of the shock and on the characteristics of both the economy and the labor market. During past crises, workers in developing countries typically faced large declines in hourly wages or employment reallocation across sectors rather than major reductions in employment.[1]

The Disconnect between the Impact of the Crisis and the Policy Responses

The experiences of the global downturn of 2008–09 highlight a common disconnect between the impact of crises on the labor market and the policy responses. Identifying the labor market channels through which the economic downturn is transmitted is a precondition for effective targeting of policy interventions (see, for

Gaurav Khanna is a PhD student at the Department of Economics, University of Michigan; David Newhouse is a Senior Economist, and Pierella Paci is a Lead Economist at the World Bank in Washington, DC.

example, Johansson *et al.* 2010. If first-round labor market adjustments are concentrated in specific jobs, sectors, or geographic areas, targeted employment interventions to protect those most immediately affected may effectively mitigate the impacts of the crisis. If, by contrast, most of the adjustment occurs through generalized wage declines, standard employment-focus policies are not the most effective instruments for easing the impact of a crisis. But lack of fast-track data to monitor changes in main labor market indicators in a timely manner often prevents well-targeted policy responses. This failure painfully highlighted the disconnect—described in some detail in chapter 4 of this volume—between the prevailing labor market adjustment during the global downturn of 2008–09 and the majority of the policy responses. The lack of adequate information on the prevailing adjustment mechanism in the developing world was mostly to blame for the disconnect. In general, most analysis of the magnitude and nature of labor market adjustments to the 2008 economic shock has been limited to countries in the Organisation for Economic Co-operation and Development (OECD), and quantitative cross-country evidence on the impact of the great recession on labor market outcomes in developing countries has been scarce.[2]

This chapter summarizes evidence from 45 middle-income countries on how the 2008 crisis affected labor markets and reaches four main conclusions:

- First, as in previous crises, adjustments occurred more through the *quality* of jobs than through their *quantity*. For the average country in the sample, earnings growth slowed by three times as much as employment growth, and unemployment changed little.
- Second, for several countries, growth in hourly wages did not collapse, and the adjustment came mainly through large reductions in hours worked.
- Third, while labor market adjustments generally tracked declines in gross domestic product (GDP), outcomes varied considerably across countries. For a given decline in GDP growth, countries with smaller manufacturing sectors, larger export sectors, and less costly redundancy regulations were better able to protect earnings.
- Finally, the responsiveness of employment growth to changes in GDP growth increased during the crisis, leading simple projections to understate the extent of employment loss during the crisis.

Data and Methodology

The chapter uses data from published quarterly labor market statistics on 45 middle-income countries. Thirty-seven of these countries have information on both GDP growth and employment growth, while 31 have information on GDP growth and earnings growth. Most of the countries lie in Latin America or in the developing countries of Europe and Central Asia. The authors divide the remaining countries into two regions: East Asia and Sri Lanka, and the Middle East and Africa.[3] The main sources of primary data on labor market and GDP are country statistics published by the relevant country statistical offices and provided, on a subscription basis, to the World Bank by three private data providers—Haver Analytics, CEIC, and EMED—that collect them daily. These data were supplemented by the LABORSTA database of the International Labour Organization (ILO).[4] Data on other country indicators—such as per capita GDP and the size of the manufacturing and export sectors—come from the World Development Indicators database.

Data coverage and sources vary across countries and indicators. GDP, employment, and unemployment statistics are available quarterly for almost all countries in the sample.[5] Many countries, however, do not report earnings, and even fewer provide hours. Moreover, hours and earnings are sometimes reported as changes in indexes rather than as levels. Since data are often missing for particular quarters, the analysis is limited to year-on-year changes for comparable quarters. Tables 2A.1 and 2A.2 in the annex list the types of surveys used to generate employment and earnings indicators. In three quarters of the countries analyzed, employment statistics were derived from labor force surveys, while in the remaining one-fourth, employment levels were obtained from surveys of registered firms or administrative data (table 2A.1). As a result, in a quarter of the countries analyzed, employment trends may refer only to formal employees. By contrast, earnings data come from establishment surveys in 70 percent of cases, and in these cases, informal or self-employed workers are not represented. In a few countries (Colombia, Mexico, and Turkey), earnings data from establishment surveys cover only the industrial or manufacturing sectors, and most countries in Eastern Europe collect earnings data only for nonagricultural workers. Finally, employment and earnings data often do not cover the full country. At least 16 percent of countries—typically China and countries in Latin America—collect employment data only in urban areas.

Results should be interpreted with appropriate caution. Much of the analysis focuses on the change in the wage bill as a convenient summary measure of the total magnitude of the labor market adjustment borne by workers. The wage bill is the product of employment and average monthly earnings. Given the nature of the data, changes in the wage bills often reflect changes in firms' earnings and total employment. Many of these countries have large informal sectors, and the cyclicality of earnings in formal and informal firms may differ, adding additional uncertainty to the estimates of the precise role of earnings in the adjustment process. It is reassuring, however, that the data on earnings from 17 middle-income countries presented in the next chapter also tend to show moderate to large earnings adjustments.

The analysis compares growth rates during the crisis year with averages over the prior two years. Focusing on the change in the growth rate, rather than on postcrisis declines, is important for an accurate measurement of the effect of the crisis relative to precrisis trends.[6] Extending back two years allows a comparison with changes immediately preceding the crisis, while mitigating the influence of the rapid price increases in food and fuel in 2008. GDP growth in crisis-affected countries fell sharply in the fourth quarter of 2008. Therefore, the postcrisis period includes the four quarters from Q4 2008 to Q3 2009, while the precrisis period includes the eight quarters from Q1 2006 to Q3 2008.[7]

The Extent and Nature of the Labor Market Adjustment

While the cost of the crisis to workers was considerable, it was delayed and gradual. As shown in figure 2.1, the average wage bill, which had been growing by nearly 10 percent over the precrisis years of 2007 and 2008, came to a near standstill in 2009, with the growth dropping to less that 1 percent. The drop was only slightly less than the fall in GDP growth over this period (9.4 percentage points), but the decline in wage bill growth began later than that of GDP and continued longer. This finding is in line with those from previous crises and suggests that the long-term impacts on workers may be deep and protracted.

Reduced growth in earnings was the main culprit for the slowdown in the wage bill.[8] Real earnings growth began to decline in the first quarter of 2008, as increases in food and fuel prices led to accelerating inflation. The sharp decline in GDP growth in the fourth quarter of 2008 was mirrored by a relatively large decline in nominal earnings growth: nearly three quarters of the 8.7 percentage point slowdown in the wage bill, among countries for which data are available, came from the reduction in earnings growth, which fell 6.5 percentage points. This number is largely consistent with evidence from past crises, as pointed out earlier (for more details, see note 1). The simultaneous drop in inflation of 2.8 percentage points, due to easing demand for commodities, prevented an even steeper drop in the wage bill and led to a small increase in the rate of real wage growth of 0.7 percentage points (figure 2.2).

Hours fell considerably in several countries. The slowdown in hours tracks closely the reduction in earnings growth (see figure 2.2).[9] On average, in the

Figure 2.1 Growth of GDP, Real Earnings, Employment, and the Wage Bill, March 2007–September 2009

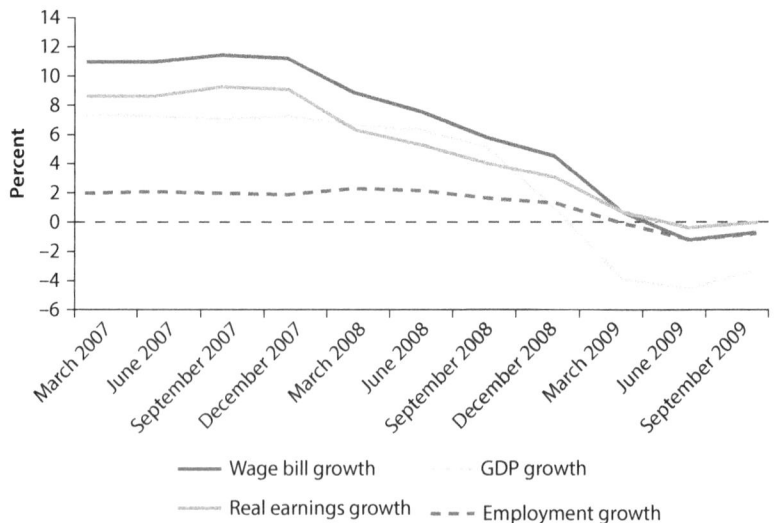

Source: World Bank staff, based on data from CEIC/EMED, Haver, ILO, and national statistical offices.
Note: Figure 2.1 is based on 24 countries that reported gross domestic product (GDP) growth, employment growth, and real earnings growth in each quarter.

Figure 2.2 Growth in Hours Worked, the Consumer Price Index, Real Earnings, and Nominal Earnings in Selected Middle-Income Countries, March 2007–September 2009

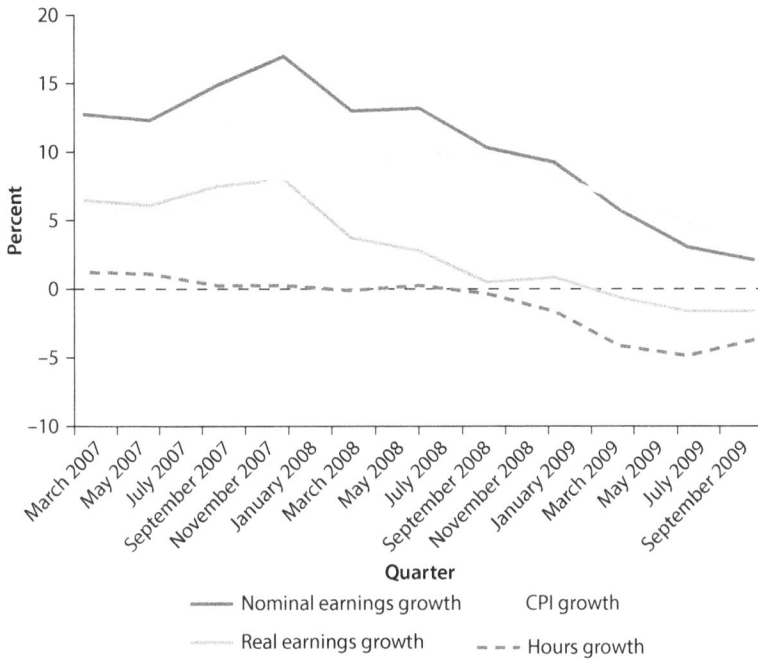

Source: World Bank staff, based on data from CEIC/EMED, Haver, ILO, and national statistical offices.
Note: CPI = consumer price index.

14 countries for which data are available, growth in hours worked fell by a striking 7 percentage points, but the drop was highly concentrated in only half these countries (figure 2.3). The decline in hours worked not only accounted for the entire decline in earnings (figure 2.4) but also allowed for a slight increase in real hourly wages (0.7 percentage points). However, the extent to which the reduction in hours was an active policy response rather than simply an adjustment mechanism is unclear. For example, an ILO survey of 54 countries (10 low-income, 10 lower-middle-income, 17 upper-middle-income, and 17 high-income countries) shows that reductions in hours worked was a common response to the downturn in countries as different as Argentina, China, Colombia, Indonesia, Jordan, Mexico, the Philippines, and Vietnam (ILO 2009a).

Because of the relatively minor impact of the downturn on employment, output per worker grew more slowly than in previous years. Among the 33 countries for which the relevant data are available, GDP growth fell by 7.9 percentage points. Of that drop, just over 6 percentage points were attributable to a decline in growth in per adult GDP, while the slower employment growth rate contributed only 1.7 percentage points and declines in labor force participation rates added very little (only 0.1 percentage points) (figure 2.5).[10] This result is consistent with the patterns for employment and hours discussed above; while employment growth slowed little, the growth rate

Figure 2.3 Change in the Growth of Hours Worked in 14 Developing Economies, Postcrisis Period vs. Precrisis Period

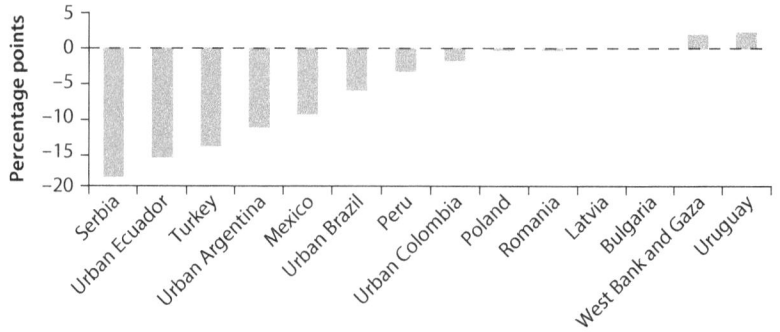

Sources: World Bank staff, based on data from CEIC/EMED, Haver, ILO, and national statistical offices.
Note: Postcrisis period covers Q4 2008 to Q3 2009. Precrisis period covers Q4 2006 to Q3 2008.

Figure 2.4 Decomposition of the Change in the Growth of the Wage Bill, Earnings, and Wage Rates in 14 Developing Countries, Postcrisis Period vs. Precrisis Period
Percent

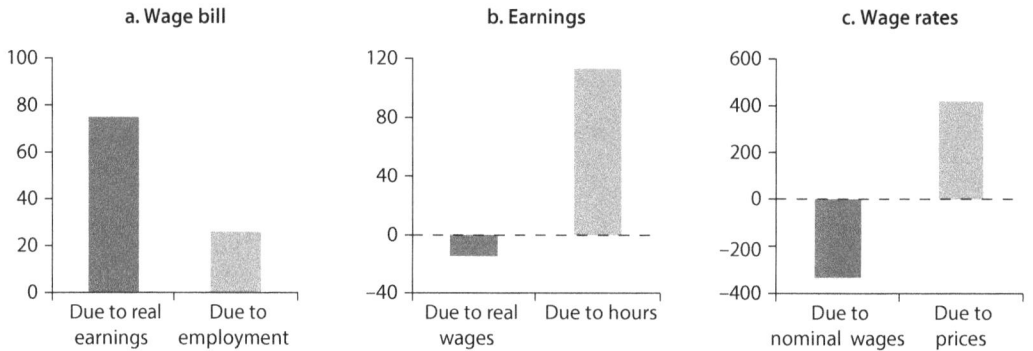

Source: World Bank staff, based on data from CEIC/EMED, Haver, ILO, and national statistical offices.
Note: Postcrisis period covers Q4 2008 to Q3 2009. Precrisis period covers Q4 2006 to Q3 2008.

of the number of hours worked dropped steeply, meaning that each worker spent less time producing output.

Employment shifts out of more productive sectors, however, also played an important role. Small aggregate employment changes masked significant shifts out of industry and into the agricultural and service sectors.[11] The fall in industrial employment is not surprising, since manufacturing exports suffered during the crisis in many countries and entry barriers are lower for family businesses in retail trade and agriculture, facilitating employment shifts into these sectors.[12] Even within the service and industrial sectors, however, the high-productivity sectors suffered most. Figure 2.6 below shows changes in employment growth across different sectors for a subsample of nine countries with the available level of disaggregation.[13] Employment growth in agriculture and low-productivity service sectors fell slightly (less than 1 percentage point), while growth in

Figure 2.5 Breakdown in the Causes of the Slowdown in the Growth of GDP per Adult in 33 Developing Countries, Postcrisis Period vs. Precrisis Period

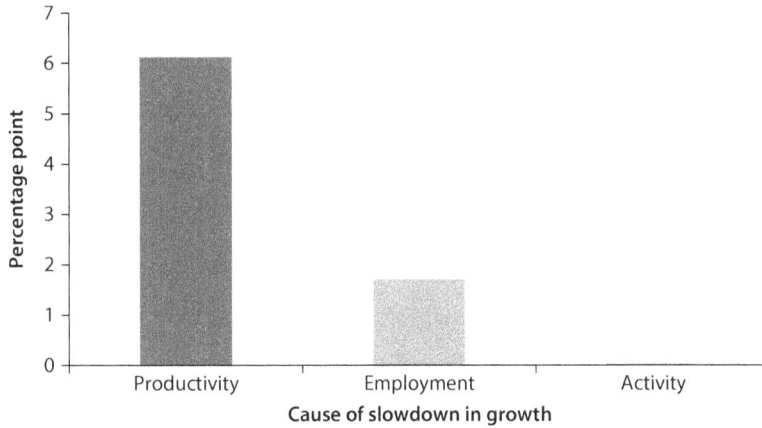

Sources: World Bank staff, based on data from CEIC/EMED, Haver, ILO, and national statistical offices.
Note: GDP = gross domestic product. Postcrisis period covers Q4 2008 to Q3 2009. Precrisis period covers Q4 2006 to Q3 2008.

Figure 2.6 Change in Employment Growth in Nine Developing Countries, Postcrisis Period vs. Precrisis Period

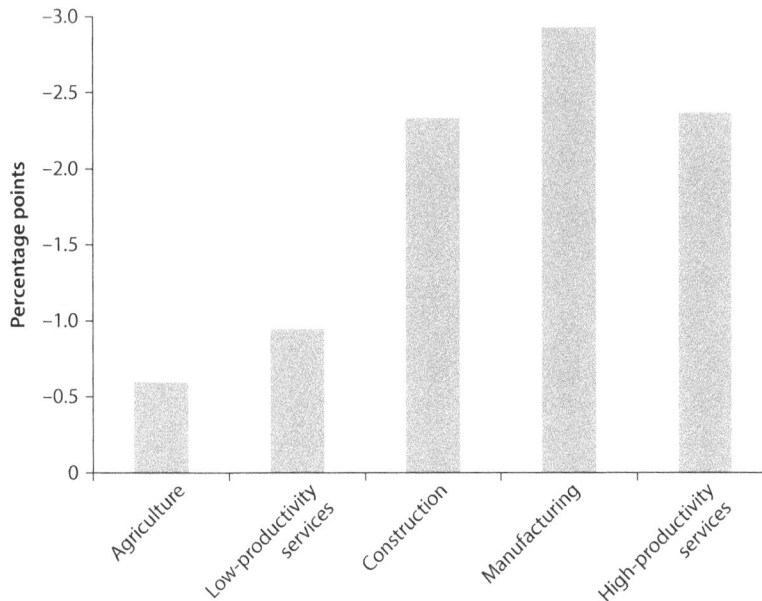

Sources: World Bank staff, based on data from CEIC/EMED, Haver, ILO, and national statistical offices.
Note: Postcrisis period covers Q4 2008 to Q3 2009. Precrisis period covers Q4 2006 to Q3 2008.

high-productivity services fell 2.5 percentage points. Evidence from a larger sample of countries on more aggregate sectors suggests similar patterns.

Both participation rates and unemployment rates, however, were largely unaffected. Contrary to evidence from previous crises, on average labor force participation rates remained almost unchanged (from 54.0 percent to 54.3 percent), suggesting that the effects of the added workers and the discouraged workers may have balanced out. Unemployment rates also hardly changed (from 9.9 percent to 10.3 percent). In other words, while very mild added-worker effects may have increased participation, a smaller share of those in the labor force were employed.[14]

In Which Countries Were Adjustments Unexpectedly Large?

Examining average labor market changes across such a varied sample of countries does not tell the whole story. While no country escaped the crisis unharmed, the way labor markets adjusted varied widely in the sample. As suggested in the introduction, much of this heterogeneity derives from fundamental differences in the severity of the shock, the structure of the economy, and the nature of labor market institutions. Figures 2.7 and 2.8 show how labor market outcomes varied according to the size of the shock. Countries more severely affected by the shock tended to adjust primarily through earnings rather than employment, as figure 2.7 shows.[15] Nevertheless unemployment increased faster in countries with larger GDP declines (figure 2.8). However, both figures clearly show

Figure 2.7 Change in Earnings and Employment Growth by GDP Growth, Postcrisis Period vs. Precrisis Period

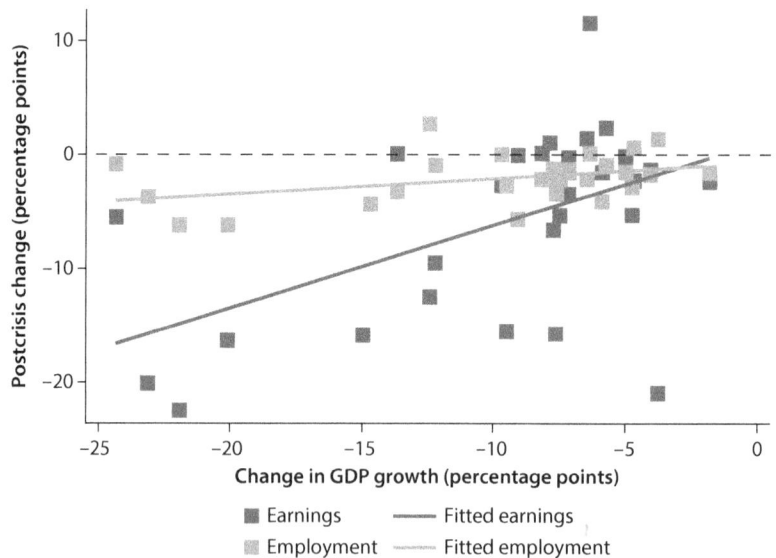

Source: World Bank staff, based on data from CEIC/EMED, Haver, ILO, and national statistical offices.
Note: GDP = gross domestic product. Postcrisis period covers Q4 2008 to Q3 2009. Precrisis period covers Q4 2006 to Q3 2008.

Figure 2.8 Change in Unemployment and Participation by GDP Growth, Postcrisis Period vs. Precrisis Period

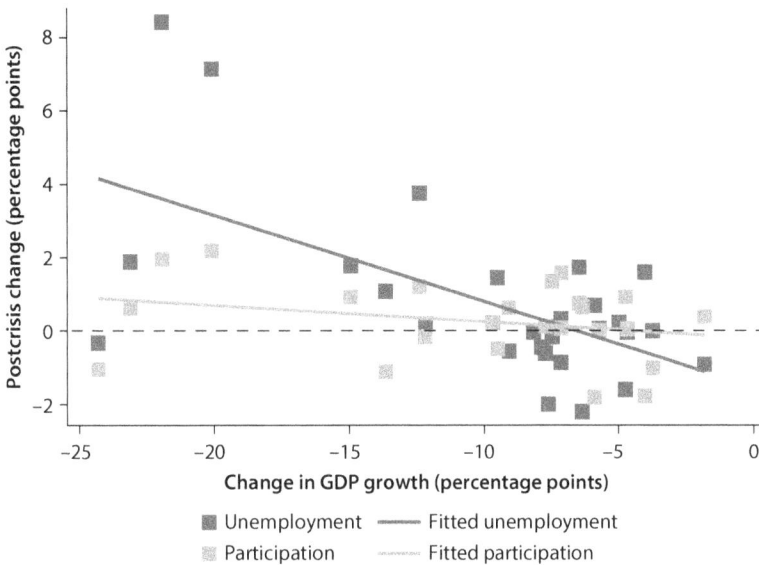

Source: World Bank staff, based on data from CEIC/EMED, Haver, ILO, and national statistical offices.
Note: GDP = gross domestic product. Postcrisis period covers Q4 2008 to Q3 2009. Precrisis period covers Q4 2006 to Q3 2008. Fitted unemployment and participation represent linear predictions.

substantial heterogeneity even for countries with identical GDP declines. This finding raises the question of which country characteristics helped cushion the labor market from the negative impact of economic shocks.

To assess the role of these other factors, this chapter classifies countries along seven dimensions. The first two are region and per capita GDP, which are intended to capture structural differences in the economy and in labor market institutions. Countries are also classified according to the relative size of the manufacturing and export sectors, two areas of the economy where crisis impacts were most severe. Exports were also affected by countries' exchange rate regimes, as those with currencies pegged to the dollar suffered larger falls in exports, since the dollar appreciated roughly 15 percent against the euro in the latter half of 2008.[16] Finally, countries are grouped according to their degree of labor regulation (high/low) to investigate the expectation that stringent labor market regulations, if enforced, discouraged employers from shedding workers during a downturn. Two measures of firing costs from the 2009 Doing Business indicators are used for this purpose: the difficulty of firing index and the firing cost.[17] Only a few of these characteristics are closely correlated with each other.[18]

Countries with larger export sectors and less stringent regulation better maintained previous trends in earnings without incurring large employment costs. Figure 2.9 shows how earnings and employment are associated with each set of country characteristics after accounting for the declines in countries' GDP growth. The most striking results are those associated with exports and firing

Figure 2.9 Correlations between Country Characteristics and Employment Loss and Earnings in 35 Developing Countries, Postcrisis Period vs. Precrisis Period

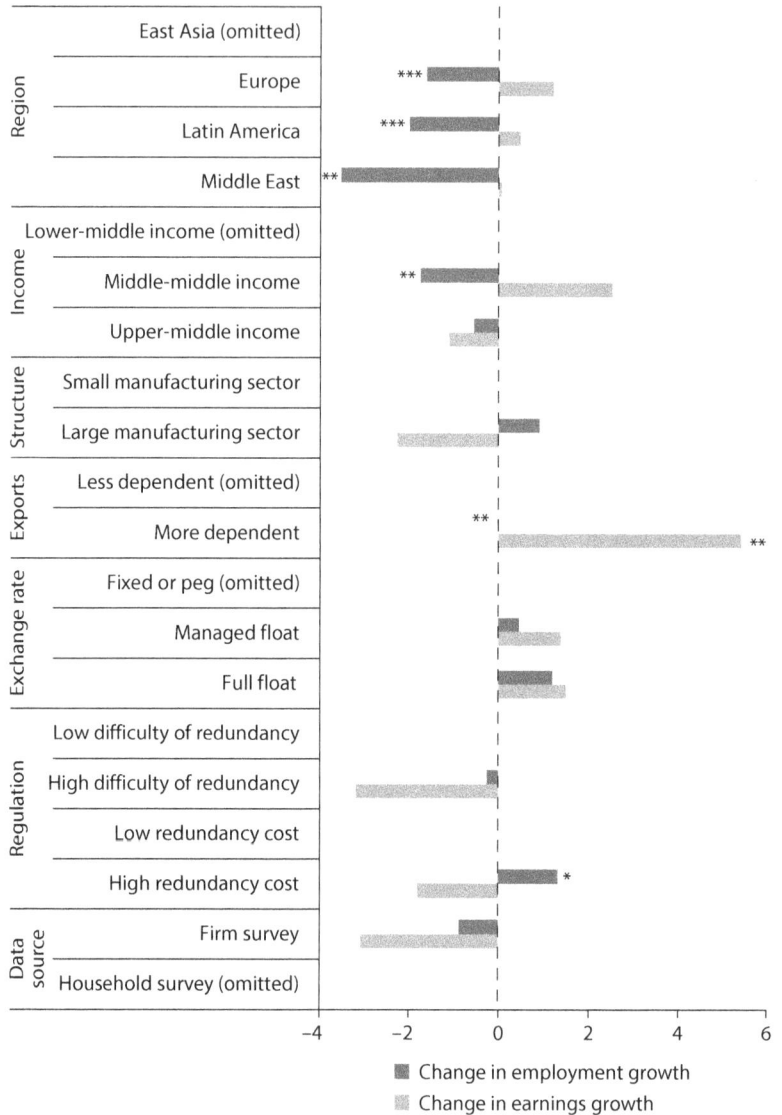

Source: World Bank staff, based on data from CEIC/EMED, Haver, ILO, and national statistical offices.
Note: Bars indicate coefficients from 14 separate cross-sectional regressions of changes in employment and earnings growth on change in GDP growth, data source, and each country characteristic. There are 35 or 36 observations in the employment regressions and 30 or 31 in the earnings regressions.
Significance level: * = 10 percent, ** = 5 percent, *** = 1 percent.

regulations. High-export countries were much better able to maintain earnings, at negligible cost to employment. Countries with higher redundancy costs were better able to protect employment, on the order of 1–2 percentage points. However, this cushion may have come partly at the expense of steeper reductions in earnings. Countries with more costly and cumbersome firing regulations had a 2–3 percentage point greater decline in earnings. The relationship between firing regulations and earnings declines, however, is only suggestive and not statistically significant, because of the imprecision of the earnings measures.

After the size of the shock was factored in, increases in unemployment were larger outside of Europe and in countries with higher redundancy costs. When GDP growth was controlled for, unemployment increases were particularly low in Eastern Europe and Central Asia (figure 2.10). This finding suggests that concerns that European institutions exacerbated unemployment increases during the crisis were exaggerated, at least for the middle-income European countries in the sample. Activity rates and unemployment rates increased in higher-income countries, as laid-off workers in these countries were more able to afford to search for work, in part perhaps because spouses or younger members of the household rejoined the labor force. Finally, countries with higher redundancy costs experienced significantly larger increases in unemployment. During the crisis, unemployment rates increased most for youth, who may have faced particular difficulty in obtaining employment in countries with higher redundancy costs.

How Accurate Were Projections of Employment Changes?

Employment became more sensitive to changes in GDP during the crisis. The authors estimated the relationship between employment growth and GDP growth before and after the crisis for the 37 countries that reported data for each of these variables. The preferred estimates control for time-invariant characteristics of the country. They indicate that the employment elasticity rose during the crisis, from 0.16 before the crisis to 0.25 after the crisis (table 2.1).[19]

This result is important since forecasts of employment changes are often based on methods that combine estimates of employment elasticities with GDP projections. The ILO, for example, predicts present and future employment based on regressions of employment rates on GDP growth, controlling for time-invariant country characteristics (ILO 2010, 79). If the relationship between GDP growth and employment growth changes during the crisis, extrapolating from the past may lead to inaccurate estimates of employment loss.

Predictions based on precrisis elasticities, which significantly underestimated employment loss during the crisis, had predicted employment growth of 0.47 percent. However, in the countries analyzed, employment actually declined on average, although slightly, by 0.08 percent. Therefore, on average the employment estimates overstated employment growth by 0.55 percentage points. This is a significant overestimate, given that employment growth in total declined about 2 percentage points.

Forecasting employment changes on the basis of GDP alone typically produces inaccurate estimates for individual countries. The extent of the discrepancy between actual and predicted employment ranged from −10.5 to 6.5 percentage points. On average across the countries, the prediction was off by a magnitude of 1.9 percentage points.[20]

Working through the Crisis · http://dx.doi.org/10.1596/978-0-8213-8967-6

Figure 2.10 Correlations between Country Characteristics and Change in Unemployment and Participation in 36 Developing Countries, Postcrisis vs. Precrisis Period

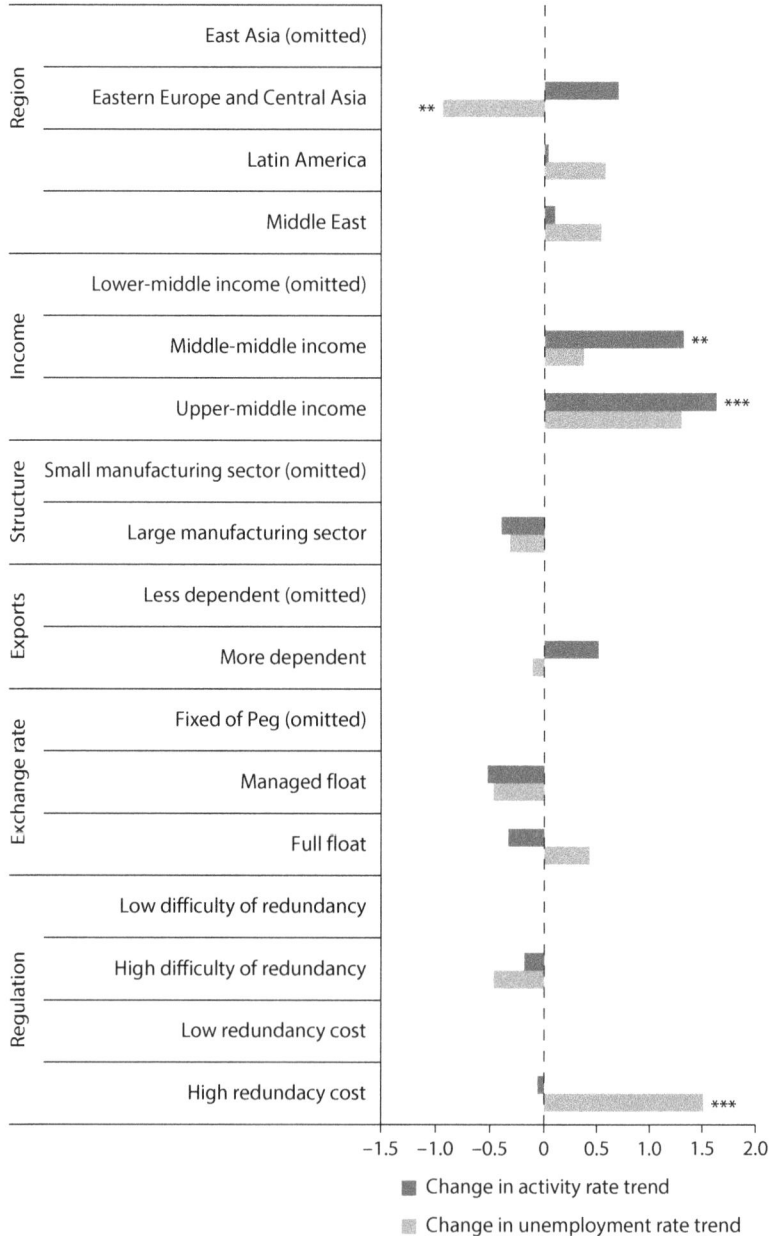

Source: World Bank staff, based on data from CEIC/EMED, Haver, ILO, and national statistical offices.
Note: All data are from household surveys. Unemployment regressions contain 36 or 37 observations, while activity regressions contain 29 observations.
Significance level: * = 10 percent, ** = 5 percent, *** = 1 percent.

Table 2.1 Employment Growth and GDP Growth in 37 Developing Countries, Precrisis Period vs. Postcrisis Period

	Precrisis	Postcrisis
Estimated elasticity of employment with respect to growth	0.16	0.25
Average projected employment growth (based on postcrisis GDP)	n.a.	0.47
Average actual employment growth	1.88	−0.08
Average overestimate of employment growth (percentage points)	n.a.	0.55
Average magnitude of discrepancy across countries (percentage points)	n.a.	1.9

Source: World Bank staff, based on data from CEIC/EMED, Haver, ILO, and national statistical offices.
Note: GDP = gross domestic product; n.a. = not applicable. Postcrisis period covers Q4 2008 to Q3 2009. Precrisis period covers Q4 2006 to Q3 2008.

From Evidence to Policy Responses

Evidence on labor market adjustments is an important input in the design of policy responses. While economic growth has bottomed out and appears to be recovering in the advanced economies, labor markets recover more slowly and can often take years to bounce back from sharp downturns (Reinhart and Rogoff 2009). In the meantime, the nature of the labor market adjustment determines winners and losers. For example, employment declines tend to concentrate losses among an unlucky few, while earnings declines spread losses more evenly among the workforce. The next chapter considers in greater detail which types of workers were more insulated from the crisis.

The appropriate mix of policies in response to the crisis depends partly on the nature of the labor market adjustment. Income replacement programs such as unemployment insurance or public works are most effective in mitigating the impact of job loss. In contrast, when the labor market adjustment occurs through earnings, then income maintenance programs—such as cash transfers or income tax credits—become particularly important. Targeting the working poor through income support programs is therefore a priority in these circumstances.[21]

Most policy responses during crisis times have concentrated on employment generation.[22] For example, employment generation programs were implemented in response to crises in Argentina, the Republic of Korea, Mexico, and Thailand. Meanwhile, wage subsidies were implemented in response to past crises in Argentina, Costa Rica, and Malaysia. Public works programs have also been implemented in response to crises, as in Indonesia in 1998. None of these programs, however, directly benefited workers in the informal sector, and relatively few provide income support to workers who maintained their jobs.[23]

The emerging evidence presented in this chapter suggests that effective policy packages should support earnings and household income. Crisis responses in European OECD countries—such as partial unemployment insurance, expanding cash transfers to poor workers, and temporary wage subsidies—may be priority interventions in those countries where hours and earnings adjustments dominated.

Working through the Crisis • http://dx.doi.org/10.1596/978-0-8213-8967-6

Sound diagnostics are also important to understanding the causes and implications of different adjustment patterns. Labor markets can adjust to downturns in different ways, with different implications for workers. The nature of these adjustments is at least partially determined by countries' labor market policies and institutions and has important implications for the welfare of the poor. Future downturns are bound to occur, and additional research based on sound labor market diagnostics can help unravel the link between policies and institutions, labor market adjustments, and outcomes for the poor.

Annex 2A

Table 2A.1 Summary of Labor Market Trends and Data Sources, by Economy, Precrisis Period vs. Postcrisis Period

Region and country	Data source Employment	Earnings	Income group	Severity group	Change in average growth rate in postcrisis period relative to precrisis period (percentage points) GDP	Wage bill	Employment	Earnings	Hours
East Asia	n.a.	n.a.	n.a.	n.a.	−5.64	−5.38	−0.14	−5.13	0.22
Urban China	Firm	Firm	LMIC	Mild	−5.00	0.88	−1.52	2.55	—
Indonesia	Household	Household	LMIC	Mild	−1.81	−3.98	−1.53	−2.39	0.22
Malaysia	Household	—	HMIC	Medium	−8.92	—	0.21	—	—
Philippines	Household	Legislated	LMIC	Mild	−4.68	−1.59	0.62	−2.26	—
Sri Lanka	Household	Legislated	LMIC	Mild	−3.76	−19.52	1.38	−20.93	—
Thailand	Household	Household	MIC	Medium	−9.68	−2.67	0.03	−2.65	—
Europe and Central Asia	n.a.	n.a.	n.a.	n.a.	−11.84	−11.30	−2.70	−8.32	−5.66
Albania	Household	—	LMIC	Mild	−0.16	—	0.89	—	—
Armenia	Household	Firm	LMIC	Severe	−24.31	−13.77	−0.84	−9.39	—
Belarus	Household	Firm	MIC	Medium	−7.48	−5.07	−2.12	−3.15	—
Bosnia and Herzegovina	Firm	—	MIC	—	—	—	−17.26	—	—
Bulgaria	Firm	Firm	MIC	Medium	−9.07	−6.29	−5.66	−0.04	−0.01
Georgia	Firm	N/A	HMIC	Severe	−13.31	—	−1.19	—	—
Kazakhstan	Household	Firm	MIC	Medium	−7.87	−1.09	−2.16	1.04	—
Kyrgyz Republic	Firm	—	LMIC	Medium	−7.82	—	−0.44	—	—
Latvia	Household	Firm	HMIC	Severe	−21.92	−28.68	−6.20	−22.47	−0.23
Lithuania	Household	Firm	HMIC	Severe	−20.08	−22.30	−6.19	−16.35	—
Macedonia, FYR	Household	Household	MIC	Medium	−6.35	12.11	0.10	11.57	—
Moldova	Household	Firm	LMIC	Medium	−7.78	−4.25	−3.28	0.08	—
Montenegro	Household	—	HMIC	—	—	—	1.31	—	—
Poland	Household	Firm	HMIC	Mild	−4.75	−8.39	−2.83	−5.31	−0.31

table continues next page

Table 2A.1 Summary of Labor Market Trends and Data Sources, by Economy, Precrisis Period vs. Postcrisis Period
(*continued*)

Region and economy	Data source Employment	Earnings	Income group	Severity group	Change in average growth rate in postcrisis period relative to precrisis period (percentage points) GDP	Wage bill	Employment	Earnings	Hours
Romania	Household	Firm	MIC	Severe	−12.20	−8.69	−0.95	−9.50	−0.28
Russian Federation	Household	Firm	MIC	Severe	−14.96	−20.11	−3.86	−15.87	—
Serbia	Household	Firm	LMIC	Medium	−7.62	−18.67	−3.42	−15.71	−18.84
Tajikistan	Household	—	LMIC	—	—	—	1.03	—	—
Turkey	Household	Household	HMIC	Severe	−12.42	−9.60	2.69	−12.49	−14.29
Ukraine	Firm	Firm	LMIC	Severe	−23.10	−23.45	−3.68	−18.90	—
Latin America	n.a.	n.a.	n.a.	n.a.	−6.82	−5.35	−1.89	−2.47	−5.08
Urban Argentina	Household	Firm	HMIC	Medium	−5.72	1.42	−0.91	2.39	−11.59
Urban Brazil	Household	Firm	MIC	Medium	−7.14	−1.60	−1.30	−0.25	−6.22
Chile	Firm	Firm	HMIC	Medium	−6.46	−0.76	−2.14	1.45	—
Urban Colombia	Household	Firm	MIC	Medium	−7.14	−5.17	−1.55	−3.46	−1.85
Dominican Republic	Firm	—	MIC	Medium	−9.10	—	−4.38	—	—
Urban Ecuador	Household	Household	LMIC	Mild	−4.05	−8.34	−0.72	−1.32	—
Jamaica	Household	—	MIC	Mild	−3.17	—	−3.75	—	—
Mexico	Household	Firm	HMIC	Medium	−9.49	−18.13	−2.73	−15.50	−9.72
Paraguay	—	Firm	LMIC	Medium	−8.40	—	—	−3.85	—
Peru	Firm	Firm	MIC	Medium	−8.17	−2.17	−2.14	0.12	−3.39
Trinidad and Tobago	Household	—	HMIC	—	—	—	0.03	—	—
Uruguay	—	Household	HMIC	Medium	−5.27	—	—	2.36	2.29
Venezuela, RB	Household	Firm	HMIC	Medium	−7.72	−8.04	−1.27	−6.61	—
Middle East and Africa	n.a.	n.a.	n.a.	n.a.	−2.80	−5.71	−2.25	0.25	1.89
Egypt, Arab Rep.	Household	—	LMIC	Mild	−2.58	—	−3.61	—	—
Jordan	—	—	HMIC	Medium	−5.76	—	—	—	—
Mauritius	Household	—	MIC	Mild	−3.31	—	−3.69	—	—
South Africa	Household	Household	MIC	Medium	−5.88	−5.71	−4.10	−1.53	—
West Bank and Gaza	—	Household	HMIC	Mild	−0.40	—	—	2.04	1.89

Source: World Bank staff, based on data from CEIC/EMED, Haver, ILO, and national statistical offices.
Note: GDP = gross domestic product; HMIC = higher-middle-income country; LMIC = lower-middle-income country; MIC = middle-income country; — = not available; n.a. = not applicable. Postcrisis period covers Q4 2008 to Q3 2009. Precrisis period covers Q4 2006 to Q3 2008.

Table 2A.2 Characteristics of Data Sources

Indicator	Coverage and source	Number of countries
Employment	Whole country	30
	Only urban	6
	Total	36
Employment	Labor force or household survey	27
	Establishment survey	9
	Total	36
Earnings	Industry/nonagriculture	9
	All sectors	19
	Unknown	3
	Total	31
Earnings	Labor force or household survey	7
	Establishment survey	22
	Legislated	2
	Total	31

Source: Metadata from CEIC/EMED, Haver, ILO, and national statistical offices.
Note: Excludes Bosnia and Herzogovina, Montenegro, Trinidad and Tobago, and Tajikistan due to lack of GDP data.

Table 2A.3 Average Annual Changes in Labor Market Indicators, Precrisis Period vs. Postcrisis Period

Indicator	Number of countries	Average % change, precrisis period	Average % change, postcrisis period	Difference (percentage points)
GDP growth	28	7.3	−2.4	−9.7
Wage bill growth	28	9.4	1.1	−8.3
Employment growth	28	1.8	−0.2	−2.0
Earnings growth	28	7.3	1.3	−6.0
Hours worked growth	14	1.7	−5.2	−6.9
Real wage growth	14	6.5	7.2	0.7
Nominal wage growth	14	12.9	12.2	−0.7
Growth in consumer price index	14	7.0	6.0	−1.0
Unemployment rate	28	9.0	9.7	0.7
Participation rate	24	53.0	53.3	0.3

Source: World Bank staff, based on data from CEIC/EMED, Haver, ILO, and national statistical offices.
Note: The precrisis period is an average of year-on-year changes over eight quarters from Q3 2006 to Q3 2008. The postcrisis period is an average of Q4 2008 and Q3 2009.

Table 2A.4 Estimates of Elasticity of Employment with Respect to Growth, by Period

	Fixed-effects regression		Pooled ordinary least-squares regression		Random effects regression	
	Precrisis	Postcrisis	Precrisis	Postcrisis	Precrisis	Postcrisis
GDP growth	0.160*	0.252***	0.0230	0.199***	0.0897	0.225***
Constant	0.726	0.282***	1.719***	0.205	1.190**	0.200
Observations	244	144	244	144	244	144
R^2	0.035	0.276	0.001	0.247		
Number of countries	37	37			37	37

Source: World Bank staff, based on data from CEIC/EMED, Haver, ILO, and national statistical offices.
Note: Robust standard errors *** = p < 0.01, ** = p < 0.05, * = p < 0.1.

Notes

1. These declines were particularly true of the East Asian crisis in the late 1990s (Betcherman and Islam 2001; Fallon and Lucas 2002), but it was also true for Mexico's "tequila" crisis, which resulted in a drop in real wages of 21 percent between 1994 and 1996, while aggregate employment increased slightly (McKenzie 2002).

2. The analysis of the present crisis in developing countries often focuses on changes in GDP (Blanchard, Faruqee, and Das 2010; Calderon and Didier 2009). Other analyses that focus on labor markets are sometimes based on simulations using precrisis data (Habib *et al.* 2010; ILO 2009b, 2010; IMF 2010).

3. The five economies from the Middle East and Africa are the Arab Republic of Egypt, Mauritius, Morocco, South Africa, and the West Bank and Gaza.

4. A detailed list of sources and comments on the data are available from the authors upon request.

5. Quarterly data are usually available. However, Indonesia and Peru have only half-yearly results.

6. A simple example makes this clear. China was far more affected by the financial crisis in 2009 than Morocco. But a simple comparison of postcrisis rates of growth would have given the false impression that Morocco suffered more. This is because Morocco's GDP grew only half as fast China's, even after the crisis, and employment growth in the two countries was nearly the same. However, in the precrisis period the Chinese economy had been growing more rapidly, so GDP growth slowed by 6 percentage points more in China than it did in Morocco. Employment growth also slowed by 3.5 percentage points more.

7. Using eight quarters of precrisis data rather than four may mitigate the impact of the food and fuel crisis of 2007–08.

8. Table 2A.3 in the annex shows that these conclusions hold when examining pre- and postcrisis average growth in a slightly larger sample of 28 countries that report quarterly, semi-annual, or annual data.

9. However, the slowdown underestimates the extent of the fall in hours, because it reflects only the eight countries that report hours quarterly.

10. In line with the findings of the authors, some high-income countries, like the United States, had sharp rises in productivity, something that the country had not seen in past crises.

11. In the sample of 15 countries that report sectoral employment, growth in agricultural employment increased by 1.5 percentage points, growth in service sector employment grew by 0.2 percentage points, and growth in industrial employment fell by 3.3 percentage points.

12. Estimates of past crises suggest a similar story: during the 1997 Asian crisis, some 30–40 percent of displaced urban workers are estimated to have moved to agricultural jobs (Manning 2000). Evidence indicates that worker reallocation and the quality of new jobs created are procyclical, rather than countercyclical (Bowlus 1993). The returns to labor in these small-scale sectors are low, but displaced workers often lack better options during downturns (Mead and Liedholm 1998).

13. High-productivity services include the following: transport and communications, real estate and financial services, and personal services. The remaining sectors—including public administration, real estate, education, hotel, retail trade, social work, and private household—are classified as low-productivity services.

14. Reduced earnings may lead to a rise in labor market participation. Some crises appear to have driven more women and children into the labor market, especially in rural areas (Ezemenari, Chaudhury, and Owens 2002; Manning 2000; McKenzie 2004). However, in others participation rates appeared unresponsive. And in some cases underemployment rates rose significantly due to decreased labor demand—for example, Mexico during the peso crisis (McKenzie 2004) and Thailand and the Republic of Korea in 1997–98 (Sarkar and Kumar 2002)—suggesting that workers had little ability to increase their labor supply.

15. Figure 2.7 shows an increasing divergence between earnings and employment effects as the size of the shock increases.

16. We use the International Monetary Fund's de facto exchange rate regime to classify countries by their currency regime, http://www.imf.org/external/np/mfd/er/2006/eng/0706.htm.

17. Countries are classified as high manufacturing, high export, difficult to fire, and high firing cost countries, based on whether the indicator exceeds the median across countries in the sample. The difficulty-of-firing index measures (1) whether redundancy is allowed as a basis for terminating workers and (2) the existence of redundancy regulations and requirements. The redundancy cost indicator measures the cost of advance notice requirements, severance payments, and penalties due when terminating a redundant worker, expressed in weeks of salary. Additional information on the redundancy indexes is available at http://www.doingbusiness.org/Methodology/Surveys/EmployingWorkers.aspx.

18. In only four cases do the pair-wise correlations between characteristics exceed 0.25. Latin American countries are most likely to be upper-middle-income and least likely to be lower-middle-income. Europe and Central Asian countries and middle-income countries tend to have larger manufacturing sectors, but Latin American countries are less likely to have large manufacturing sectors. Finally, countries with high redundancy costs are far more likely to be in East Asia or Latin America than Europe and are less likely to be middle-income countries. Somewhat surprisingly, the correlation between a high difficulty of redundancy and high redundancy cost is weak and negative.

19. These estimates come from regressions, based on quarterly data, of annual percentage change in employment growth on annual percentage change in employment, controlling for country fixed effects. Separate regressions were run for the eight quarters before the crisis and for the four during the crisis. Results are shown in annex table 2A.4. The increase in the employment elasticity from 0.16 to 0.25 is not statistically significant but leads to economically meaningful discrepancies between predicted and actual employment.

20. In other words, the average of the absolute value of the discrepancy across countries and quarters is 1.9.

21. Surprisingly little is known about how well passive and active labor market programs work during severe downturns, despite the large literature on the impact of these programs on labor market outcomes (Auer, Efendioglu, and Leschke 2005; Betcherman, Olivas, and Dar 2004; Fretwell, Benus, and O'Leary 1999).

22. For more detail, see Johansson *et al.* (2010) and chapter 5 of this volume.

23. Argentina and Mexico concentrate on employment generation, while Brazil had a large unemployment insurance scheme (Marquez 2000). Argentina and Costa Rica also had wage subsidy programs. Argentina's Jefes program promoted employment in Argentina's private sector to recover lost jobs in companies with sufficient capacity

(Marshall 2004). In Mexico, although there were not many legal reforms of labor market policies, changes took place largely through collective bargaining. Social security reform was implemented in 1995 but did not involve changes in employer-level contributions (Marshall 2004). In Korea, job creation and a wage claim guarantee were the thrust of the policy response to the East Asian crisis (Phang and Kim 2001). The country also had a job training program to encourage reemployment (Hur 2001). An employment insurance scheme that was active from 1995 was extended to cover all enterprises in 2008 (Phang and Kim 2001). Even in Thailand, the emphasis of labor market policies in response to the crisis was direct job creation rather than self-employment. Informal workers were not protected but were likely to benefit from "income support activities" such as tax reductions on value-added tax, price supports for rice, and the like (Betcherman and Islam 2001). In Indonesia, public works were mainly to provide emergency income and create social capital, with the ultimate goal of creating a total of 226 million person-days of employment. While Malaysia already had a public works program in place, it initiated wage subsidies in August 1998. In response to the 1997 crisis, the Philippines initiated an emergency loans program, while providing wage subsidies and training (Betcherman and Islam 2001).

References

Auer, P., U. Efendioglu, and J. Leschke. 2005. *Active Labour Market Policies around the World.* Geneva, Switzerland: International Labour Organization.

Betcherman, G., and R. Islam. 2001. *East Asian Labor Markets and the Economic Crisis: Impacts, Responses, and Lessons.* Washington, DC: World Bank and the International Labour Office.

Betcherman, G., K. Olivas, and A. Dar. 2004. "Impacts of Active Labor Market Programs: New Evidence from Evaluations with Particular Attention to Transition Countries." Social Protection Paper 0402, World Bank, Washington, DC.

Blanchard, O., M. Das, and H. Faruqee. 2010. "The Impact of the Crisis on Emerging Market Countries." Working paper, International Monetary Fund, Washington, DC.

Bowlus, A. J. 1993. "Job Match Quality over the Business Cycle." In *Panel Data and Labour Market Dynamics*, edited by. H. Bunzel, P. Jensen, and N. Westergård-Nielsen, 21–41. Amsterdam: Elsevier.

Calderon, C., and T. Didier. 2009. "Severity of the Crisis and Its Transmission Channels." Latin America Crisis Brief Series, World Bank, Washington, DC.

Ezemenari, K., N. Chaudhury, and J. Owens. 2002. "Gender and Risk in the Design of Social Protection Interventions." Social Protection Discussion Paper 0231, World Bank, Washington, DC.

Fallon, P., and R. Lucas. 2002. "The Impact of Financial Crises on Labour Markets, Household Incomes, and Poverty: A Review of Evidence." *World Bank Research Observer* 17 (1): 21–43.

Fretwell, D., J. Benus, and C. O'Leary. 1999. "Evaluating the Impact of Active Labor Programs: Results of Cross Country Studies in Europe and Central Asia." Social Protection Discussion Paper 9915, World Bank, Washington, DC.

Habib, B., A. Narayan, S. Olivieri, and C. Sanchez-Paramo. 2010. "Assessing Ex-ante the Poverty and Distributional Impact of the Global Crisis in a Developing Country: A Micro-Simulation Approach with Application to Bangladesh." Policy Research Working Paper 5238, World Bank, Washington, DC.

Hill, H., and T. Shiraishi. 2007. "Indonesia after the Asian Crisis." *Asian Economic Policy Review* 2 (1): 123–41.

Hur, J. J. 2001. "Economic Crisis, Income Support, and Employment Generating Programs: Korea's Experience." Paper prepared for the United Nations Economic and Social Commission for Asia and the Pacific seminar "Evaluation of Income/Employment Generating Programs to Alleviate Socio-Economic Impacts of the Economic Crisis," Bangkok, May 23–25.

ILO (International Labour Organization). 2009a. *Protecting People, Promoting Jobs: A Survey of Country Employment and Social Protection Policy Responses to the Global Economic Crisis.* Geneva, Switzerland: ILO.

———. 2009b. *Global Employment Trends.* Geneva, Switzerland: ILO.

———. 2010. *Global Employment Trends.* Geneva, Switzerland: ILO.

IMF (International Monetary Fund). 2010. *World Economic Outlook.* Washington, DC: IMF.

Johansson, S., P. Paci, A. Revenga, and B. Rijkers. 2010. "Avoiding the Eye of the Storm: How to Deal Effectively with Crises," Economic Premise 40, World Bank, Washington DC.

Manning, C. 2000. "Labour Market Adjustment to Indonesia's Economic Crisis: Context, Trends and Implications." *Bulletin of Indonesian Economic Studies* 36 (1): 105–36.

Marquez, G. 2000. "Labor Markets and Income Support: What Did We Learn from the Crises?" Working paper 425, Inter-American Development Bank, Washington, DC.

Marshall, A. 2004. "Labour Market Policies and Regulations in Argentina, Brazil and Mexico: Programmes and Impacts." Working paper, International Labour Organization, Geneva, Switzerland.

McKenzie, D. 2002. "How Do Households Cope with Aggregate Shocks? Evidence from the Mexican Peso Crisis." *World Development* 31 (7): 1179–99.

———. 2004. "Aggregate Shocks and Urban Labor Market Responses: Evidence from Argentina's Financial Crisis." *Economic Development and Cultural Change* 52 (4): 719–58.

Mead, D., and C. Liedholm. 1998. "The Dynamics of Micro and Small Enterprises in Developing Countries." *World Development* 26 (1): 61–74.

Phang, H., and D-H. Kim. 2001. "Policy Options for Income Support and Active Labor Market Programs: A Synthesis of the Korean Experience." Paper prepared for the conference "Labor Market Policies: Its Implications to East and Southeast Asia," Manila, March 1–2.

Reinhart, C., and K. Rogoff. 2009. "The Aftermath of Financial Crises." *American Economic Review* 99 (2): 466–72.

Sarkar, H., and R. Kumar. 2002. *Protecting Marginalized Groups during Economic Downturns: Lessons from the Asian Experience.* New York: United Nations.

CHAPTER 3

How Did the Great Recession Affect Different Types of Workers? Evidence from 17 Middle-Income Countries

Yoonyoung Cho and David Newhouse

About This Study

This chapter examines which groups of workers in developing countries were most affected by labor market retrenchment during the great recession. The analysis sets aside other important dimensions affecting income and household well-being, such as changes in transfers, remittances, and consumption patterns, and focuses only on changes in labor market outcomes. Labor market outcomes are a critical determinant of household well-being during an economic crisis, especially in developing countries where labor is usually the main source of income. Understanding how labor market outcomes changed for different groups during the most recent downturn is therefore an important first step in crafting appropriate and well-targeted policies to respond to future crises.

The vulnerability of different types of workers to economic downturns remains subject to debate, and targeted policies in response to the crisis were typically based on ad hoc or institutional considerations. Labor market assessments and anecdotal evidence typically emphasize the vulnerability of young, unskilled, or female workers. Although it is widely accepted that youth suffered disproportionate increases in unemployment during the latest downturn, less is

Social Protection and Labor Team, World Bank, Washington, DC, and the Institute for the Study of Labor (IZA), Bonn, Germany. The findings, interpretations, and conclusions expressed here are personal and should not be attributed to the World Bank, its management, its Executive Board of Directors, or any of its member countries. This chapter is part of a larger project monitoring the labor market impacts of the financial crisis, carried out jointly by the Social Protection and Poverty Reduction and Economic Management anchor units. We thank David Robalino and Arup Banerji for their support and insights, seminar participants at the 2010 World Bank/IZA conference for additional suggestions, and Ursula Casabonne, Christopher Handy, Andy Mason, Eliana Matulevich, Ririn Purnamasari, Martin Reichhuber, and Eduardo Zylberstajn for their assistance in acquiring the data.

known about youths' adjustment along other dimensions, and there is no similar consensus regarding the relative vulnerability of female and unskilled workers. Furthermore, conclusions are often inferred from past crises, data from advanced countries, or data from particular developing countries. Few studies have examined the impact of a recession on different types of workers across a wide range of developing countries. This is the first that compares disparities in labor market outcomes across several potentially vulnerable groups.

The authors examine changes in labor market trends during the crisis for different types of workers, defined by their gender, age, education, and urban or rural residence. They take data from 17 middle-income countries that field household surveys at least once a year. The outcomes measure aspects of individuals' main labor market activities and job quality. In particular, the indicators capture labor market activity, as measured by the ratios of employment, unemployment, and nonparticipation to total population and unemployment among the active labor force. Proxies for job quality include the share of the labor force employed in the agricultural sector and, significantly, wage employment. Changes in wages, hours worked, and earnings among workers are also presented when available. The authors focus on how labor market trends for each group changed during the crisis and how these changes affected their relative performance. For example, youth are almost always less likely to be employed than adults, but if the employment gap between youth and adults widened more rapidly after the crisis than before, the authors conclude that the crisis disproportionately affected youth employment.

Main Findings

The main findings are as follows: first, youth generally suffered the largest adverse impacts on employment, unemployment, and wage employment, particularly relative to older adults. Youth experienced greater percentage reductions in employment within each sector and status of employment but did not experience disproportionate reductions in earnings or wages.[1] This finding is consistent with the decisions of firms, when facing declining revenue and economic uncertainty, to let go or not hire relatively inexperienced young workers.

Second, a substantially larger share of men than women suffered adverse labor market impacts. Men's greater employment loss stems primarily from their higher employment rates and partly from their greater concentration in the hard-hit industrial sector. Gender differences in employment and wage employment, as a share of the population, were surprisingly high, comparable in size to the gap between youth and adults. Among active workers, however, increases in unemployment were only moderately greater for men than for women. Unlike youth, men and women experienced roughly equal percentage reductions in employment within each sector, suggesting that individual employers were neither more nor less likely to shed workers of either gender.

Third, relatively few women entered the labor force as a result of declines in household income. Labor force participation declined slightly more for men than for women. Furthermore, gender disparities in participation were roughly equal for less and more educated workers, suggesting that, unlike in past crises, the added-worker effect was not particularly strong for less educated workers.

Finally, less educated and urban workers fared unexpectedly well. Although data on urban and rural outcomes are limited, the available evidence shows few systematic differences. In general, differences between less and more educated workers are also smaller than those by age and gender, although very highly educated workers were better protected from employment loss.

These findings suggest two main policy lessons. First, policies targeting youth that increase labor demand and facilitate informed employment decisions can help mitigate employment loss during a financial shock. Potential policy options for youth range from active labor market programs, such as job search assistance and the dissemination of labor market information, to subminimum wages and wage subsidies. Second, since programs targeting unskilled or female workers may not benefit the majority of affected workers, expanding or maintaining these programs in response to a crisis should be done with appropriate caution and strong empirical support based on timely country data.

This chapter is organized as follows. The next section reviews existing studies that investigate explanations of why labor market adjustments vary for different types of workers. The following section describes the data and methodology used in the analysis. Then, the chapter presents basic descriptive statistics on the size of the shock and the nature of the adjustments in aggregate labor market indicators, while the next section presents and analyzes disparities in the outcomes of different groups of workers. The final section offers some conclusions.

What Explains Differential Impacts across Groups?

Studies of past crises and the current great recession typically refer to three potential explanations for the vulnerability of particular groups to economic downturns. They point to the differences in workers' initial exposure to the shock, firms' employment decisions during a downturn, and workers' labor market behavior in response to declines in household income.

Differences in Exposure to the Shock

Sectoral employment differences are particularly salient for women.[2] Worldwide, women are moderately more likely than men to work in the service sector rather than in the industrial sector (ILO 2010b).[3] Initially, the brunt of the current crisis was borne by workers in heavily affected sectors such as manufacturing, construction, and financial services. Partly as a result of occupational segregation, both current and past recessions in the United States have caused greater job losses for men, who are disproportionately represented in vulnerable sectors (Elsby, Hobijn, and Sahin 2010). In Canada and Finland, initial reductions in employment during the current recession were also greater in male-dominated sectors such as manufacturing, construction, and finance (ILO 2010b). However, several studies emphasize the potential vulnerability of women, based on women's increasing participation in the globalized workplace (Sabarwal, Sinha, and Buvinic 2011), or assert that women are overrepresented in export-oriented manufacturing sectors hit hardest by the crisis (Ghosh 2010; ILO 2010b; Walby 2009). In fact, for 16 of the 17 countries in this analysis, men were more concentrated in the industrial sector than women (see figure 3.1).

In contrast to gender, less evidence exists on occupational segregation by age, education, and region. In the 17 countries in the sample, differences in sectoral employment patterns between youth and adults tended to be small (figure 3.2). This finding is consistent with a study of several European and North American countries that found mixed evidence of a link between precrisis patterns of youth employment and subsequent increases in youth unemployment; a marked relationship for construction was apparent but none for manufacturing (Verick 2009). With respect to differences in education and region, less educated and rural workers are more likely to participate in agriculture, which may help insulate them from this and other downturns. No study, however, has emerged that describes in detail how sectoral employment patterns depend on education and region of residence.

The second main mechanism that can explain differential impacts is firms' perceptions of the productivity and likelihood of remaining in the labor force of different type of workers. This perception could affect young workers in particular, who are often correctly perceived to have acquired fewer important firm-specific skills and are therefore the easiest to forgo (World Bank 2009). There are also concerns that firms could shed female workers first because they may be more likely to leave due to child-rearing career disruptions or because they are less likely to be bread winners (Seguino 2009). Little evidence, however, either substantiates or refutes claims that prevailing social norms lead to substantially greater layoff rates for female workers in developing countries.[4]

Another possibility is that labor regulations affect firms' demand for certain groups during a crisis. Minimum wages, for example, may reduce firms' downward wage flexibility for young and unskilled workers, who tend to earn lower wages. This factor could lead to greater reductions in employment and increases in unemployment among these groups. Finally, existing employment protection legislation such as severance pay, restrictions on collective dismissals, and conditions for term contracts can also disproportionally affect new workers over incumbent ones. Indeed, the proportion of youth in temporary contracts, who would have limited benefit packages, is rising in the advanced economies (Scarpetta, Sonnet, and Manfredi 2010). However, little evidence exists on the impacts of labor market regulations on particular groups during a crisis. While one study suggested that employment protection legislation may have prevented a surge of layoffs among young workers in Europe (Verick 2009), evidence on how these regulations affect different types of workers during a crisis is limited.

The third main contributor to differential impacts on employment and unemployment is household labor supply decisions. The most commonly invoked pattern is the added-worker effect, where women compensate for decreases in household income by rejoining the workforce. Studies suggest that female labor force participation is countercyclical, especially for poorer, less educated workers in low-income economies (Sabarwal, Sinha, and Buvinic 2011; Signorelli,

Figure 3.1 Sectoral Employment Shares by Gender, 2007

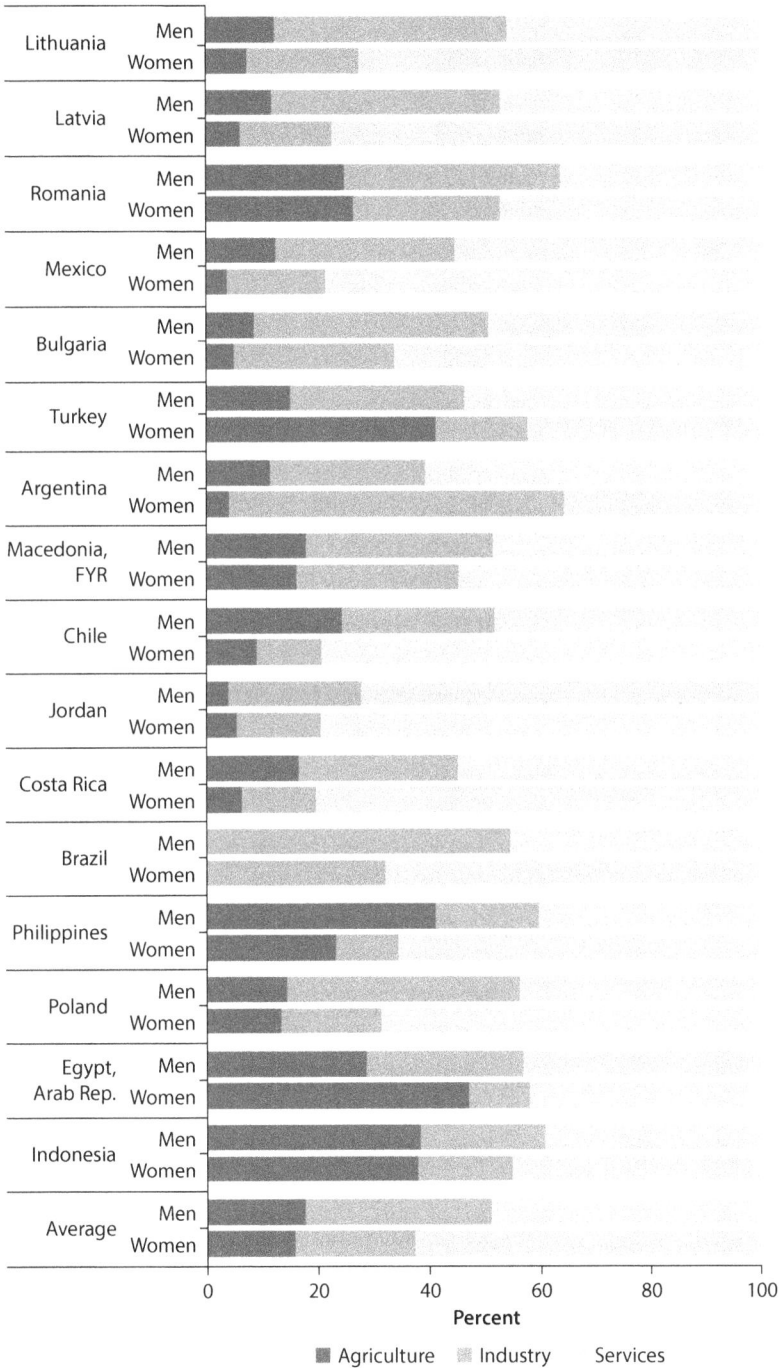

Source: World Bank staff.

Figure 3.2 Sectoral Employment Shares by Age Group, 2007

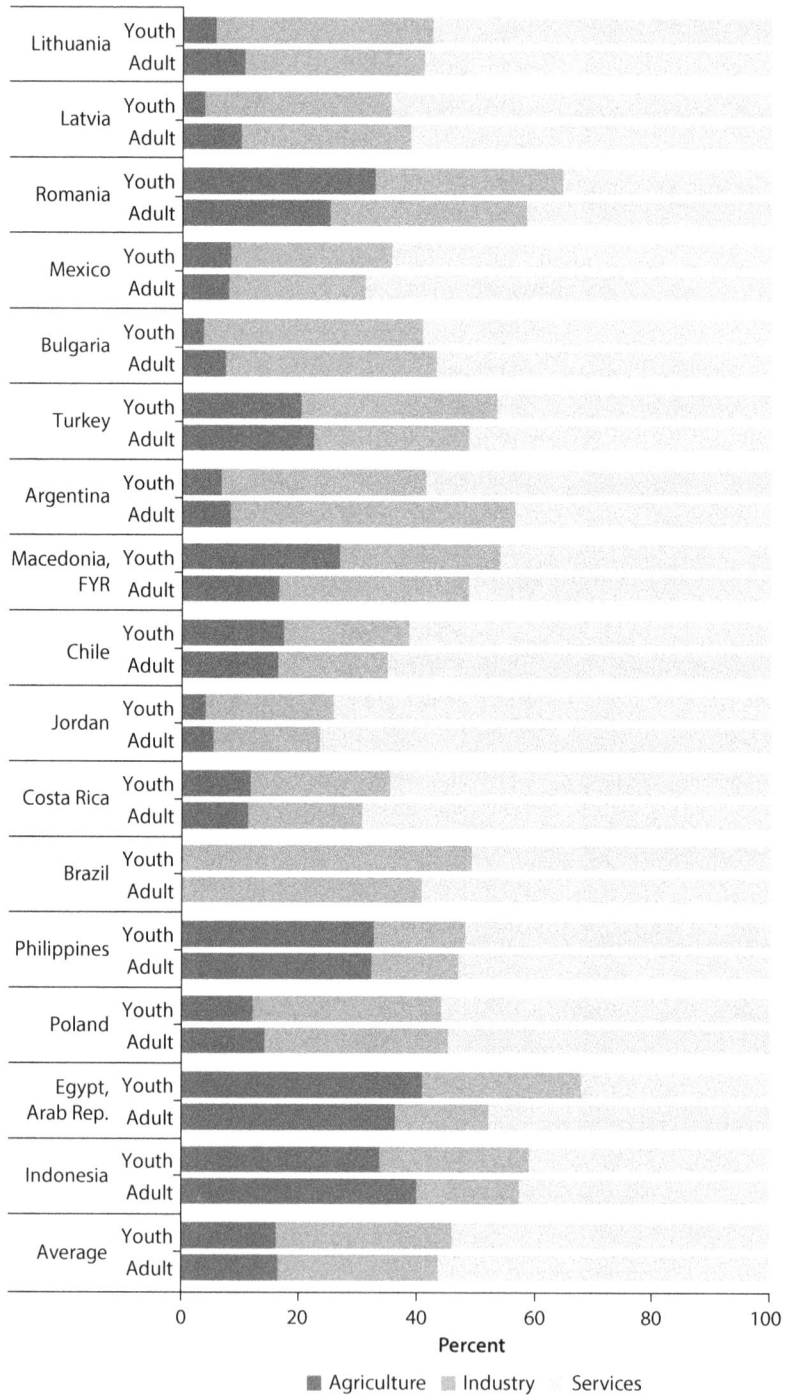

Source: World Bank staff.

Choudhry, and Marelli 2012). During Argentina's financial crisis, for example, job exits increased for both men and women, but women experienced smaller employment losses due to an increase in job entry (see McKenzie 2004). In theory, youth could face similar pressures; families facing job loss or a fall in real income may withdraw youth from school, or idle youth may be forced to work. Evidence from the Mexican "tequila" crisis, however, indicates that most of the burden of the adjustment in increased labor force participation fell on wives rather than on children (Skoufias and Parker 2006). In rural areas, employment declines may be smaller, if women and youth joining the workforce find it particularly convenient to enter family businesses, which are more common in rural areas.

Key Studies of Different Groups during Downturns

How have these three factors affected the vulnerability of different groups during downturns? While several studies have examined households' vulnerability to crises, fewer have documented their effects on individual workers.[5] Most studies of crisis impacts focus on Europe and the United States (Elsby, Hobijn, and Sahin 2010; Scarpetta, Sonnet, and Manfredi 2010; Verick 2009) or highlight the experience of particular groups or countries (Ha *et al.* 2010; ILO 2010a; 2010b; Leung, Stampini, and Vencatachellum 2009; Sabarwal, Sinha, and Buvinic 2011).

The best existing evidence on the effect of past crises on workers' income and employment exploits longitudinal data from urban Argentina and Indonesia. Men and women experienced equally destructive falls in real wages in both countries. Employment patterns were different, however. In Indonesia, female employment fell markedly less than male employment, as women entered self- and family employment to offset job losses in the formal sector (Smith *et al.* 2002). Employment in medium and large manufacturing firms also declined more for men than for women, as women were overrepresented in larger and exporting firms, which were more resilient to the crisis (Hallward-Driemeier, Rijkers, and Waxman 2010). During Argentina's 1995 crisis, however, employment fell equally for men and women (McKenzie 2004).

Most preliminary studies of the current crisis have emphasized large increases in youth unemployment.[6] Most of this evidence is from countries in the Organisation for Economic Co-operation and Development (OECD) and indicates that youth unemployment skyrocketed in 2009. In addition, according to some indications, youth were more likely to shift to informal sector employment in six Latin American countries (Ha *et al.* 2010). This finding appears to be more consistent with past experience in Indonesia than Argentina. In Indonesia, employment declined slightly more for youth than for adults, largely because older women rejoined the labor force in large numbers. Young workers, particularly women, experienced somewhat larger wage declines than their older counterparts. In Argentina, meanwhile, young and old workers experienced similar wage and employment changes.

Existing analyses of the labor market effects of the current crisis on men and women are mixed. Preliminary International Labour Organization (ILO) estimates suggest that men and women have experienced roughly equal increases in unemployment, from which the ILO authors conclude that the downturn has affected male and female outcomes more or less equally (ILO 2010b). Other studies, drawing mostly on data from Europe and the United States, suggest that men suffered larger unemployment increases than women due to their concentration in banking and finance and in export-oriented industry sectors (Barakat *et al.* 2010; Elsby, Hobijn, and Sahin 2010; World Bank 2010b).

The experience of educated workers depends on the nature of the crisis, although some studies suggest that the current crisis has led to larger employment reductions for less educated workers. In the United States, the current recession reduced employment more for less educated workers (Elsby, Hobijn, and Sahin 2010). Similarly, in South Africa, additional education substantially reduced the risk of employment loss (Leung, Stampini, and Vencatachellum 2009). Finally, preliminary evidence from China in chapter 6 suggests that the crisis disproportionately affected unskilled migrant workers.[7] This pattern is different from the Indonesian and Argentine crises, where employment and earnings losses were greatest for better educated women. In both countries, declines in incomes were similar for less educated and better educated men, but significantly larger for educated women than for less educated women. Educated women were also particularly likely to lose their job or to exit employment.

The authors know of no analysis of the effects of the current crisis on urban and rural workers. During the East Asian crisis, the initial impact was felt particularly hard in the urban manufacturing and construction sectors (see Fallon and Lucas 2002). In Indonesia, both overall and salaried employment declines were larger in urban areas, and urban women suffered substantially larger wage declines than rural women.

In summary, existing empirical evidence from past and present crises suggests four hypotheses:

- Men and women experienced roughly equal falls in income and employment, although in some settings, the added-worker effect may have led to smaller employment declines among women.
- Young workers experienced greater increases in unemployment and informal employment than adult workers.
- Impacts on less educated workers were more severe than those on better educated workers, but the results depended on the country context and the nature of the shock.
- The shock may have reduced employment and earnings more for urban workers than for rural workers.

Evidence on the vulnerability of different types of workers to this shock remains quite limited. Past crises in Argentina and Indonesia may not be relevant to the current great recession, since the macroeconomic causes and consequences are very different and most initial evidence on the current crisis has focused on unemployment and is often limited to OECD or European countries.[8]

Data and Methodology

This analysis draws on repeated cross-sectional household data from 17 countries (table 3.1).[9] These include five Latin American and Caribbean countries (Argentina, Brazil, Chile, Costa Rica, and Mexico), seven countries in the Europe and Central Asia region (Bulgaria, Latvia, Lithuania, the former Yugoslav Republic of Macedonia, Poland, Romania and Turkey), two countries in East Asia and Pacific (Indonesia and the Philippines), two countries in the Middle East and North Africa (the Arab Republic of Egypt and Jordan), and one country in Sub-Saharan Africa (South Africa). Countries differ in the indicators collected, in the span and frequency of data, and in the coverage of rural areas: countries in Europe and Central Asia do not report hours and earnings and include only the means of key variables by demographic cell rather than individual workers' outcomes; three countries in Latin America and the Caribbean (Argentina, Brazil, and Chile) cover only urban areas. In addition, earnings are often reported only for salaried workers (Chile and Indonesia). The size of the shock is measured as a change in gross domestic product (GDP) growth rates and varies widely, from 1.7 percentage points in Indonesia to 21.3 percentage points in Lithuania.[10] European and Latin American countries are overrepresented in the data, but these were the two regions most affected by the shock.

Data

The data cover a wide variety of job and worker characteristics. Labor market indicators include job status (for example, wage employment, self-employment, or family work), sector (agriculture, industry, or service), participation, employment, unemployment, hours, and earnings.[11] The activity indicators are the share of the population employed, unemployed, and out of the labor force, as well as the standard unemployment rate. Meanwhile, the analysis focuses on four key worker characteristics—gender, age, education, and region (urban or rural)—which are present in most surveys.[12]

Changes in the evolution of these indicators shed light on how different groups were affected by the downturn. For example, group differences in employment loss could reflect both firm employment decisions and household labor supply decisions. Firm employment decisions, however, are more consistent with increases in unemployment, while household labor supply decisions could be explained by smaller declines in participation. To measure job quality, the authors examine employment status (the share of the labor force working as the wage employed, self-employed, or family worker) and sector (the share of those working in the agricultural, industrial, and service sector), as well as average earnings, hours, and wage rates where available. The self-employed working poor constitute a significant portion of workers in many developing countries, earning small profits as smallholder farmers or street retailers. Unemployed or idle adults may be forced to take these low-paying jobs to cope with the downturn and mitigate losses to household income during recessions, which would appear as an increase in the share of the labor force in self-employed or agricultural work.

Table 3.1 Data Used for the Analysis

Region	Country	Slowdown in GDP growth (%)	Source	Period	Frequency	Note
Latin America and the Caribbean						
	Argentina	−6.9	Household survey (EPH)	Q4 2006–Q2 2009	Quarterly	Urban only; rotational panel; self-employed and family worker combined
	Brazil	−4.7	Monthly Survey of Employment (PME)	Jan 2006–Aug 2009	Monthly	Urban only; rotational panel; no agricultural sector
	Chile	−5.7	National Survey of Employment (ENE)	Q1 2006–Q3 2009	Quarterly	Urban only; no earnings data
	Costa Rica	−5.4	Multipurpose Household Survey (EHPM)	2006–09	Annually	
	Mexico	−11.2	National Survey of Occupation and Employment (ENOE)	Q1 2007–Q1 2009	Quarterly	Rotational panel
East Asia and Pacific						
	Indonesia	−1.7	Indonesian Labor Force Survey (Sakernas)	Feb 2006–Feb 2009	Biannually	Earnings only for wage and salary workers
	Philippines	−4.5	Philippines Labor Force Survey	2006–09	Biannually	Daily wage rate for earnings
Middle East and North Africa						
	Egypt, Arab Rep.	−2.5	Egyptian Labor Force Survey (ELFS)	2006–09	Quarterly	Rotational panel
	Jordan	−5.6	Jordanian Employment and Unemployment Survey (JEUS)	2006–09	Quarterly	

table continues next page

Table 3.1 Data Used for the Analysis *(continued)*

Region	Country	Slowdown in GDP growth (%)	Source	Period	Frequency	Note
Europe and Central Asia						
	Bulgaria	−10.7	Eurostat	2006–09	Annually	Cell means by gender, education, and age reported by Eurostat; urban/rural breakdown available only for selected outcomes; no earnings and hours information
	Latvia	−20.7				
	Lithuania	−21.3				
	Macedonia, FYR	−6.1				
	Poland	−4.2				
	Romania	−12.2				
	Turkey	−7.4				
Sub-Saharan Africa						
	South Africa	−8.2	Labor Force Survey and Quarterly Labor Force Survey	2006–09	Biannually	Earnings not available; urban/rural information not available; sector information not available

Sources: National Statistical Offices, Eurostat, World Bank staff.

Note: Slowdown in GDP growth rate due to the recession is calculated as GDP growth rate in 2009 compared with the average GDP growth rates in 2007–08. For detailed numbers, see annex table 3A.1.

Need for Careful Interpretation

Normative interpretation of the results requires care because indicators can have ambiguous welfare implications. Changes in economic activities, in particular, do not lend themselves to straightforward interpretation. Greater employment declines for men than for women, for example, do not imply that men were more disadvantaged during the crisis, if, for example, a large increase in female employment came about because of economic distress. Compared with changes in employment and unemployment, declines in wage employment, nonagricultural employment, and wage rates can more confidently be interpreted as a welfare loss, largely because wage and salaried jobs and nonagricultural jobs tend to be more productive and offer greater access to benefits.[13] Changes in earnings and wage rates can also be interpreted normatively with greater confidence than employment changes, since they directly affect workers' income. Unfortunately, the coverage and accuracy of earnings data raise important concerns. Fewer countries collect earnings data than employment data, and some countries collect earnings data only for salaried workers. The profits of self-employed workers are notoriously difficult to measure accurately, and inaccurate measures of inflation can also introduce additional noise into earnings data.[14]

Methodology

To better understand which groups were most affected, the analysis divides workers into 16 categories, based on their gender, age, education, and location of residence. Only workers between ages 15 and 64 are included in the sample. Age is broken into youth (ages 15–24) and adults (ages 25–64), and education is grouped into the least educated (those that completed elementary or junior high) and more educated (secondary level and above). Average indicators are taken for each category, country, and survey, weighted according to their sample weights. With the exception of education groupings in the European countries, the dataset is defined consistently for all 17 countries.[15]

Labor market activity and type of job indicator are considered both as a ratio of the population and as a ratio of the labor force. Indicators of interest include the labor market activities throughout the population (employment, unemployment, and nonparticipation ratios), the share of the labor force in each sector, and status (such as self-employed or wage employed), and earnings and hours information for workers (earnings, wages, and hours). First, the trends in employment, unemployment, and nonparticipation rates as a share of the population are considered. Population trends may be relevant for policies, such as cash transfers provided directly to households that are delivered outside the labor market. To better understand changes among potential workers and to inform the design of labor market programs, the analysis then examines labor market outcomes for the active labor force, with an emphasis on shifts in sectors, employment status, and unemployment. Finally, in countries where the data are available, the authors report changes in average earnings, wages, and hours of work.

The focus is on how disruptions in labor market trends during the crisis varied for different groups of workers. A simple way of looking at that impact is to compare pre- and postcrisis outcomes for each group. However, this comparison may be misleading if baseline trends and initial labor market performance vary across groups. Even before the crisis, socioeconomic changes in each country were affecting different groups in different ways. For example, in many countries, employment rates were growing faster for women than for men, because of trends in educational achievement and cultural norms that encourage greater female employment. To take this factor into account, the analysis examines how each group's trend changed, relative to its precrisis trend. In other words, the key indicator is the rate at which changes in each indicator slowed down or sped up, compared across groups.

The method used to calculate changes in trends is illustrated using data from Mexico. Section A of table 3.2 gives the employment ratios for low-educated male youth in urban areas for each quarter between 2007 and 2009. The authors then calculate the change in the employment ratio relative to the same quarter in the previous year. The employment ratio changed from 57.3 percent in the first quarter of 2007 to 57.8 percent in the same quarter in 2008, yielding a slight increase of 0.5 percentage points. For each cell, the authors then take the average of these changes across all precrisis periods (up until the fourth quarter of 2008) and all postcrisis periods (from the first quarter of 2009 onward). In this cell, the average year-on-year change in the employment rate after the crisis is −3.6 percentage points, and the average precrisis trend is −0.3 percentage points, indicating that, for this cell, growth in the employment ratio slowed by 3.3 percentage points. Taking a weighted average over all 16 cells, with weights equal to the cell population in this case, gives the overall change in the employment ratio. Among all Mexican workers, the employment ratio slowed by 1.7 percentage points (section B of table 3.2). The difference between the precrisis and the postcrisis averages of year-on-year changes in the indicator is used to measure workers' labor market adjustment throughout this chapter.

Group Comparison

The analysis examines differences in labor market adjustment by group, controlling for selected observable characteristics. In particular, the authors regress the change in the trend, described above, for each cell in each country on dummy variables for the four characteristics, separately for each outcome and country.[16] There are therefore 16 observations in each regression. Using regression coefficients rather than simple tabulations isolates changes in the returns to a single characteristic, while holding the other three constant; for example, a rise in the coefficient on youth unemployment cannot be attributed to higher education levels among youth. That is, the authors estimate the following equation (3.1) (see the annex for more details on the specification):

$$\tilde{Y}_i = \gamma_0 + \gamma_1 Men_i + \gamma_2 Young_i + \gamma_3 LowEdu_i + \gamma_4 Urban_i + \tilde{v}_i, \qquad (3.1)$$

Table 3.2 Changes in Employment Trends from Pre- to Postcrisis in Mexico

Year/quarter	Employment ratio (%)				Year-on-year change (percentage points)				Average precrisis trend (percentage points) 2007–08	Average postcrisis trend (percentage points) 2009	Difference between post- and precrisis (percentage points)
	Q1	Q2	Q3	Q4	Q1	Q2	Q3	Q4			
A. One cell: Low-educated male youth in urban areas											
2007	57.3	57.4	58.2	60.8	n.a.	n.a.	n.a.	n.a.	n.a.	n.a.	n.a.
2008	57.8	58.3	57.8	57.0	0.5	0.9	−0.4	−2.2	−0.3	n.a.	n.a.
2009	54.2	53.9	54.1	—	−3.6	−4.4	−2.7	n.a.	n.a.	−3.6	−3.3
B. All: Weighted average of 16 cells											
2007	61.3	61.7	61.6	63.0	n.a.	n.a.	n.a.	n.a.	n.a.	n.a.	n.a.
2008	61.8	62.4	62.0	61.4	0.5	0.7	0.4	−1.6	0.0	n.a.	n.a.
2009	60.2	60.4	60.6	—	−1.6	−2.0	−1.4	—	n.a.	−1.7	−1.7

Source: World Bank staff, based on ENOE survey.

Note: — = not available; n.a. = not applicable.

where $\tilde{Y}_i$ is the difference in the trend for each cell i in each country, and *Men, Young, LowEduc,* and *Urban* represent dummy variables for each group.

The coefficients from the linear regressions capture the difference between groups. The sign and magnitude of each coefficient indicate each group's relative vulnerability to the crisis compared to its counterparts. For example, an estimated value of -1 for γ_1 from the employment ratio regression indicates that, conditional on the other characteristics, the share of men employed slowed one percentage point more than the share of women employed. Meanwhile, the relative magnitudes of the coefficients indicate which groups were most exposed to the shock. For example, a value of γ_2 that is greater in absolute value than γ_3 would indicate that age disparities were larger than education disparities in the employment adjustment.

Decompositions

Two Shapley decompositions are employed to better highlight the factors that account for group disparities in adjustments.[17] A natural first step is to decompose the changes in the employment ratio into portions explained by changes in the employment rate and labor force participation.[18] In other words, a decline in the share of the population working can be attributed either to increased unemployment or to reduced labor force participation. Formally, using $emp_t = erate_t * lfp_t$ where *emp, erate,* and *lfp* denote the employment ratio, employment rate, and labor force participation, respectively, the change in employment ratio can be decomposed as shown in equation (3.2),

$$\Delta emp_t = \underbrace{emp_{t-1} - emp_t}_{1} = \underbrace{\Delta erato_t \overline{lfp}}_{2} + \overline{erate}\Delta lfp_t, \qquad (3.2)$$

where $\overline{lfp}$ and $\overline{erate}$ denote the average value over t and $t + 1$.[19] The first term represents the portion explained by the change in the employment rate, while the second part represents the portion explained by the change in labor force participation over time. This decomposition is calculated for each gender, age, and education group.

The second and more novel decomposition builds on the discussion in the previous section to better determine which mechanisms explain group differences in crisis response. The authors decompose group disparities in the slowdown in employment ratios into three components: differences in the initial level of employment, differences in the sectoral distribution of employment, and differences in percentage changes in employment within the three sectors.[20] The first of these—the portion of employment change due to initial differences in employment levels—indicates the extent to which absolute disparities would result from an equal percentage reduction in each group's probability of working. The second component—the portion of the group disparity due to different distributions across sectors—gives an indication of the importance of occupational segregation in explaining group disparities. Finally, the third component—the percentage change in employment within firms—reflects both firms' decisions and workers' supply-side decisions. For example, a small third component for gender might suggest that firms reduce employment proportionally for men and women. However, since men typically comprise a disproportionate share of the workforce, proportional reductions for men and women will lead to a greater absolute reduction in employment rates for men, which will be captured by the first component. The decomposition, while far from definitive, provides a useful summary of the relative importance of these three factors in explaining, in an accounting sense, differential adjustments among groups.

So that this decomposition can be carried out, the difference in the trend of each indicator for a particular group is rewritten as follows:

$$\Delta emp_t = emp_{t-1} - emp_t = emp_t r_t = emp_t \sum_i s_{it} r_{it}, \qquad (3.3)$$

where r_{it} is the percentage employment growth rate within sector i, emp_t is an initial employment level, and s_{it} is the share of the group in sector i (see the annex for a detailed explanation of the decomposition). Three factors may explain the difference between men and women in the change of employment: the initial level of employment ratio (emp_t), the sectoral distribution (s_{it}), and the employment change within each sector (r_{it}). Applying the decomposition to gender differences in employment from equation (3.3) leads to equation (3.4):[21]

$$\Delta emp_t = \underbrace{(emp_m - emp_f) \sum_i s_{im} r_{im}}_{1} + \underbrace{emp_f \sum_i (s_{im} - s_{if}) r_{im}}_{2} + \underbrace{emp_f \sum_i s_{if} (r_{im} - r_{if})}_{3}.$$

$$(3.4)$$

The first part is the portion due to gender differences in the initial employment level, the second part is the portion due to occupational segregation, and the third part is the portion due to the differential growth rate within the sector. Equation (3.4) is one of six potential ways to carry out the decomposition, and the authors use the average across all six. Of course, the same decomposition methodology can be applied to examine age, education, and locational differences. The authors also calculate a variant that examines the role of segregation among wage or self-employed workers in accounting for group disparities.

Aggregate Labor Market Adjustments

The analysis first presents basic results on the extent of the shock and the overall nature of the labor market adjustment in the 17 countries. To illustrate how a country's exposure to the crisis affected the labor market adjustments of different groups, figures 3.3 and 3.4 plot the magnitude of the adjustment, on the vertical axis, against the size of the slowdown in GDP. These two figures show the labor market adjustments for all individuals (figure 3.3), labor force participants (figures 3.3 and 3.4), and workers (figure 3.4), sorting by the magnitude of the shock.[22] The horizontal axis in each figure indicates the severity of the crisis, as shown in table 3.1. The vertical axis is defined as the slowdown in each indicator as explained in the previous section.[23]

Figure 3.3 Aggregate Adjustment among Labor Force in Unemployment Rate and Employment Sector, 2006–09

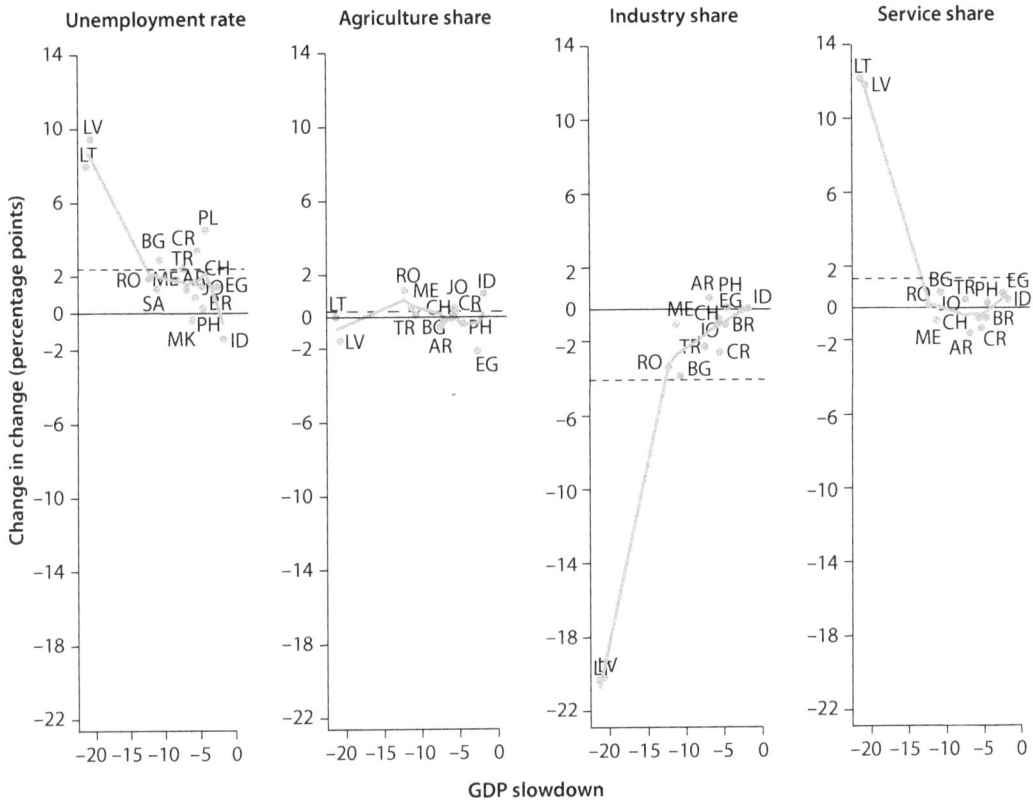

Source: World Bank staff.

Note: The horizontal axis represents the slowdown in real GDP growth rate as defined in table 3A.1. The vertical axis is analogously defined as slowdown in the indicator. Two-letter codes represent countries: AR = Argentina; BG = Bulgaria; BR = Brazil; CH = Chile; CR = Costa Rica; EG = Arab Republic of Egypt; ID = Indonesia; JO = Jordan; LT = Lithuania; LV = Latvia; ME = Mexico; MK = former Yugoslav Republic of Macedonia; PH = Philippines; PL = Poland; RO = Romania; SA = South Africa; TR = Turkey.

Variations in the Effects of the Crisis across Countries

While each country suffered declines in economic growth, the severity of the shock varied substantially from one country to the next. Countries in Asia tended to be less affected by the crisis, while countries in Europe suffered the largest declines in growth. Latvia and Lithuania, in particular, suffered tremendous economic disruptions, as growth rates in these countries slowed by roughly 20 percentage points in 2009, compared to the average growth rates in the two prior years. Bulgaria, Mexico, Romania, and Turkey also suffered severe slowdowns in growth because of a decline in exports to Western Europe and the United States. In contrast, a larger group of seven countries—including the non-Mexican Latin American countries, Jordan, the Philippines, Poland, and South Africa—were only moderately affected. Finally, Egypt and Indonesia escaped the brunt of the crisis, as growth fell only around 2 percentage points.

Figure 3.4 Aggregate Adjustments among Workers in Earnings, Hours, and Wage Rates, 2006–09

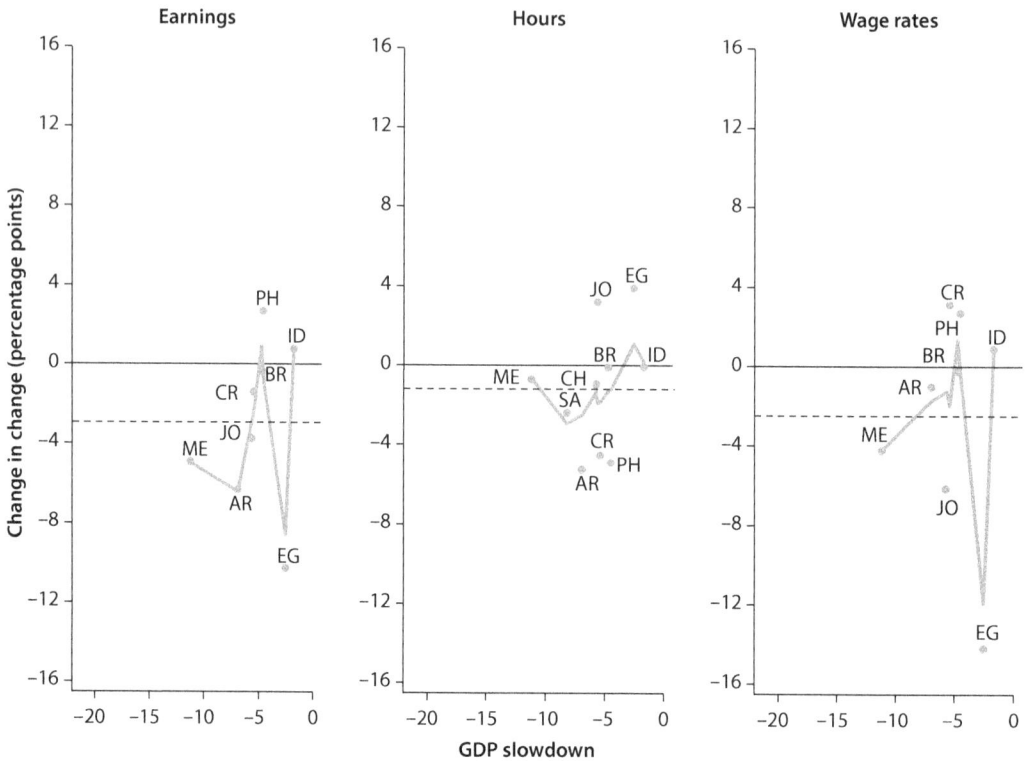

Source: World Bank staff.
Note: The horizontal axis represents the slowdown in real GDP growth rate as defined in table 3.1. The vertical axis is analogously defined as slowdown in the indicator. Two-letter codes represent countries (see note for figure 3.3).

Differences in Labor Market Institutions

The size of the adjustment in employment and unemployment may be related to countries' labor market institutions. Employment losses varied considerably across countries. Bulgaria, Costa Rica, and Poland, for example, experienced unexpectedly large employment losses, given their moderate decline in growth, while Romania and Turkey experienced larger slowdowns in growth but substantially smaller employment reductions (figure 3.3).[24] These patterns suggest that countries with more rigid labor markets fared somewhat better in maintaining employment during the crisis. For example, growth in employment and wage employment fell relatively little in Romania and Turkey, even though Turkey is probably among the most regulated labor markets in the OECD, with a low Doing Business ranking in employing workers and 40 percent of Romanian workers belong to a union.[25] Bulgaria and Costa Rica, where employment fell more, have relatively free labor markets among countries analyzed here: both countries score relatively high on the Fraser index of labor market freedom, and only 13 percent of Costa Rican workers belong to a union (Freeman 2009). If labor markets with high firing costs responded to the crisis by reducing hours rather than by shedding employment, employment loss may have been smaller in more rigid countries.[26] This finding is line with evidence presented in chapter 2 that employment during the crisis fell slightly less in countries with higher firing costs and other studies that also cast doubt on the link between existing measures of institutions and worse employment outcomes (Baker *et al.* 2004; Freeman 2005).

The Effects of Declines in Employment on Unemployment and Participation

Employment declines translated into increased unemployment, as workers continued to search for jobs, more than reducing participation (figure 3.3).[27] However, the extent of this adjustment also varied across countries. Bulgaria and Poland, for example, experienced greater employment losses than would be expected based on the severity of the shock. While Bulgaria's employment losses were largely explained by an increase in nonparticipation, large employment losses in Poland were entirely linked to unemployment increases. These patterns may be related to their labor market policy such as unemployment insurance. Poland's unemployment insurance has relatively high coverage and impacts compared to other Eastern European countries, which may reduce the incentive of unemployed workers to leave the labor market (Vodopivec 2009).

Substantial declines in the share of wage employment among the labor force led to greater increases in unemployment than in self-employment (figure 3.4). Declines in the share of wage employment and corresponding increases in unemployment were greater for more severely affected countries. Latvia and Lithuania experienced large declines in wage employment and slight shifts to self-employment. In other countries, declines in wage employment did not lead to an increase in self-employment. This finding suggests that self-employment did not serve as an informal safety net by absorbing displaced workers, except to a limited extent in the most severely affected countries.[28]

Declines in industrial sector employment, in most cases, were not absorbed by the service or the agricultural sector. The service sector did expand in Latvia and Lithuania, absorbing 60 percent of the decline in industrial employment (the remainder was absorbed by increases in unemployment). Excluding Latvia and Lithuania, agriculture and the service sector saw little change, and large decreases in industry tended to be reflected in increased in unemployment.

Earnings slowed because of declines in both hours and wage growth, but there was no discernible relationship between these indicators and the severity of the GDP shock. Figure 3.4 shows changes for earnings, hours, and wage rates, which unfortunately are limited to eight countries. In some countries, such as Argentina and Costa Rica, earnings decreases were driven by declines in hours, while in other countries such as Egypt, Jordan, and Mexico, earnings declines were due mainly to decreased wage rates. Wage rate declines do not appear to be systematically related to shifts to less productive self-employment and agricultural employment. Self-employment rates changed little in Jordan, despite a large decline in wage rates. Egypt, however, experienced even larger declines in wage rates despite falling into self-employment and agricultural employment, illustrating that the extent to which declines in labor demand translate into wage declines varies from country to country.

Overall, the aggregate indicators suggest that retrenchment reduced employment, particularly in the industrial sector, and increased unemployment. Little evidence suggests that the agricultural sector or self-employed jobs increased dramatically during the crisis or that the crisis led workers to withdraw from the labor force.

Group Differences in Labor Market Adjustments

This section examines how adjustments varied for different types of workers: that is, how trends in indicators changed, conditional on gender (men relative to women), age (young relative to older workers), education (less educated relative to more educated workers), and location (urban relative to rural workers). A key distinction is whether labor market changes are measured relative to the population, as in the employment-to-population ratio, or relative to the active labor force. The former shows which groups were most affected by the shock overall, while the latter measures how the crisis affected different types of active workers. Finally, the section investigates how initial differences in employment rates, systematic differences in sector of work, and percentage employment reductions within sectors contributed to group differences in employment rates.

Group Differences in the Population

The differences between different groups' employment, wage employment, and unemployment outcomes are striking. Figures 3.5, 3.6, and 3.7 show how these three indicators varied for different groups. As in the previous section, the vertical axis shows the percentage point adjustment in a particular labor market indicator, and the horizontal axis shows the slowdown in GDP growth. Each point represents a coefficient from a regression for a particular country, in which the dependent variable is the difference in the rate in which the indicator slowed or accelerated during the crisis, as indicated in equation (3.1). The independent variables are dummy variables for men, youth, less educated, and urban residence.[29] For convenience, throughout this section these are referred to as changes for particular groups as if they were simple unconditional trends, even though they are in fact conditional regression coefficients.[30] Also for simplicity, the terms *slowdown, fall, acceleration, rise, change,* and *adjustment* all refer to the change in the rate of year-on-year change.[31]

Effects on Men and Youth

As a proportion of the population, employment and wage employment slowed most for men and youth. The two left panels of figure 3.5 show that both men and youth experienced larger falls in employment, as a share of population, in 13 of the 17 countries. This finding is reflected in the average disparity across the 17 countries, which is about 1 percentage point for youth and slightly greater for men. The labor market impacts on men and youth are even more apparent when

Figure 3.5 Group Comparisons: Employment-to-Population Ratio, 2006–09

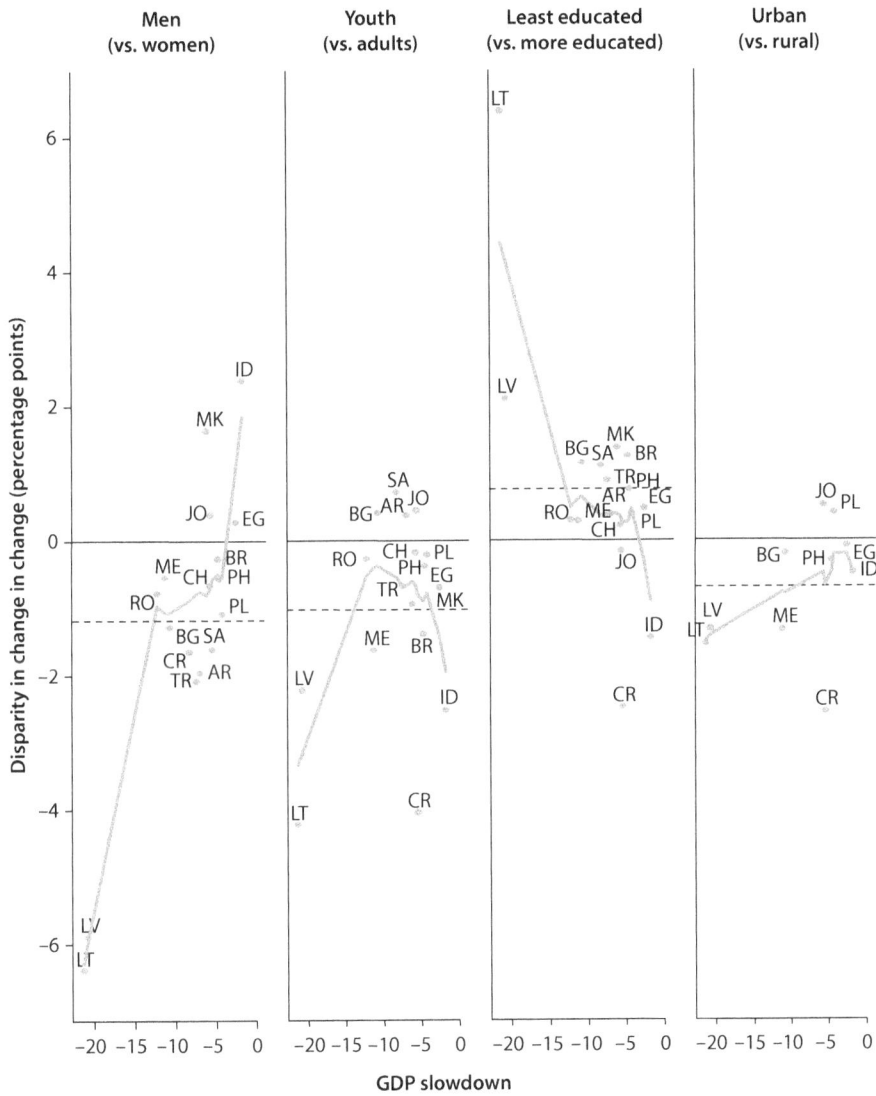

Source: World Bank staff.
Note: The dotted line indicates mean value and the solid line indicates running line smooth. The figure shows the disparity between groups, controlling for other characteristics, in the slowdown in the employment-to-population ratio. The plotted number is the coefficient from regression for each country (equation 3.1). The horizontal axis represents the slowdown in real GDP growth rate as defined in table 3A.1. Two-letter codes represent countries (see note for figure 3.3).

examining wage employment (figure 3.6). A greater percentage of women than men lost wage jobs in only two countries—Egypt and Jordan—and wage employment fell noticeably more for adults than for youth only in South Africa. Age disparities are even greater when comparing youth with older adults aged 45–65 (see figure 3.8), as firms retained their most experienced workers.

Figure 3.6 Group Comparisons: Wage Employee–to-Population Ratio, 2006–09

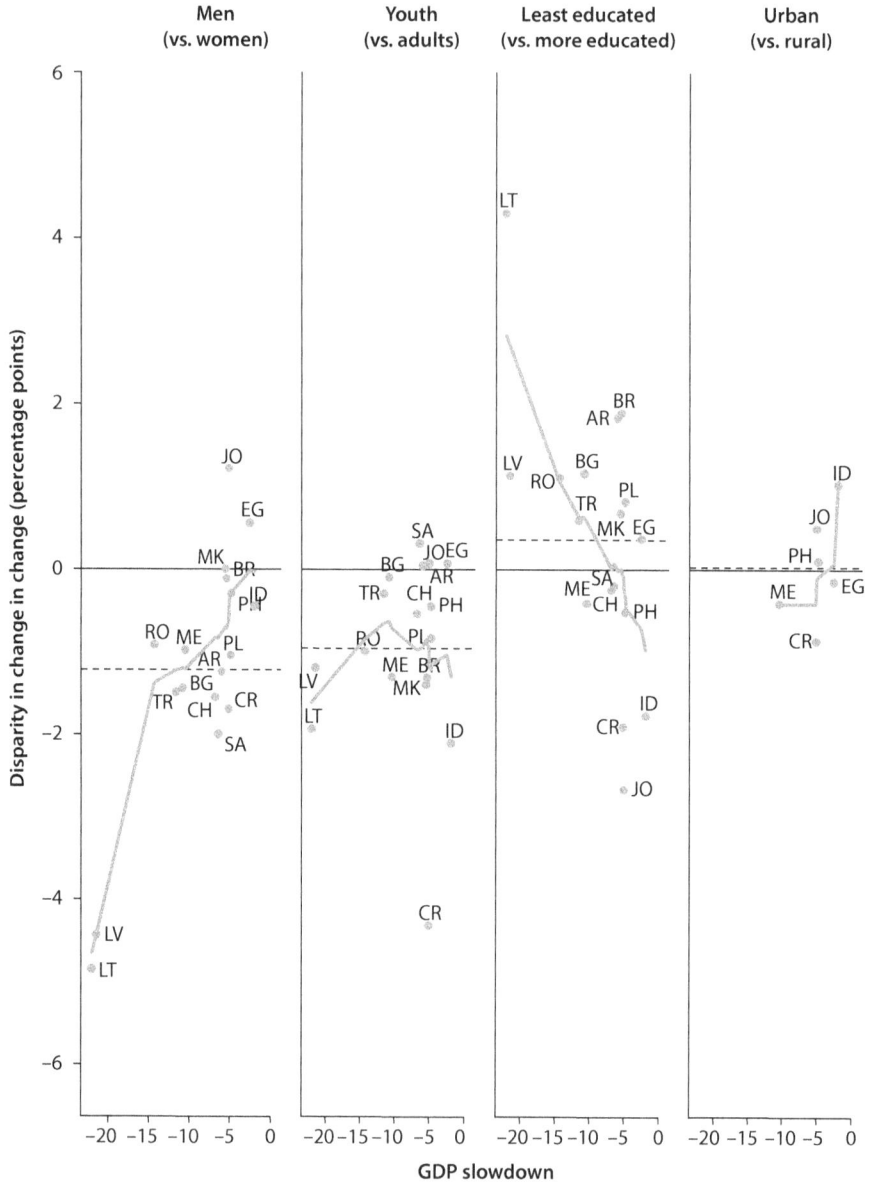

Source: World Bank staff.
Note: The dotted line indicates mean value and the solid line indicates running line smooth. The figure shows the disparity between groups, controlling for other characteristics, in the slowdown in the employment to population ratio. The plotted number is the coefficient from regression for each country (equation 3.1) in the annex. The horizontal axis represents the slowdown in real GDP growth rate as defined in table 3.1. Two letter codes represent countries.

Figure 3.7 Group Comparisons: Nonparticipation-to-Population Ratio, 2006–09

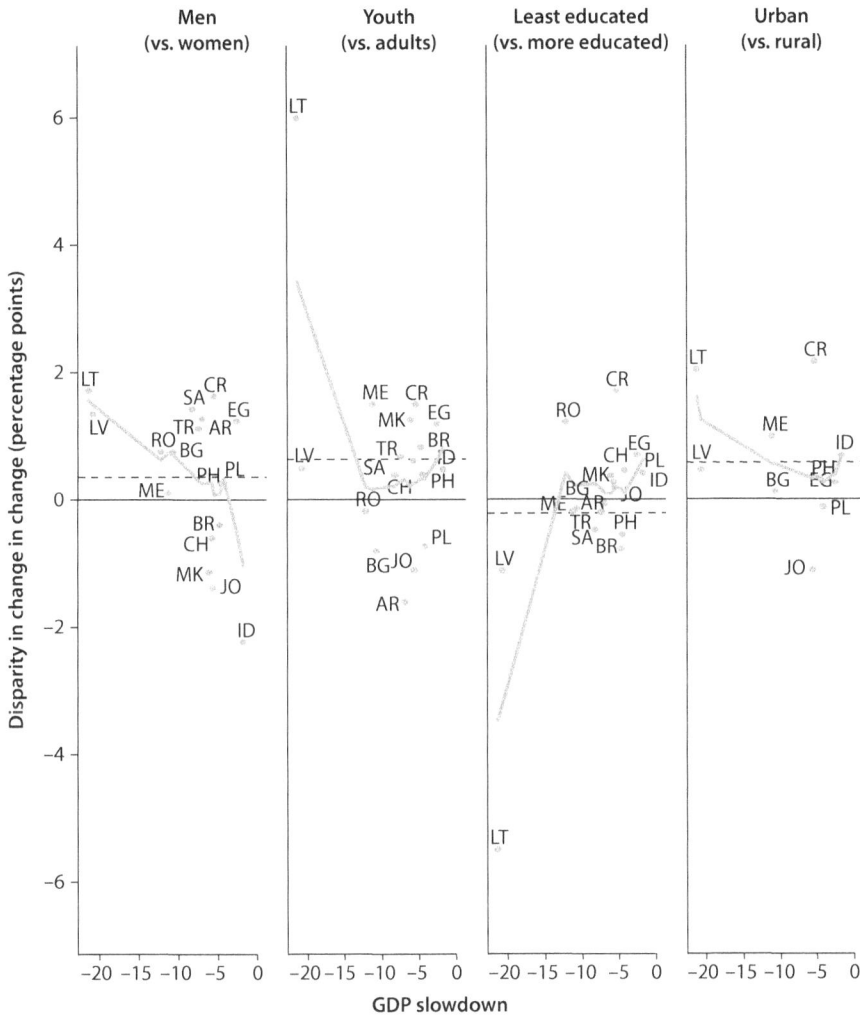

Source: World Bank staff.

Note: The dotted line indicates mean value and the solid line indicates running line smooth. The figure shows the disparity between groups, controlling for other characteristics, in the slowdown in the employment to population ratio. The plotted number is the coefficient from regression for each country (equation 3A.1) in the annex. The horizontal axis represents the slowdown in real GDP growth rate as defined in table 3.1. Two letter codes represent countries.

Effects on More Educated Workers and on Urban Residents

Better educated and urban residents, to a lesser extent, also suffered disproportionate employment losses. The third panel of figure 3.5 tells a similar story for better educated workers, where employment slowed more than it did for less educated workers in 14 of 17 countries. Breaking education into three groups, as shown in figure 3.8, shows a slightly more nuanced story. The best educated and least educated workers experienced the smallest employment losses, while it was the workers in the middle of the education distribution, typically with a junior high education, that experienced the greatest losses in employment.[32] Finally,

Figure 3.8 Age and Gender Comparisons with Three Groups: Employment Ratio, 2006–09

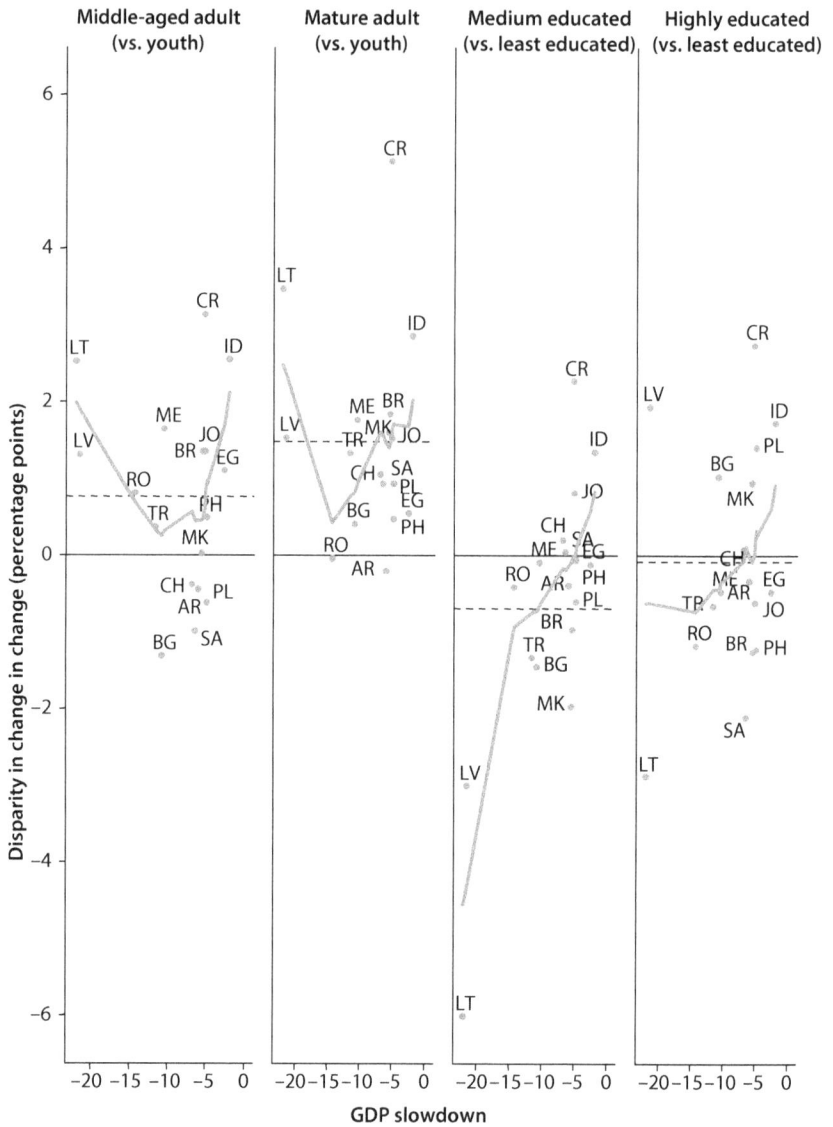

Source: World Bank staff.
Note: The dotted line indicates mean value and the solid line indicates running line smooth. The figure shows the disparity between groups, controlling for other characteristics, in the slowdown in the employment to population ratio. The plotted number is the coefficient from regression for each country (equation 3A.1) in the annex. The horizontal axis represents the slowdown in real GDP growth rate as defined in table 3.1. Two letter codes represent countries.

the far right panel of figure 3.7 shows that in 8 of 10 countries, employment slowed more in urban areas than in rural areas, although differences were small in several cases.[33]

Disparities in employment adjustments between groups were sizable, in comparison with overall employment declines. This finding holds true even in Latvia and Lithuania, where overall employment rates fell by a hefty 5–9 percentage points (figure 3.3). In these two countries, employment, for example, fell by 6 percentage points more for men, 2–4 percentage points more for youth, and 2–6 percentage points more for the least educated. In Costa Rica, where overall employment fell by about 2.5 percentage points, the 4 percentage point disparity faced by young workers is very large in comparison.

Added-worker effects for women appear to be mild. Men, youth, and urban workers experienced slightly larger increases in nonparticipation (figure 3.7). For youth, this finding suggests that increased school attendance and discouragement slightly outweighed any added-worker effect. Women, however, were slightly less likely to drop out of the labor force than men, reflecting small added-worker effects. Group differences in participation, however, tend to be small, as employment declines for males and youth were reflected mostly in increased unemployment rather than in nonparticipation.

Even among less educated women, no evidence suggests a strong added-worker effect. Experiences from past crises indicate that better educated women tend to exit and less educated women tend to enter the labor market during crises (Sabarwal, Sinha, and Buvinic 2011). Figure 3A.1 shows gender disparities in employment, wage employment, and nonparticipation for less educated and better educated women. For each of the three indicators, the differences between less and better educated women are few, suggesting that, in contrast to previous crises, in this sample of middle- and upper-middle-income countries, the added-worker effects even among less educated women were weak.[34]

Group Differences among Active Workers

The previous section focused on labor market effects on the entire population, whether people were in the labor force or not. This section turns to different impacts across different types of active workers, which is more relevant for policies, such as wage subsidies, that benefit workers.

Unemployment

Overall, youth experienced by far the largest rise in unemployment. Unemployment rates also increased more for men and urban workers, but the differences were much smaller than those by age. The second panel of figure 3.8 shows large disparities in the increase of the youth unemployment rate relative to the adult rate, averaging about 3 percentage points. A disproportionate unemployment increase for youth occurred in all countries except in Egypt. There is no clear relationship between the size of the shock and the increase in youth unemployment, however. Disparities were largest in Latvia and Lithuania, but they were also large in Costa Rica, Indonesia, and Poland—countries that escaped the full brunt of the crisis. Gender disparities in unemployment rates were not as large, with male increases typically a half to 1 percentage point greater. Urban workers also experienced larger rises in unemployment, in 7 of the 10 countries for which data are available, but the disparity tended to be small.

Wage Employment

A large percentage of active youth also shifted out of wage employment (figure 3.9). In 15 of 17 countries, wage employment rates, as a proportion of the active labor force, declined more for youth than for adults. Differences between youth and adults were particularly large, as increases exceeded 3 percentage points in seven countries. Although declines were larger for men than women in 13 countries, gender differences tended to be small. The average gender and education disparities are largely driven by Latvia and Lithuania, and education

Figure 3.9 Group Comparisons: Share of Wage Employment among Labor Force, 2006–09

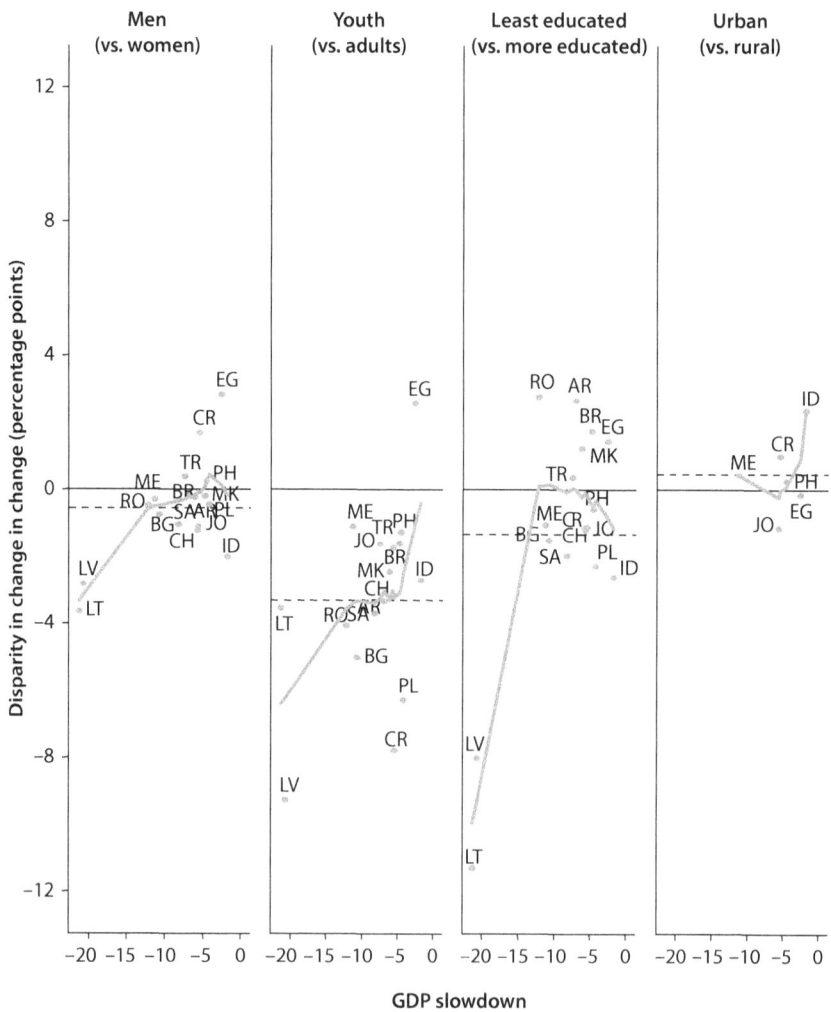

Source: World Bank staff.
Note: The dotted line indicates mean value and the solid line indicates running line smooth. The figure shows the disparity between groups, controlling for other characteristics, in the slowdown in the employment to population ratio. The plotted number is the coefficient from regression for each country (equation 3A.3 in the annex. The horizontal axis represents the slowdown in real GDP growth rate as defined in table 3.1. Two letter codes represent countries (see note for figure 3.3).

disparities in other countries are less clear. Similarly, differences in wage employ-ment between urban and rural residents are not systematic.

Unemployment

Men and, to a lesser extent, less educated workers also experienced larger increases in unemployment and declines in wage employment. Unemployment rose at least as much for men as for women in 16 of the 17 countries, although differences tended to be small, particularly compared to the age disparities. Education dispari-ties are more muddled, as in several countries unemployment and wage employ-ment outcomes were worse for better educated workers. On average, however, in large part because of significant disparities in Latvia and Lithuania, unemploy-ment increases were higher for less educated workers. While group disparities in Latvia and Lithuania are larger than others in most indicators, the education gap in wage employment declines was particularly wide, reflecting the extreme dis-tress experienced by less educated workers in these severely hit countries.

Earnings, Hours, and Wages

Disparities in earnings, hours, and wages across groups are less pronounced than those in activity, sector, and status of employment. Youth, despite greater reduc-tions in employment and wage employment, did not experience a larger earnings reduction than adults, and there is no sign of a decrease in the wage rate of youth. This finding, with a large increase in youth unemployment, suggests that down-ward wage rigidity impinged on labor flexibility and denied youth the opportu-nity of remaining employed at lower wages.[35]

Explaining Disparities in Employment Loss

This section presents results from two decompositions that seek to better deter-mine how changes in employment, as a share of the population, differed across groups. As explained in the methodology section above, the first one decomposes the change in the employment-to-population ratio into portions explained by changes in employment rates (as a proportion of the labor force) and participa-tion rates within each group. The second one revisits group disparities and decomposes differences in employment ratios with differences in initial level of employment, employment patterns in sector (or status), and within sector (or status) employment growth.

Increased Unemployment

For all types of workers, drops in employment led mainly to increased unemploy-ment rather than to reduced participation. Recall that declines in employment, as a percentage of the population, can lead either to increased unemployment or to withdrawal from the labor force. Table 3.3 shows the result of this decomposition for different groups.[36] For example, in the average country, men's employment ratio slowed by 2.5 percentage points, of which 2 percentage points (about 80 percent) were due to accelerating unemployment and the remaining 0.5 percentage points (about 20 percent) was due to slowing participation. The results reinforce the aggregate trends displayed in figure 3.1, which shows larger

Table 3.3 Decomposition of Employment Ratio between Changes Due to Employment Rate and Those Due to Labor Force Participation

Group	(1) Precrisis (2006–08)			(2) Postcrisis (2008–09)			(3) Difference between (1) and (2)		
	Employment ratio change	Changes due to employment rate	Changes due to participation	Employment ratio change	Changes due to employment rate	Changes due to participation	Employment ratio change	Changes due to employment rate	Changes due to participation
Men									
Average	0.7	0.4	0.3	−1.9	−1.6	−0.3	−2.5	−2.0	−0.5
%	100.0	56.8	43.2	100.0	86.4	13.6	100.0	78.6	21.4
Women									
Average	1.0	0.5	0.6	−0.4	−0.7	0.4	−1.4	−1.2	−0.2
%	100.0	44.1	54.9	100.0	202.8	−100.0	100.0	85.5	14.5
Young									
Average	0.7	0.5	0.2	−1.9	−1.5	−0.5	−2.6	−2.0	−0.7
%	100.0	69.9	30.1	100.0	76.5	23.5	100.0	74.7	25.3
Old									
Average	0.8	0.3	0.5	−1.0	−1.1	0.2	−1.7	−1.5	−0.3
%	100.0	43.0	57.0	100.0	118.1	−18.1	100.0	84.4	15.6
Low education									
Average	0.4	0.2	0.1	−1.1	−1.1	−0.1	−1.5	−1.3	−0.2
%	100.0	60.5	39.5	100.0	95.1	4.9	100.0	86.2	13.8
High education									
Average	0.8	0.5	0.3	−1.3	−1.2	−0.1	−2.1	−1.7	−0.4
%	100.0	63.5	36.5	100.0	95.4	4.6	100.0	82.9	17.1

Source: World Bank staff.

Note: Numbers are for average of all 17 countries. Each proportion of change explained by employment rate and labor force participation is presented as a percentage.

changes in unemployment than in participation. Over the six groups, on average, 82.9 percent of the slowdown in employment as a share of the population was due to increased unemployment, while only 17.1 percent was due to declines in participation.

Lower Participation

Declines in participation were surprisingly large for youth. Youth may have reacted to the downturn by remaining in or returning to school, while the opportunity cost of schooling is lower. Although data on educational attendance are unavailable, changes in participation rates are consistent with a delay of youth's entrance into the labor market or the exit from it. In particular, more than a quarter of youth's employment slowdown is attributable to the slowdown in participation, which is slightly higher than the average 17.1 percent for all workers (table 3.3). In other words, displaced youth are more likely to leave the labor market than displaced adults are. Men, meanwhile, also experienced slightly larger reductions in participation rates than women, in line with the mild added-worker effect shown in figure 3.7.

Men's Employment Loss

The particularly large slowdown in men's employment can be primarily attributed to higher initial levels of employment. Table 3.4 decomposes the gender disparities in employment loss into three components: the initial employment gap, differences in sector (status) of employment, and differences in employment growth rates within sector (status).[37] The first component, shown in the second column of table 3.4, is what the gender disparity would be if men and women experienced the same percentage reductions in employment. Because men have higher initial rates of employment, an equivalent percentage reduction will lead men to greater reductions in employment, as a share of the population. The large part of the average gender disparity in employment—roughly 58 percent—can be explained by men's higher rates of initial employment (second column of the top row).

Men's greater presence in the industrial sector, however, also led to significant employment losses. The third column of table 3.4 gives the portion of the gender employment disparity attributable to different sectoral work patterns. This finding indicates what the employment disparity would be if men and women had the same initial level of employment and the same percentage employment reductions in each sector, while maintaining their actual precrisis sectoral employment patterns. On average, the difference in sectoral employment patterns accounted for 37 percent of the total gender disparity, mostly because of the greater percentage of men that work in the industrial sector, as seen in figure 3A.1, and because of the industrial sector's large employment loss.

Women's Employment Loss

Scant evidence indicates that women suffered greater employment losses than men within sectors. The fourth column of table 3.4 shows what the disparity would have been had men and women had the same initial rates of employment and the same propensity to work in the three main sectors. This decomposition

Table 3.4 Decomposition of Gender Disparities in Employment Ratio Changes by Sector and Status

Region and country	Sector				Status			
	Differences in employment ratio change	Changes due to employment level gap	Changes due to sectoral distribution	Changes within sector growth rate	Differences in employment ratio change	Changes due to employment level gap	Changes due to status distribution	Changes within status growth rate
Latin America and the Caribbean								
Argentina	-0.82	0.03	-1.10	0.26	-0.82	0.07	0.15	-1.03
Brazil	-0.99	-0.39	-0.15	-0.45	-0.99	-0.41	-0.05	-0.52
Chile	-0.92	-1.25	-0.50	0.83	-0.92	-1.19	-0.66	0.92
Costa Rica	-0.29	-1.93	-1.47	3.11	-0.29	-0.98	-3.79	4.47
Mexico	-0.79	-1.00	-0.35	0.55	-0.79	-0.84	-0.05	0.10
East Asia and the Pacific								
Indonesia	2.22	-0.63	0.02	2.83	2.22	-0.69	-1.17	4.08
Philippines	-0.72	0.32	-0.26	-0.78	-0.72	0.25	-0.03	-0.93
Middle East and North Africa								
Egypt, Arab Rep.	0.26	-1.82	1.36	0.72	0.26	-1.67	1.56	0.37
Jordan	-0.10	-2.27	0.06	2.11	-0.10	-2.16	0.28	1.78

table continues next page

Table 3.4 Decomposition of Gender Disparities in Employment Ratio Changes by Sector and Status *(continued)*

Region and country	Sector				Status			
	Differences in employment ratio change	Changes due to employment level gap	Changes due to sectoral distribution	Changes within sector growth rate	Differences in employment ratio change	Changes due to employment level gap	Changes due to status distribution	Changes within status growth rate
Europe and Central Asia								
Bulgaria	−0.92	−0.57	−1.21	0.86	−0.92	−0.56	0.14	−0.50
Latvia	−5.80	−0.83	−1.67	−3.29	−5.80	−0.87	0.85	−5.78
Lithuania	−6.31	−0.05	−0.76	−5.50	−6.31	−0.05	0.83	−7.08
Macedonia, FYR	n.a.	n.a.	n.a.	n.a.	1.16	0.00	−0.07	1.24
Poland	n.a.	n.a.	n.a.	n.a.	−1.18	−0.52	0.05	−0.72
Romania	−0.68	−0.12	−0.71	0.16	−0.68	−0.12	−0.03	−0.52
Turkey	−2.23	0.10	0.06	−2.40	−2.23	−0.33	−0.59	−1.32
Africa								
South Africa	n.a.	n.a.	n.a.	n.a.	−1.66	−0.93	−0.51	−0.22
Average	−1.29	−0.74	−0.48	−0.07	−1.16	−0.65	−0.18	−0.33
Percent	100.0	57.6	36.9	5.5	100.0	55.8	15.6	28.6

Source: World Bank staff.
Note: n.a. = not applicable.

gives an indication of whether percentage reductions in each sector's employment favored men or women. Considering only percentage changes in sectoral employment, on average men would have had about a 0.1 percentage point greater reduction in employment, accounting for 6 percent of the total disparity in employment. The results are similar for the decomposition by employment status. With a few exceptions, gender disparities caused by within-sector (status) differences in employment growth rates were generally small.[38] In other words, percentage changes in employment did not consistently favor men or women, and in most countries they were close to gender neutral.

Youth's Employment Loss

Unlike men, youth suffered far larger employment losses than adults within each sector and status of employment. Table 3.5 shows the same decomposition of the large age disparity in employment by status (the left half of table 3.5). Overall, percentage employment reductions within status were much larger for youth than for adults, and this finding accounted for an enormous average employment disparity equal to 2.8 percentage points. A larger proportion of adults than youth work, however, which mitigates these age disparities as a share of the population. Finally, differences in employment status played only a marginal role in explaining differences by age group. Similar results were found for decompositions by sector. Overall, the results are consistent with firms in each sector reducing employment disproportionately for youth.

Employment Loss and Educational Level

Higher initial employment rates, as well as a greater tendency to work in wage employment, contributed to greater employment reductions among the better educated. Although the differences were not as stark as the gender and youth disparities, better educated persons experienced surprisingly large reductions in employment rates. The right half of table 3.5 sheds some light on the factors causing the larger employment reductions among the better educated. Like youth, but to a lesser extent, less educated workers experienced greater percentage reductions in employment within both wage and self-employed work. Like men, however, people with more education are more likely to work than those with less education. This fact alone would have negated the employment disadvantage faced by less educated workers within each sector. The deciding factor in this case is that better educated workers tended to be clustered in wage employment jobs; since employment reductions were greater in wage employment than in self-employment, greater employment reductions took place among better educated workers.

Conclusion

This chapter identifies groups in 17 middle-income countries that experienced the greatest labor market dislocations during the 2009 financial crisis. Most conjectures about the vulnerability of different groups are based on three potential

Table 3.5 Decomposition of Age and Education Disparities in Employment Ratio Changes by Status

Region and country	Youth (vs. adults)				Least educated (vs. more educated)			
	Differences in employment ratio change	Changes due to employment level gap	Changes due to status distribution	Changes within status growth rate	Differences in employment ratio change	Changes due to employment level gap	Changes due to status distribution	Changes within status growth rate
Latin America and the Caribbean								
Argentina	0.68	−0.29	−0.32	1.28	−1.05	0.00	0.02	−1.08
Brazil	−1.28	0.70	0.26	−2.24	0.77	0.21	−0.14	0.70
Chile	−0.47	1.81	−1.23	−1.05	0.27	0.15	1.53	−1.41
Costa Rica	−4.01	1.67	−1.66	−4.01	−0.92	0.13	1.54	−2.59
Mexico	−1.48	0.97	−0.40	−2.06	0.71	0.21	0.13	0.37
East Asia and the Pacific								
Indonesia	−2.40	0.98	0.85	−4.23	−0.98	−0.16	0.29	−1.11
Philippines	0.00	−0.58	−0.54	1.13	0.91	0.16	0.75	−0.01
Middle East and North Africa								
Egypt, Arab Rep.	−1.00	1.45	0.11	−2.56	0.37	0.21	−2.87	3.02
Jordan	0.51	0.51	−0.44	0.43	−0.39	0.39	−0.20	−0.57
Europe and Central Asia								
Bulgaria	1.31	4.27	−0.10	−2.87	1.73	3.16	0.23	−1.66
Latvia	−1.42	7.95	−0.75	−8.62	0.91	7.20	0.20	−6.48
Lithuania	−4.03	7.88	−0.68	−11.23	3.58	3.95	1.59	−1.96

table continues next page

Table 3.5 Decomposition of Age and Education Disparities in Employment Ratio Changes by Status *(continued)*

Region and country	Youth (vs. adults)				Least educated (vs. more educated)			
	Differences in employment ratio change	*Changes due to employment level gap*	*Changes due to status distribution*	*Changes within status growth rate*	*Differences in employment ratio change*	*Changes due to employment level gap*	*Changes due to status distribution*	*Changes within status growth rate*
Europe and Central Asia								
Macedonia, FYR	−0.91	0.92	0.73	−2.56	1.43	0.31	1.68	−0.56
Poland	0.08	2.48	0.07	−2.47	0.40	2.71	0.76	−3.07
Romania	−0.01	0.84	0.52	−1.37	0.97	−0.20	1.34	−0.18
Turkey	−0.86	0.50	−0.60	−0.75	0.58	0.20	1.41	−1.03
Africa								
South Africa	0.29	4.37	0.19	−4.27	0.58	0.58	1.13	−1.13
Average	−0.88	2.14	−0.23	−2.79	0.58	1.13	0.55	−1.10
Percent	100.0	−242.8	26.6	316.2	100.0	194.6	95.2	−189.8

Source: World Bank staff.

factors: uneven exposure to the shock across sectors or status of employment, firms' employment decisions, and households' labor supply decisions in response to the crisis. Previous findings from the recent and previous crises, particularly the two well-documented cases in Argentina and Indonesia, suggested four hypotheses:

- Employment outcomes were similar for men and women.
- Youth experienced greater increases in unemployment.
- Adjustments for less educated workers were more severe.
- The shock reduced employment more in urban areas.

Youth experienced the greatest employment dislocations. As in past crises, young workers experienced large reductions in employment, and their shift from wage employment to unemployment during this crisis was particularly striking. For most dislocated youth, self-employment did not provide a buffer to compensate for fewer wage jobs. Supply-side factors may also have contributed to increases in youth unemployment during the downturn. For example, youth may have less access to information about the labor market than adults, leading them to delay adjusting their expectations downward regarding the wages they could expect. Youth likely benefited more than adults from their parents' financial support during the downturn, which may have also contributed to youth unemployment.

Unlike past crises, in which men and women experienced similar employment changes, overall employment rates declined markedly more for men. Men experienced substantially larger declines in the percentage of the population employed. Unlike for youth, however, percentage employment declines within sectors were nearly equal for men and women. No evidence suggests that firms systematically discriminated against women when reducing employment.

Women were only slightly more likely to remain in the labor force than men, and they did not enter self-employment except in the worst-hit countries. Gender differences in participation were small, even among the less educated. In this respect, added-worker effects during this crisis were generally more similar to the past crisis in urban Argentina, where female self-employment increased little, than to Indonesia, where female self-employment increased substantially. The exceptions are Latvia and Lithuania, which experienced GDP slowdowns exceeding 20 percentage points, and women experienced much larger increases in self-employment.

There were few striking differences by education or urban residence. Disparities between less and more educated groups tended to be small, partly because of offsetting responses among middle and highly educated workers. Workers with medium levels of education—typically junior high school graduates—were affected most by the crisis, as measured by declines in employment and increases in unemployment, while workers at the extremes of the education distribution suffered smaller declines. The evidence for urban and rural disparities is mixed, although in most countries urban workers experienced greater decreases in employment but greater increases in hours and earnings than rural workers.

Firm decisions, initial employment rates, and occupational segregation can all contribute to group disparities. In absolute terms, youth and men experienced the largest declines in employment and wage employment as a percentage of the population, which is arguably the indicator most relevant for assessing mitigation policies that apply to the entire population. For youth, larger percentage reductions in employment were partially mitigated by the fact that a larger percentage of adults work. For men, however, both their concentration in the industrial sector and, even more important, their higher initial employment rates contributed to greater employment reductions.

Significance of Findings for Policy Response

To address the decline in youth employment, policies can either seek to increase labor demand for youth or assist youth in making better career decisions. Youth experienced declines in employment in each sector and status of employment, but the limited evidence available shows no systematic declines in hours and wages. This finding suggests that firms reacted to reports of economic instability by laying off or freezing the hiring of their least experienced employees. Subminimum wages and job subsidies for youth can partially counteract these layoffs by encouraging firms to retain or hire youth during the downturn. Educational subsidies can also encourage youth to respond by acquiring additional schooling, rather than remaining idle, during periods of declining employment opportunities. Finally, job search assistance, including the dissemination of accurate information on labor market conditions, can help youth make more informed decisions during tumultuous economic times.

Scaling up existing programs targeting disadvantaged groups, such as unskilled, female, or urban workers, may not benefit those most affected by job loss due to crisis. Training or other active labor market programs often target youth, unskilled, and female workers, who are perceived to be at a disadvantage in the labor market. However, with the exception of youth, these programs are not always well-targeted to the industrial and wage workers who suffered the largest employment contractions during the crisis. Turkey, for example, responded to the crisis in part by extending a wage subsidy program that reduces working women's social security contributions. Although this subsidy may have been effective in boosting low participation rates before the crisis, it did not benefit the majority of those who suffered job loss and may have exacerbated employment loss for Turkish men.

Finally, the results confirm the importance of country-specific information when targeting policy responses to crises. Latvia and Lithuania aside, the size of disparities between groups was usually weakly related to the size of the shock. Although the patterns across countries for many indicators and groups were not consistent, disparities were often large. While the analysis focused on general patterns, groups in each country responded differently to the shock, meaning that country-specific data are critical to helping policy makers gauge the optimal policy response. Furthermore, this study covers only 17 countries, selected on the basis of data availability, and the patterns of adjustment in other countries may be different. Further development of data collection and dissemination systems will enable the policy response to this and future crises to better serve the needs of the most severely affected workers.

Annex 3A

Table 3A.1 GDP Growth Rates and Their Slowdown, 2007–09

	Annual GDP growth rates			Average GDP growth rates		
	2007	2008	2009	2007–08	2009	Slowdown
Argentina	8.7	6.8	0.9	7.8	0.9	−6.9
Brazil	6.1	2.8	−0.2	4.5	−0.2	−4.7
Bulgaria	6.2	5.1	−5.0	5.7	−5.0	−10.7
Chile	4.6	3.7	−1.5	4.2	−1.5	−5.7
Costa Rica	7.9	0.7	−1.1	4.3	−1.1	−5.4
Egypt, Arab Rep.	7.1	7.2	4.7	7.1	4.7	−2.5
Indonesia	6.3	6.0	4.5	6.2	4.5	−1.7
Jordan	8.9	7.8	2.8	8.3	2.8	−5.6
Latvia	10.0	−4.6	−18.0	2.7	−18.0	−20.7
Lithuania	9.8	2.8	−15.0	6.3	−15.0	−21.3
Macedonia, FYR	5.9	4.8	−0.7	5.4	−0.7	−6.1
Mexico	3.3	6.0	−6.5	4.7	−6.5	−11.2
Philippines	7.1	3.8	0.9	5.5	0.9	−4.5
Poland	6.8	5.0	1.7	5.9	1.7	−4.2
Romania	6.3	3.8	−7.1	5.1	−7.1	−12.2
South Africa	5.5	7.3	−1.8	6.4	−1.8	−8.2
Turkey	4.7	0.7	−4.7	2.7	−4.7	−7.4

Source: World Economic Outlook Database.
Note: GDP = gross domestic product.

Technical Note

Regression
The analysis in this chapter is based on the estimated coefficients from descriptive regressions of year-on-year changes in outcome on worker characteristics for each outcome of interest. Each regression is conditioned on four worker characteristics: their gender, age group (youth aged 15–24 or adult aged 25–64), education group (least educated or better educated), and urban or rural residence.[39]

$$\Delta Y_{i,t} = \alpha + \beta_{1,t} Men_i + \beta_{2,t} Age_i + \beta_{3,t} Educ_i + \beta_{4,t} Rural_i + \upsilon_{i,t}, \tag{1}$$

where $\Delta Y_{i,t}$ is an average year-on-year change in labor market outcome for a cell i and time t in each country. When annual data are used and $t = 2008$, $Y_{i,2008} = Y_{i,2008} - Y_{i,2007}$. If quarterly data are used, then the authors used average year-on-year change, and $t = 2008$,

$$\Delta Y_{i,2008} = \sum_{q=1}^{4} (Y_{i,2008,q} - Y_{i,2007,q}) / 4.$$

Table 3A.2 Labor Market Adjustments by Gender, 2006–09

| | | Among population | | | | | | Among active labor force | | | | | | | | Among workers | | | | | |
| | | Employment | | Unemployment | | Nonparticipation | | Unemployment | | Wage employment | | Self employment | | Agriculture | | Earnings | | Hours | | Wage rates | |
Region	Country	Men	Women	Men	Women	Men	Women	Men	Women	Men	Women	Men	Women	Men	Women	Men	Women	Men	Women	Men	Women
LAC	Argentina	−0.59	0.81	1.31	0.70	−0.72	−1.51	1.45	1.56	−1.29	−2.17	−0.17	0.61	−0.92	−0.06	−9.20	−5.67	−5.72	−7.39	−3.48	1.73
	Brazil	−1.65	−0.81	1.28	0.59	0.37	0.22	1.72	0.96	−1.14	−0.50	−0.57	−0.46	—	—	−0.99	−0.12	−0.18	−0.18	−0.81	0.06
	Chile	−2.51	−1.47	1.57	0.34	0.94	1.13	2.36	1.17	−3.79	−2.76	1.42	1.59	−0.42	−0.49	—	—	−0.96	−1.44	—	—
	Costa Rica	−3.15	−1.37	2.25	2.17	0.90	−0.80	3.27	5.44	−4.53	−6.28	1.26	0.85	0.55	−1.52	−5.27	−2.20	−6.25	−7.43	0.98	5.23
	Mexico	−1.95	−1.24	1.09	0.56	0.86	0.68	1.53	1.31	−1.70	−1.43	0.17	0.12	0.42	−0.45	−5.24	−4.54	−0.91	−0.30	−4.33	−4.24
EAP	Indonesia	0.71	−1.75	−1.25	−1.05	0.54	2.80	−1.04	−1.48	−0.46	1.30	1.49	0.17	1.81	−0.45	3.33	−4.47	0.14	−0.35	3.19	−4.12
	Philippines	0.14	0.90	0.33	0.15	−0.48	−1.06	0.39	−0.06	−1.18	−0.88	0.79	0.94	−0.79	−0.03	3.63	2.12	−5.07	−4.95	3.63	2.12
MENA	Egypt, Arab Rep.	−0.74	−0.93	0.02	1.44	0.73	−0.51	0.14	5.11	1.18	1.32	−1.32	−6.42	−2.13	−6.00	−8.64	−13.25	3.11	8.79	−11.75	−22.04
	Jordan	−0.03	−0.39	0.36	−0.03	−0.33	0.43	0.26	0.30	−0.95	−0.35	0.69	0.06	0.12	0.00	−2.83	−4.12	3.37	2.56	−6.20	−6.68
ECA	Bulgaria	−4.68	−3.40	2.02	1.48	2.66	1.92	3.19	4.08	−3.54	−4.00	0.36	−0.08	—	—	—	—	—	—	—	—
	Latvia	−12.24	−6.46	9.14	4.63	3.10	1.83	14.14	8.69	−14.15	−10.52	0.01	1.83	—	—	—	—	—	—	—	—
	Lithuania	−7.86	−1.63	7.98	3.38	−0.11	−1.75	12.29	5.52	−12.63	−7.65	0.34	2.13	—	—	—	—	—	—	—	—
	Macedonia, FYR	0.60	−0.88	−0.56	−0.26	−0.03	1.14	−0.90	0.70	−1.07	−0.81	1.97	0.11	—	—	—	—	—	—	—	—
	Poland	−2.94	−1.85	3.30	2.47	−0.36	−0.63	5.40	4.72	−5.02	−4.19	−0.39	−0.52	—	—	—	—	—	—	—	—
	Romania	−0.85	−0.05	1.28	1.15	−0.43	−1.10	1.75	1.73	−2.54	−1.71	0.79	−0.01	—	—	—	—	—	—	—	—
	Turkey	−1.79	0.39	1.83	0.78	−0.04	−1.17	2.56	2.41	−2.92	−3.19	0.36	0.78	—	—	—	—	—	—	—	—
SSA	South Africa	−3.83	−2.21	0.56	0.37	3.27	1.83	2.57	2.42	−4.70	−3.87	2.13	1.45	—	—	—	—	−4.41	−2.81	—	—

Source: World Bank staff.

Note: The table contains the difference between the annual percentage point change in 2009 and the average annual change between 2006 and 2008. — = data unavailable; EAP = East Asia and Pacific; ECA = Europe and Central Asia; LAC = Latin America and the Caribbean; MENA = Middle East and North Africa; SSA = Sub-Saharan Africa.

To estimate how the great recession changes the effect of each worker characteristics on the trend of outcomes, the authors estimate the following equation pooling all periods for each country:

$$\Delta Y_i = \tilde{\alpha} + \tilde{\beta}_1 Men_i + \tilde{\beta}_2 Age_i + \tilde{\beta}_3 Educ_i + \tilde{\beta}_4 Rural_i$$
$$+ I(crisis = 1) \times (\gamma_1 Men_i + \gamma_2 Age_i + \gamma_3 Educ_i + \gamma_4 Rural_i) + \tilde{\upsilon}_i, \qquad (2)$$

where $I(\text{crisis}=1)$ indicates the experience of the recession, that is, $t \geq 2009$. Each γ is the coefficient of interest that reflects the change in the relationship between worker characteristics and outcomes. In figures 3.5 through 3.9, the authors plot all γ's for each country and labor market outcome.

Given the linearity of the equations above, note that estimating γ's from the equation (3A.2) is equivalent to the following equation:

$$\tilde{Y}_i = \gamma_0 + \gamma_1 Men_i + \gamma_2 Age_i + \gamma_3 Educ_i + \gamma_4 Rural_i + \tilde{\upsilon}_i, \qquad (3)$$

where $\tilde{Y} = \overline{\Delta Y_i} \,|\, (crisis = 1) - \overline{\Delta Y_i} \,|\, (crisis = 0)$. Note that $\overline{\Delta Y_i} \,|\, (crisis = 1)$ is an average of ΔY_{it} over $t \geq 2009$, and $\Delta \bar{Y}_i \,|\, (crisis = 0)$ is an average of $\Delta Y_{i,t}$ over $t \leq 2008$.

Observations are weighted according to the product of the cell's survey weights and the number of observations used to generate the average, when available.[40] The outcomes are the ratio of the employed, unemployed, and non-participants among population; the proportion of unemployed, wage employed, and self-employed among the labor force; and hourly wage, hours of work, and monthly earnings for the employed.

The authors repeat the same exercise of estimation separately by gender, assuming that the effects of demographic characteristics on outcomes may vary by gender. Based on the results for each country separately by gender, table 3A.2 presents the median of each γ's.

Decompositions

The main outcome of interest is $(\Delta emp_t|_{m,post} - \Delta emp_t|_{m,pre}) - (\Delta emp_t|_{f,post} - \Delta emp_t|_{f,pre})$, where emp denotes the employment ratio for each gender (m, f) for each time period of pre- and postcrisis as defined in the text, and $\Delta X_t = X_{t+1} - X_t$ for all variables.

The authors first examine the extent to which the change in employment ratio is explained by changes in employment rate and labor force participation:

$$\Delta emp_t = emp_{t+1} - emp_t$$

$$\Delta emp_t = \Delta erate_t lfp_{t+1} + erate_t \Delta lfp_t \qquad (3A.1)$$

$$\Delta emp_t = \Delta erate_t lfp_t + erate_{t+1} \Delta lfb_t, \qquad (3A.2)$$

Figure 3A.1 Gender Comparisons by Education: Employment Ratio, Unemployment Ratio, and Nonparticipation Ratio

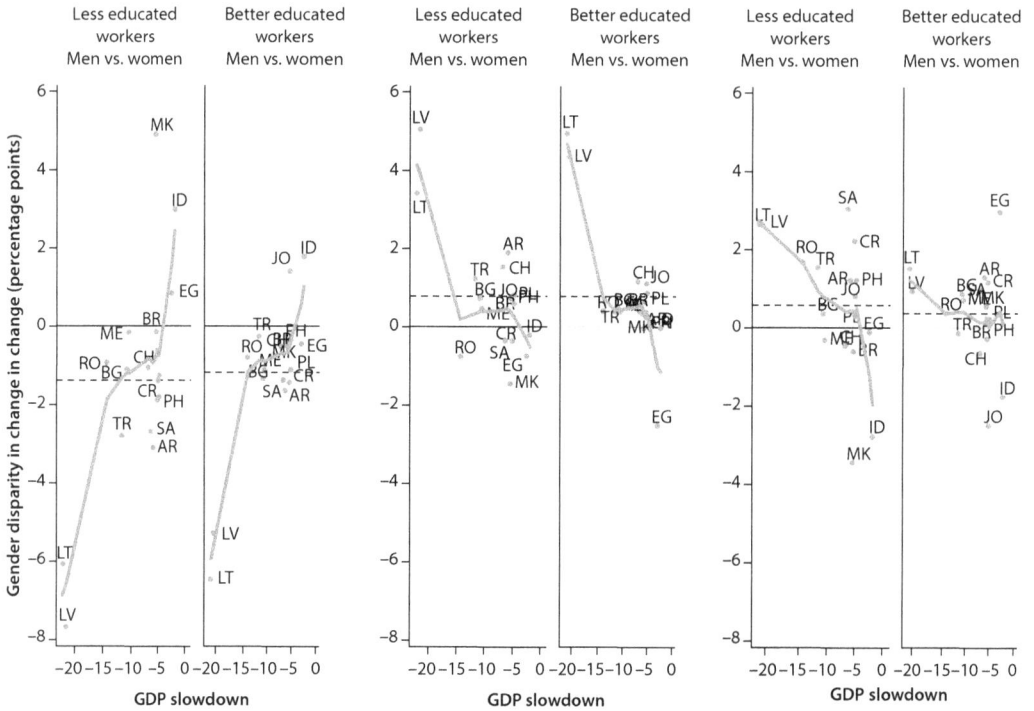

Source: World Bank staff.
Note: Lines indicate mean value and running line smooth. The figure shows the disparity between groups, controlling for other characteristics, in the slowdown in the employment to population ratio. The plotted number is the coefficient from regression for each country (equation 3A.3). The horizontal axis represents the slowdown in real GDP growth rate as defined in table 3A.1. Two letter codes represent countries (see note for figure 3.3).

where *emp*, *erate*, and *lfp* denote employment ratio, employment rate, and labor force participation, respectively, using $emp_t = erate_t * lfp_t$. Taking an average of equations (3A.1) and (3A.2) yields

$$\Delta emp_t = \underbrace{\Delta erate_t \overline{lfp}}_{①} + \underbrace{\overline{erate}\Delta lfp_t}_{②}. \tag{3A.3}$$

The first term is the portion of the change in the employment ratio that is explained by the change in employment rate, while the second term is the portion explained by the change in labor force participation. This decomposition is shown for each group for gender, age, and education.

Examining differences across groups is another type of decomposition exercise, one in which the initial level of employment and distribution across sector and status for employment varies by group.

Let $S_{it} = \dfrac{EMP_{it}}{EMP_t}$ be a share of sector i for each gender at t, where $\Sigma s_{it=1}$. The relationship between an employment ratio in each sector and the overall employment ratio is

$$emp_{it} = s_{it}emp_t, \tag{3A.4}$$

where $emp_{it} = \dfrac{EMP_{it}}{Pop_t}$, the share of the population employed in sector i, and $emp_{it} = \dfrac{EMP_{it}}{Pop_t}$, the employment-to-population ratio.

The growth rate of overall employment and sector-specific employment are denoted by r_t and r_{it} respectively: $r_t = (emp_{t+1}-emp_t)/emp_t$ and $r_{it} = (emp_{it+1}-emp_{it})/emp_{it}$.

Using equation (3A.3), the following relationship holds for each gender:

$$r_{it}+1 = \frac{S_{it}+1}{S_{it}}(r_t+1) \xrightarrow{\ yields\ } S_{it}(r_{it}+1) = S_{it+1}(r_t+1).$$

Given that $\Sigma s_{it} = 1$, taking summation in both sides, $\Sigma_i s_{it}(r_{it+1}) = \Sigma_i s_{it+1}(r_t+1)$, yields

$$r_t = \Sigma_i s_{it}r_{it}. \tag{3A.5}$$

Equation (3A.5) indicates that the percentage change in the employment-to-population ratio is equal to the weighted average of each sector's percentage employment changes, as a share of total employment. The employment change in each period can then be expressed as

$$\Delta emp_t = emp_{t+1} - emp_t = emp_t r_t = emp_t \Sigma_i s_{it}r_{it}. \tag{3A.6}$$

Each term represents three factors that combine to explain the difference between groups' employment change: different initial employment level (emp_t), different sectoral distributions (s_{it}), and different percentage employment changes within each sector (r_{it}).

Since there are three factors whose product is the change in employment, the authors use a Shapley decomposition to examine the contribution of each factor in explaining group disparities. This involves averaging the contribution of each of three factors over six unique permutations in which one variable is varied while others are held constant. The first permutation involves first varying initial employment rates (using male values for sectoral distribution and within-sector changes), then varying the sectoral distribution, and finally varying the within-sector percentage employment changes.

For simplicity, the time subscript t is omitted, and the gender difference is decomposed as

$$\Delta emp_m - \Delta emp_f = \underbrace{(emp_m - emp_f)\sum_i s_{im} r_{im}}_{①} + \underbrace{emp_f \sum_i (s_{im} - s_{if}) r_{im}}_{②}$$

$$+ \underbrace{emp_f \sum_i s_{if}(r_{im} - r_{if})}_{③}. \qquad (3A.7)$$

Then ① is the difference due to the initial employment gap, ② is due to the differences in sectoral distributions, and ③ is due to differences in within-sector employment growth rates.

There are a total of six permutations of the decomposition, which are listed below:

$$\Delta emp_m - \Delta emp_f = emp_m \sum_i s_{im} r_{im} - emp_f \sum_i s_{if} r_{if}$$

$$= (emp_m - emp_f)\sum_i s_{im} r_{im} + emp_f \sum_i (s_{im} - s_{if}) r_{im} + emp_f \sum_i s_{if}(r_{im} - r_{if})$$

$$= (emp_m - emp_f)\sum_i s_{im} r_{im} + emp_f \sum_i (s_{im} - s_{if}) r_{if} + emp_f \sum_i s_{im}(r_{im} - r_{if})$$

$$= (emp_m - emp_f)\sum_i s_{if} r_{if} + emp_m \sum_i (s_{im} - s_{if}) r_{if} + emp_m \sum_i s_{im}(r_{im} - r_{if})$$

$$= (emp_m - emp_f)\sum_i s_{if} r_{if} + emp_m \sum_i (s_{im} - s_{if}) r_{im} + emp_m \sum_i s_{if}(r_{im} - r_{if})$$

$$= (emp_m - emp_f)\sum_i s_{if} r_{im} + emp_m \sum_i (s_{im} - s_{if}) r_{im} + emp_f \sum_i s_{if}(r_{im} - r_{if})$$

$$= (emp_m - emp_f)\sum_i s_{im} r_{if} + emp_f \sum_i (s_{im} - s_{if}) r_{if} + emp_m \sum_i s_{im}(r_{im} - r_{if}).$$

$$(3A.8)$$

For the decomposition exercise in the text, the authors report the average share for each of the three components of these six equations.

Notes

1. It is also possible that the wage differences between groups are also mitigated by selection rather than rigidity. For example, average wages could rise for youth despite greater declines in demand if the lowest-wage youth were rationed out of jobs.
2. See, for example, Polachek (1979) and other references in Altonji and Blank (1999).

3. The International Labour Organization (ILO) estimates that, in 2009, 47 percent of women worldwide worked in services, while 37 percent worked in agriculture and 16 percent in manufacturing. The corresponding percentages for men are 40, 33, and 27. Unfortunately, the ILO's key indicators of the labor market do not disaggregate sectoral employment by age, education, or region.

4. Two papers report that during the Asian financial crisis, layoff rates were seven times higher for women in the Republic of Korea than for men (Seguino 2009; Singh and Zammit 2000), but this claim is difficult to substantiate. According to the Korean Employment Insurance Information Service, however, men accounted for roughly two-thirds of layoffs in 1998, a significantly higher share than in 1996. While these data exclude many marginal workers, they cover 75 percent of the workforce, and women make up only a slight majority of irregular workers in Korea.

5. Households' vulnerability and response to economic crises have been explored in Peru (Glewwe and Hall 1998); Mexico (Cunningham and Maloney 2004; McKenzie 2003); the Russian Federation (Lokshin and Ravallion 2000); Indonesia (Strauss *et al.* 2004); and Argentina (Corbacho, Garcia-Escribano, and Inchauste 2007), among others.

6. Examples include Ha *et al.* (2010), Barakat *et al.* (2010), IMF and ILO (2010), Bell and Blanchflower (2010), Verick (2009), and Scarpetta, Sonnet, and Manfredi (2010).

7. Mixed results are also found when looking at household income or consumption. Households with better educated heads experienced smaller consumption drops in Argentina and Peru (Corbacho, Garcia-Escribano, and Inchauste 2007; Glewwe and Hall 1998) but larger income and consumption reductions in Mexico (McKenzie 2004).

8. In particular, exchange rates have changed relatively little during this crisis, while both Argentina and Indonesia experienced extraordinary currency devaluations during their crises.

9. For European countries, the authors use Eurostat Survey data instead of individual countries' Labor Force Survey data, which were not available. Eurostat provides the mean of key labor market indicators by demographic cells. For European countries, age, education, and gender estimates rely on data from the eight cells defined by the three characteristics, while urban/rural estimates rely on a separate set of eight cells defined by residence, age, and gender.

10. The slowdown is calculated as the difference between the GDP growth rate in 2009 and the average GDP growth rates over 2007–08. See annex table 3A.1 for the calculation of the slowdown in GDP growth rates in each country.

11. In some countries, these data also contain information on household responses to the crises and individuals' labor market transitions during the crisis, but these topics are left for future research.

12. For detailed information on data construction for this analysis, refer to the technical note in the annex.

13. This does not imply or assume that all self-employed workers are unproductive or that all self-employed workers are excluded from wage employment, as many workers are self-employed by choice. Workers often choose to start a business, for example, because they have acquired sufficient assets to earn greater profits in self-employment or because they value time flexibility. The use of wage employment as a proxy for changes in job quality during the crisis is based on the plausible assumption that the downturn, rather than raising preferences for self-employment among workers, reduced demand

for wage workers. If wages are rigid, then reductions in demand would ration workers out of wage employment jobs, forcing them to enter self-employment.

14. Comparing changes in urban and rural earnings is also problematic in countries that collect only price indexes in urban areas.

15. In the developing countries of Europe and Central Asia, the least educated group includes those with secondary education or below, as their education level is higher than other regions.

16. Observations are weighted both by the population weight for that cell and by the number of unweighted observations used to generate the average to adjust for heteroscedasticity in the cell mean outcomes.

17. The Shapley approach decomposes the product of several factors by taking the simple average of factors' contribution over all permutations, where one factor is varied while others are held constant. See the annex and Shorrocks (2013) for further details.

18. To fix terminology, the *employment ratio* refers to the employment-to-population ratio, while the *employment rate* refers to employment as a proportion of the active labor force, which of course is the complement of the unemployment rate.

19. The decomposition actually averages the results of two decomposition equations, of which equation (3.2) is one. More detail can be found in the annex.

20. The three main sectors are agriculture, industry, and services.

21. See equations (3A.3) and (3A.4) in the annex for a more detailed derivation.

22. The labor market adjustments for all individuals, labor force participants, and workers, disaggregated by gender in each country, are presented in table 3A.2 in the annex.

23. Recall that the indicator of interest is the difference between precrisis and postcrisis averages for changes in outcomes.

24. This is consistent with findings from previous studies. See World Bank (2010a). Two letters in the figures represent each country: AR (Argentina), BG (Bulgaria), BR (Brazil), CH (Chile), CR (Costa Rica), EG (the Arab Republic of Egypt), ID (Indonesia), JO (Jordan), LT (Lithuania), LV (Latvia), ME (Mexico), MK (FYR Macedonia), PH (the Philippines), PL (Poland), RO (Romania), SA (South Africa), and TR (Turkey).

25. Each year, the World Bank Group's Doing Business report provides objective indicators of business regulations for local firms in 183 countries. Turkey ranked 145 out of 183 countries in "employing workers" in the *2010 Doing Business*, which reflects labor market rigidity with substantial hiring and firing costs.

26. Unfortunately, information on hours in these rigid countries mentioned is not available.

27. Note by definition that the share of employed, unemployed, and out of labor force workers sums up to one, and the changes of each share sum up to zero.

28. Egypt is an outlier where wage employment increased, and the share of self-employment and agricultural employment decreased. Given the openness of Egypt to the international financial market, the economic slowdown in Egypt must be largely affected by the food price crisis rather than by the financial crisis, which may explain a large slowdown in agriculture. A decrease in agriculture is probably highly associated with a decline in self-employment and a slight increase in wage employment.

29. As mentioned above, there are 16 observations in each regression, one for each of the 16 cells defined by these four characteristics. In European countries, the full 16 cells are unavailable. In these countries, cells defined by gender, age, and education are used

for those three groups, while cells defined by urban residence, age, and gender are used to generate urban and rural disparities.

30. The authors also generated unconditional results, and the patterns are qualitatively similar to the conditional results in all cases.

31. For example, a negative coefficient on the youth dummy in the employment regression is described as "youth employment fell" or "youth employment slowed."

32. In the European countries, the middle education group has a high school education.

33. See figure 3A.1 in the annex for three group comparisons in age and education groups.

34. See figure 3A.1 in the annex for the patterns of gender disparities in employment, unemployment, and nonparticipation ratios disaggregated by education group.

35. Given the cross-sectional nature of the data, it is also possible that higher-wage youth were better able to maintain employment during the crisis, masking the drop in earnings due to declining wages. However, this appears less likely for two reasons: first, the regressions control for education, gender, and urban/rural location; second, it is not clear a priori why selection on unobservables would differ between youth and adults.

36. In table 3.3, unemployment increases are shown as declines in the share of the labor force employed, which is the same thing.

37. Note that the average gender gap in employment as a share of population of the 17 countries is –1.16 percentage points, indicating that employment slowed 1.16 percentage points more for men than for women. This finding is consistent with figure 3.5. Since sector information is missing among three countries (FYR Macedonia, Poland, and South Africa), the average gender gap in the remaining 14 countries, –1.29 percentage points, are used for decomposition by sector.

38. The exceptions include three countries—Latvia, Lithuania, and Turkey—where men experienced a much larger employment slowdown within sector (status) than women, and three countries—Costa Rica, Jordan, and Indonesia—where the within-sector (status) employment slowdown was significantly larger for women.

39. Relatively well-educated workers are those who graduated from junior secondary or above, except in Eastern European countries. In these countries, the vast majority of workers attended junior high school. Therefore, well-educated workers are those who graduated from high school or college.

40. Weighting by the number of unweighted observations corrects for heteroscedasticity in the dependent variable, which is a cell mean. In countries where the number of unweighted observations is unavailable, the authors assume that they are proportional to the group's population proportion.

References

Altonji, Joseph, and Rebecca Blank. 1999. "Race and Gender in the Labor Market." In *Handbook of Labor Economics*, Vol. 3, edited by Orley Ashenfelter and David Card, 3143–59. Amsterdam: Elsevier.

Baker, Dean, Andrew Glyn, David Howell, and John Schmidt. 2004. "Labor Market Institutions and Unemployment." In *Questioning Liberalization: Unemployment, Labor Markets, and the Welfare State*, edited by D. Howell, 72–118. Oxford, U.K.: Oxford University Press.

Barakat, Bilal, Johannes Holler, Klaus Prettner, and Julia Schuste. 2010. "The Impact of the Crisis on Labour and Education in Europe." Working Paper, Vienna Institute of Demography, Vienna.

Bell, David, and David Blanchflower. 2010. "Youth Unemployment: Déjà Vu." IZA Discussion Paper 4705, Institute for the Study of Labor (IZA), Bonn, Germany.

Corbacho, Ana, Mercedes Garcia-Escribano, and Gabriela Inchauste. 2007. "Argentina: Macroeconomic Crises and Household Vulnerability." *Review of Development Economics* 11 (1): 92–106.

Cunningham, Wendy, and William F. Maloney. 2004. "The Distribution of Income Shocks during Crises: An Application of Quantile Analysis to Mexico, 1992–95." *World Bank Economic Review* 18 (2): 155–74.

Elsby, Michael, Bart Hobijn, and Aysegul Sahin. 2010. "The Labor Market in the Great Recession." Working Paper 15979, National Bureau of Economic Research, Cambridge, MA.

Fallon, Peter, and Robert Lucas. 2002. "The Impact of the Financial Crisis on Labor Markets, Household Incomes, and Poverty: Review of Evidence." *World Bank Research Observer* 17 (1): 21–45.

Freeman, Richard. 2005. "Labour Market Institutions without Blinders: The Debate over Flexibility and Labour Market Performance." Working Paper 11286, National Bureau of Economic Research, Cambridge, MA.

———. 2009. "Labor Regulations, Unions, and Social Protection in Developing Countries: Market Distortions or Efficient Institutions." Working Paper 14789, National Bureau of Economic Research, Cambridge, MA.

Ghosh, Jayati. 2010. "Financial Crises and the Impact on Women." *Development* 53 (3): 381–85.

Glewwe, Paul, and Gillette Hall. 1998. "Are Some Groups More Vulnerable to Macro Shocks than Others? Hypothesis Tests Based on Panel Data from Peru." *Journal of Development Economics* 56: 181–206.

Ha, Byung-jin, Caroline McInerney, Steven Tobin, and Raymond Torres. 2010. "Youth Employment in Crisis." Discussion Paper 201, International Labour Organization, Geneva, Switzerland.

Hallward-Driemeier, Mary, Bob Rijkers, and Andrew Waxmen. 2010. "Women in Crisis: Firm Level Evidence on the Labor Market Impacts of the Indonesian Crisis." Policy Research Working Paper 5789, World Bank, Washington, DC.

ILO (International Labour Organization). 2010a. *Global Employment Trends: 2010.* Geneva, Switzerland: ILO.

———. 2010b. *Women in Labour Markets: Measuring Progress and Identifying Challenges.* Geneva, Switzerland: ILO.

IMF (International Monetary Fund) and ILO. 2010. "The Challenges of Growth, Employment, and Social Cohesion." Background discussion paper, IMF, Washington, DC; ILO, Geneva.

Leung, Ron, Marco Stampini, and Désiré Vencatachellum. 2009. "Does Human Capital Protect Workers against Exogenous Shocks? South Africa in the 2008–2009 Crisis." IZA Working Paper 4608, Institute for the Study of Labor (IZA), Bonn, Germany.

Lokshin, Michael, and Martin Ravallion. 2000. "Welfare Impacts of the 1998 Financial Crisis in Russia and the Response of the Public Safety Net." *Economics of Transition* 8 (2): 269–95.

McKenzie, David. 2003. "How Do Households Cope with Aggregate Shocks? Evidence from the Mexican Peso Crisis." *World Development* 31 (7): 1179–99.

———. 2004. "Aggregate Shocks and Urban Labor Market Responses: Evidence from Argentina's Financial Crisis." *Economic Development and Cultural Change* 52: 719–58.

Polachek, Solomon. 1979. "Occupational Segregation among Women: Theory, Evidence, and a Prognosis." In *Women in the Labor Market*, edited by Cynthia Lloyd, Emily Andrews, and Curtis Gilroy. New York: Columbia University Press.

Sabarwal, Shwetlena, Nistha Sinha, and Mayra Buvinic. 2011. "How Do Women Weather Economic Shocks: What We Know." Economic Premise 46, World Bank, Washington, DC.

Scarpetta, Stefano, Anne Sonnet, and Thomas Manfredi. 2010. "Rising Youth Unemployment during the Crisis: How to Prevent Negative Long Term Consequences on a Generation?" Social Employment and Migration Papers 106, Organisation for Economic Co-operation and Development, Paris.

Seguino, Stephanie. 2009. "The Global Economic Crisis: Its Gender Implications and Policy Responses." Paper prepared for the "Gender Perspectives on the Financial Crisis" panel at the 53rd Session of the Commission on the Status of Women, United Nations, New York.

Shorrocks, Anthony. 2013. "Decomposition Procedures for Distributional Analysis: A Unified Framework Based on the Shapley Value." *Journal of Economic Inequality* 11(1).

Signorelli, Marcello, Misbah T. Choudhry, and Enrico Marelli. 2012. "The Impact of Financial Crises on Female Labour." *European Journal of Development Research*, http://www.palgrave-journals.com/ejdr/journal/vaop/ncurrent/abs/ejdr20123a.html.

Singh, Ajit, and Ann Zammit. 2000, "International Capital Flows: Identifying the Gender Dimension." *World Development* 28 (7): 1249–68.

Skoufias, Emmanuel, and Susan Parker. 2006. "Job Loss and Family Adjustment in Work and Schooling during the Mexican Peso Crisis." *Journal of Population Economics* 19: 163–81.

Smith, James P., Duncan Thomas, Elizabeth Frankenberg, Kathleen Beegle, and Graciela Teruel. 2002. "Wages, Employment, and Economic Shocks: Evidence from Indonesia." *Journal of Population Economics* 15 (1): 161–93.

Strauss, John, Kathleen Beegle, Agus Dwiyanto, Yulia Herawati, Daan Pattinasarany, Elan Satriawan, Bondan Sikoki, Sukamdi, and Firman Witoelar. 2004. *Indonesian Living Standards: Before and After the Financial Crisis.* Santa Monica, CA: Rand Corporation.

Verick, Sher. 2009. "Who Is Hit Hardest during a Financial Crisis? The Vulnerability of Young Men and Women to Unemployment in an Economic Downturn." IZA Discussion Paper 4359, Institute for the Study of Labor (IZA), Bonn, Germany.

Vodopivec, Milan. 2009. "Introducing Unemployment Insurance in Developing Countries." Social Protection Discussion Paper 0907, World Bank, Washington, DC.

Walby, Silvia. 2009. "Gender and the Financial Crisis." Lancaster University, http://www.lancs.ac.uk/fass/doc_library/sociology/Gender_and_financial_crisis_Sylvia_Walby.pdf.

World Bank. 2009. *Averting a Human Crisis during the Global Downturn: Policy Options from the World Bank's Human Development Network.* Washington, DC: World Bank.

———. 2010a. *Household Welfare in the Face of Economic Slowdown: Results from Five Urban City Centers in Turkey.* Washington, DC: World Bank.

———. 2010b. "Coping Well or Barely Coping: Household and Government Responses to the Great Recession in Europe and Central Asia." In *The Jobs Crisis: Household and Government Responses to the Great Recession in Eastern Europe and Central Asia*, edited by M. Ihsan Ajwad and Jesko S. Hentschel. Washington, DC: World Bank.

CHAPTER 4

Labor and Social Protection Policies during the Crisis and the Recovery

David A. Robalino, David Newhouse, and Friederike Rother

Many governments in both rich and poor countries intervened to mitigate the impact of the recent financial crisis, in part through fiscal stimulus packages aiming to revive aggregate demand. But contrary to past crises, countries also implemented policies to protect incomes, support labor demand, and connect individuals to jobs. Although high-income countries were more active and more likely to implement comprehensive packages than developing countries, the extent of government intervention in the latter remains remarkable.

This chapter takes stock of countries' policy responses, assesses their rationale, and identifies areas for improvement. The analysis is based on a unique inventory of programs implemented during the crisis, covering 52 low- and middle-income countries and 22 high-income countries. Clearly, very few of these programs, most of them emergency responses, have been subject to rigorous evaluations. Still, it is possible to provide some general insights into their rationale and potential impacts. We do this first by assessing policy interventions in light of the nature of the shock and the type of labor market adjustment. Second, we rely on what is known about the structure of social protection and labor policies in middle- and low-income countries, as well as past evaluations of programs, to discuss the effectiveness of alternative interventions in protecting different types of workers.

The main finding is that, in general, policies that countries implemented had limited scope, often depended on the programs that were already in place, and had weak links with macroeconomic and labor market adjustments. For example, the prevalence of most types of interventions was not systematically related to countries' growth in output or employment. As a result, many of the policies adopted in response to the crisis did not directly address important labor market challenges or the needs of the most vulnerable groups. Most important, the

This chapter was based on inputs provided by Vera Brusentsev, Mario di Filippo, Arvo Kuddo, Maria Laura Sanchez-Puerta, and Wayne Vroman.

limited data on cost and beneficiaries suggest that most policy responses were too small to make a difference.

Many of the policies that were implemented focused on addressing employment losses, even though labor markets often adjusted through reductions in earnings. Indeed, with the exception of cash transfers for the poor, the bulk of policies adopted focused on protecting jobs and the unemployed. Outside the countries of the Organisation for Economic Co-operation and Development (OECD), over half of all countries implemented policy interventions designed to support labor demand (excluding public works), job search assistance and training, and, in a few countries, the extension of unemployment benefits. Essentially, these policies aimed to prevent dismissals in the formal sector or to protect those who lost formal sector jobs. Savings schemes, which could be a more appropriate response to declining earnings, are largely underdeveloped in middle- and lower-income countries.

Countries' heavy reliance on employment services and training programs also raises concerns, given design problems and the potential for low impact during a downturn. Nearly 40 percent of all middle- and low-income countries implemented at least one of these policies, while around half the OECD countries did. Even though expenditures on these programs were generally limited, efforts to implement them may have diverted precious administrative resources from programs with wider coverage. Based on evidence from international experiences, both types of programs can be effective in helping workers get jobs but only if they are designed and implemented well. In the developing world, with a few exceptions, employment services are underdeveloped and suffer from low institutional capacity, while training programs are supply driven and have low external efficiency (see Almeida, Behrman, and Robalino 2012). And while intermediation services have an important role to play during the recovery when job vacancies start to grow, their role during a downturn appears to be limited.

In most cases, the policies implemented may have benefited adults more than youth, the group most affected by the crisis. As discussed in chapter 3, in those countries where information is available, youth employment rates declined more than those of adults, particularly in countries where the crisis was more severe, such as Latvia and Lithuania. Yet, youths are less likely to benefit from standard interventions for four reasons:

- First, many enter the labor market through the informal sector and move frequently between jobs (unemployment rates are often high because of a high turnover rather than long unemployment spells).
- Second, even those who enter through the formal sector are less likely to be eligible for unemployment benefits or an adequate severance package because of short vesting periods (one of the design problems of current systems).
- Third, youths are also less likely to benefit from programs that support the self-employed (for example, credit) and that target individuals with working and managerial experience.

- Fourth, most of the policies also had a bias toward formal sector workers, while many in the informal sector, possibly facing higher risks during a downturn, relied on self-insurance.

Indeed, with the exception of cash transfers and public works, most of the other interventions benefited formal sector workers. Wage subsidies or credit to enterprises are tailored to formal sector firms. Unemployment insurance or severance pay is available only to formal sector workers (insurance arrangements, in general, cover around 30–40 percent of the labor force in middle-income countries, mainly formal sector workers). Even employment services and training programs are more likely to benefit formal sector workers, since the links of the programs are with formal sector firms. The self-employed, a large share of the informal workforce, are unlikely to have benefited from any kind of support unless they were not poor.

The main conclusion from the chapter is that for better response to future crises countries need to improve the design of their social protection systems. Systems can be strengthened by (1) institutionalizing and integrating targeted cash transfers and public works programs that can expand and contract in response to business cycle fluctuations; (2) expanding the coverage of social insurance programs to include the unorganized sector—including unemployment benefits systems—that would reduce the demand for discretionary transfers during a downturn; and (3) optimizing the design of programs that deal with labor market failures related to limited information, mobility constraints, skills mismatches, and limited access to credit, before expanding them. To support these efforts, countries should invest in labor market information and early warning systems that can be used to design and adapt policies along the economic cycle and to evaluate their impacts.

The remainder of the chapter is organized in three sections. The next section, "The Role of Labor and Social Protection Policies during a Downturn," proposes a conceptual framework to guide the design of social protection and labor policies that provide adequate protection against idiosyncratic and aggregate shocks. "Social Protection and Labor Policies and Their Link to the Type of Shock and Labor Market Adjustment" reviews the instruments available for addressing different types of market failures, as well as the institutional constraints that can affect implementation. The final section—"What Can Be Done to Be Better Prepared in the Future?"—takes stock of policy responses across countries, discusses their rationale, and provides general guidelines for strengthening current social protection and labor market policies to improve their ability to respond to crises.

The Role of Labor and Social Protection Policies during a Downturn

This section discusses the objectives of labor and social protection policies during a downturn, the set of instruments available, and the economic and institutional factors that should be taken into account when designing interventions. Specific programs will, of course, depend on local conditions. The goal here is simply to outline general principles to guide policy.

Market and Government Failures That Require Attention

There is still no consensus on the role of governments during an economic downturn. Most specialists would agree that governments have to set up safety nets to protect workers who lose their jobs or see their earnings decline—although they hold different views on the optimal design of such programs. Beyond that, however, things are murkier. Several economists, for instance, consider that debt-financed government spending during a downturn has only a small short-term effect, if any, on economic growth and yet can be damaging over the medium term when the debt has to be repaid through higher taxes.[1] Others, however, consider fiscal stimulus fundamental to mitigating the impact of demand shocks and downplay current concerns about the high public debt and calls for austerity.[2] The empirical evidence, meanwhile, is mixed (see Auerbach, Gale, and Harris 2010).

There is even less consensus on the use of policies that aim to protect or create jobs directly. Some argue that protecting jobs may delay necessary adjustments to the economy and thus negatively affect the recovery and medium-term productivity growth. They recommend that governments not interfere with "creative destruction" during a recession, provided that workers receive adequate protection (see, for instance, Caballero and Hammour 1994, 1996). Others believe that job protection can help avoid unnecessary firing and hiring costs and the depreciation of skills among the newly unemployed (see Messenger and Rodriguez 2010; Verho 2008). According to defenders of these protective measures, evidence of an increase in allocative efficiency during downturns is limited; on the contrary, they argue, jobs created during contractions are often of lower quality (see Baily, Hulten, and Campbell 1992; Barlevy 2002, 2003). They advocate wage subsidies and work-sharing arrangements, sometimes coupled with training, and also the direct creation of jobs through public works (for a discussion, see ILO 2009; OECD 2010).

In this chapter, we argue that social protection and labor market policies should be designed to address market and regulatory failures that, while always present, are aggravated during a recession (see also Paci, Revenga, and Rijkers 2009). These failures can be grouped in three categories: (1) those that affect the ability of individuals to self-insure, (2) those that affect job search, and (3) those that affect labor demand. All involve problems of information, access to credit, budgetary constraints, and individuals' "myopia."

Constraints to Self-Insurance

Many individuals, particularly the less educated, are likely to fail to self-insure properly against unemployment or a fall in earnings. The first reason is that insurance markets can break down due to lack of information. Companies do not have information about the unemployment risk of each individual and therefore set premiums that reflect average risks. Low-risk individuals prefer not to enroll in the system, which drives premiums up until they become unaffordable.[3] In addition, selling unemployment insurance can be challenging. It can be difficult for companies to accommodate the costs of an economic downturn, when many individuals lose their jobs simultaneously. Two other reasons people may fail to self-insure are their lack of access to appropriate financial instruments and their budget constraints. Indeed, at least in the case of middle- and low-income countries, many individuals lack access to formal savings or insurance instruments or cannot afford to save enough. A final obstacle to self-insurance is myopia. Individuals may simply lack information or the necessary cognitive and noncognitive skills to pick the right insurance plan or devise and implement the right savings plan.

Constraints to Job Search

Information problems and lack of access to credit also affect the labor market. Individuals have limited information about where the jobs that match their skills are. Surveys in developing countries show that most find jobs through personal contacts (see World Bank 2013). Similarly, employers seeking to fill vacancies have limited information about the distribution of skills among job seekers and even applicants. It is particularly difficult to gauge so-called soft skills (team work, creativity and leadership) that are not certified by diplomas. The process of job searching can thus be time consuming and inefficient and still result in imperfect matches. During a recession, when most firms are shedding jobs and the ratio of job seekers to vacancies shoots up, this may be less of an issue. But an inefficient job search can unnecessarily slow down employment creation during a recovery (see Cunningham, Sanchez-Puerta, and Wuermli 2010; Robalino and Sanchez-Puerta 2012).

The problem can be aggravated when long unemployment spells lead to a depreciation of skills or if the recession induces structural changes in the demand for skills. In this case, for some, finding jobs involves investing in the right type of training. These investments can fail to materialize if individuals do not have the right information about market demands and the quality of training providers or if they face liquidity constraints and lack access to credit (see Almeida, Behrman, and Robalino 2012).

Constraints to Employment Creation

The same imperfections in financial markets that led to the last recession can affect firms and their ability to access credit, retain workers, or create jobs. For instance, during an economic slowdown, solvent firms may prefer to keep workers on the payroll rather than incurring dismissal and hiring costs. But when facing a drop in revenues from sales, they can do so only if they have access to credit. Unfortunately, in middle- and low-income countries, small firms have limited or no access to credit even during normal times—and during a downturn credit gets even tighter (see Beck and Demirguc-Kunt 2011).

While labor market regulations generally have modest effects on aggregate outcomes, inappropriate regulations can exacerbate downturns by hampering workers' ability to switch jobs. Most governments aim to protect workers by enforcing adequate working conditions (health and safety, working hours, and leave policies, for example), setting minimum wages, and regulating hiring and dismissal procedures. The bulk of the evidence from developing countries suggests that in most cases reforms to these regulations have minor impacts on aggregate employment outcomes.[4] Regulations can, however, limit the ability of first-time entrants, who are disproportionately youth and women, to enter good jobs (see Kahn 2010; Montenegro and Pages 2004). Furthermore, excessively rigid regulations also limit workers' mobility between jobs,[5] which can in turn reduce productivity growth.[6] During a recession, regulations may prevent workers from escaping the hardest-hit sectors and could also reduce firms' incentives to restructure.

Programs that attempt to address these potential market and regulatory failures fall into three categories: (1) programs to support and stimulate labor demand; (2) programs to support job search and preserve skills; and (3) income support programs (see figure 4.1). Setting aside specific issues of design, the last two types are uncontroversial. Programs to support job search are needed for dealing with the information problems discussed above that pervade labor markets. They include intermediation and counseling, job search assistance, training, and skills certification. Meanwhile, income protection systems that bring together social insurance and social assistance programs are also necessary to complement self-insurance. The existence of these programs may also be a precondition to facilitating the reform of labor regulations. The more controversial programs are those aiming to create and protect jobs. Facilitating access to credit, as discussed above, is of course important when capital markets are not working well. But beyond policies to stimulate aggregate demand, it is unclear whether governments should be implementing employer-linked wage subsidies or

Figure 4.1 Typology of Policies to Mitigate the Impact of the Financial Crisis

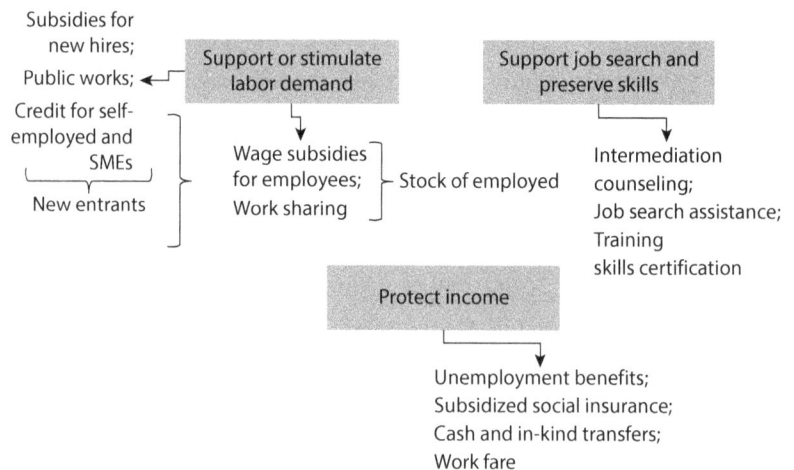

Source: World Bank staff.
Note: SMEs = small and medium enterprises.

work-sharing arrangements to protect jobs. The next section will discuss some of the issues involved.

Linking Policies to Labor Market Adjustments

As seen in chapter 2, the impacts of the recent financial crisis depended on the structure of the economy and its degree of openness, transmission channels, and labor regulations. Recessions start in a given region or economic sector but spread rapidly throughout the economy (see Manning 2000; McKenzie 2004). Usually, the impact on labor markets will vary by economic sector and geographic region. Three issues that need to be taken into account are whether adjustments take place through employment levels or through earnings, whether they are temporary or permanent, and how they affect different workers.

Whether labor markets adjust through employment levels or earnings affects which policy response is most appropriate. Policies to protect jobs or encourage the creation of new jobs, for instance, are less suitable when the adjustment is taking place through earnings. The same applies to income protection policies; unemployment based on risk pooling[7] is important when adjustments take place through reductions in employment, but if earnings are falling, insurance schemes based on savings and cash transfers are needed instead. Employment services and training programs are also more relevant when the problem is unemployment as opposed to lower earnings, although it can be argued that these programs can also help move workers from low- to high-paying jobs. Ultimately, whether employment or income effects dominate will depend on several factors, including the extent of labor regulations, the role of unions, production technologies, and how competitive the labor market is for particular skills (see Fallon and Lucas 2002). It is an empirical question that needs to be addressed case by case, which implies having access to timely labor market data.

A second issue is whether demand shocks in a given sector are temporary or permanent. In the first case, employment and earnings would ultimately recover and converge to their precrisis levels. Appropriate unemployment benefits, savings arrangements, or cash transfers can be enough to help workers smooth consumption during the transition period. In some instances, policy makers could also consider policies to protect jobs by ensuring that credit is available: the idea being to reduce the social costs associated with firing and hiring and potential skills depreciation. In the second case, either earnings will not recover or lost jobs will not come back, or both. Insurance and savings arrangements may then need to be combined with employment services and training programs that help individuals move to other sectors or regions.

Policies that attempt to protect jobs when adjustments are permanent can be counterproductive and compromise the speed of the recovery and productivity growth over the medium term.[8] The problem, unfortunately, is that it is difficult to assess ex ante whether the effect of a shock in a given industry or sector is temporary or permanent. For this reason, both chapters 2 and 3 in this volume have said little about the issue. The implication is that, even if some of the evidence discussed above suggests that efficiency gains from reallocations of labor and capital during a downturn are limited, policy makers should be careful with programs that aim to protect jobs. And if used, these programs should likely be short-lived.

The third issue is the vulnerability of different workers to the type of labor market adjustment. This vulnerability can be assessed along several dimensions, including workers' age, gender, and skills and whether they are engaged in formal or informal activities. Chapter 3 showed, for instance, that youth were more affected by the recent financial crisis than adults. Among labor force participants, low-skilled workers can also be more vulnerable because the demand for their skills is more elastic and because they tend to be lower-income workers with less capacity to self-insure. In addition, other things being equal, workers in informal activities may face higher risks of being laid off and unemployed (see, for example, the evidence from Brazil in figure 4.2), given that informal production units are often smaller and less able to accommodate a fall in demand or that they are not affected by unions and labor regulations.

On both equity and efficiency grounds, there are compelling reasons to target limited resources to the poor, particularly with respect to income-support programs. For labor market programs, this fact suggests prioritizing the informal

Figure 4.2 Risk of Unemployment of Formal and Informal Sector Workers in Brazil, March 2002–September 2009

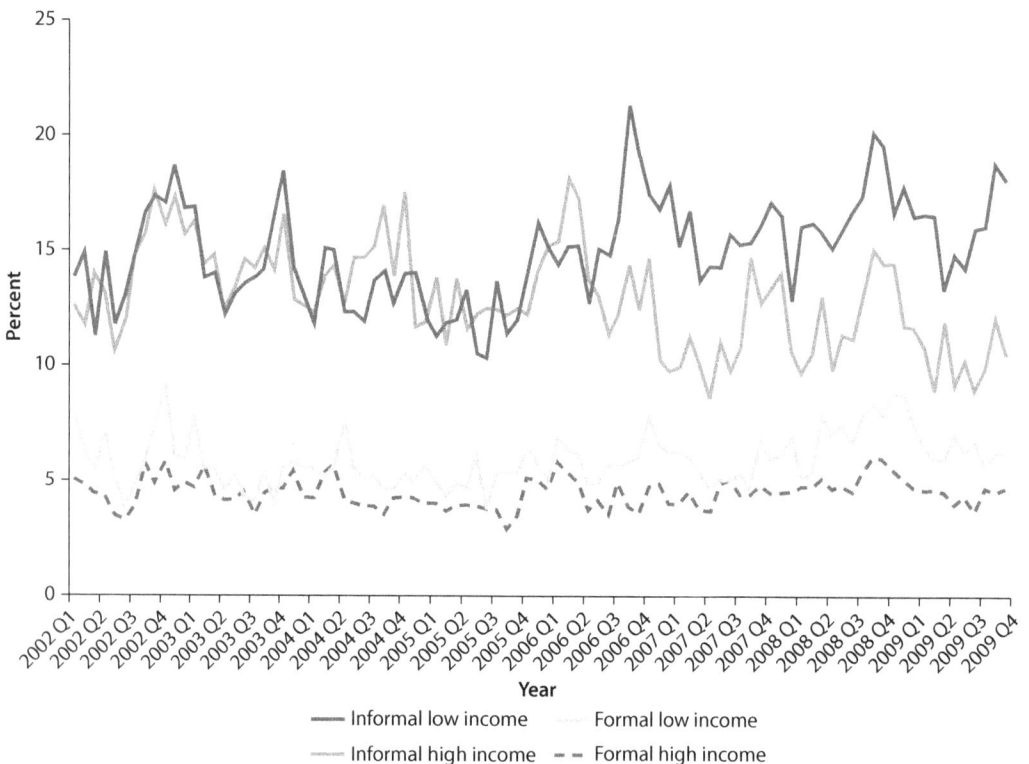

Source: Calculations based on the Brazilian Pesquisa Mensal de Emprego (PME).

sector, where low-skilled and low-income workers concentrate. These programs can also benefit youth, who also tend to enter the labor market through the informal sector. The use of public subsidies in the formal sector, however, could concentrate in sectors and regions that have been more affected by a given economic shock.

Social Protection and Labor Policies and Their Link to the Type of Shock and Labor Market Adjustment

Whether rich or poor, many of the countries implemented at least one of the policies described in the previous section.[9] Among the 52 low- and middle-income countries for which data are available, 1,130 interventions were implemented between 2008 and 2009, while about 635 were implemented in the 22 high-income countries. The most common interventions focused on supporting labor demand, followed closely by income protection. Intermediation, training, and other active labor market programs (ALMPs), though less numerous, were still prevalent. Below we provide an overview of policy responses. We first look at the prevalence, cost, and coverage of different types of programs. Then, we examine the links between the implementation of policies and the changes in output and employment growth. Then, for each of the three types of policy interventions identified above, we review international responses and discuss their effectiveness based on the results of past evaluations and what is known about program design and coverage.

The Nature of the Policy Response

Low- and middle-income countries responded differently than high-income countries. Not surprisingly, high-income countries were more likely to implement almost all types of specific interventions. One notable exception was in-kind transfers, which were more likely to be implemented by low- and middle-income countries. For developed countries, the most popular policy was the expansion of unemployment benefits (implemented by over 80 percent of the countries), followed by support to enterprises (implemented by around 60 percent). Low-income countries also tended to provide support to small and medium enterprises (SMEs) but focused more on training and income-support programs, followed by public works and in-cash or in-kind transfers (see figure 4.3, panel c).

Most programs instituted in response to the crisis were new (see figure 4.4). Overall, roughly two-thirds of all programs were new, rather than expansions of previous programs. Measures to increase labor demand were particularly likely to be new. Meanwhile, unemployment benefits, employment services, and public works programs were most likely to be expansions of initial programs, as these types of programs are more difficult to establish in the short term.

Budgetary allocations for labor demand and intermediation programs tended to be negligible. Despite the popularity of labor demand measures such as programs designed to provide credit and support to SMEs, budget allocations to these programs were tiny. Figure 4.5 shows the average country expenditure, as a share

Figure 4.3 Percentage of Countries Adopting Labor or Social Protection Policies, 2008–09

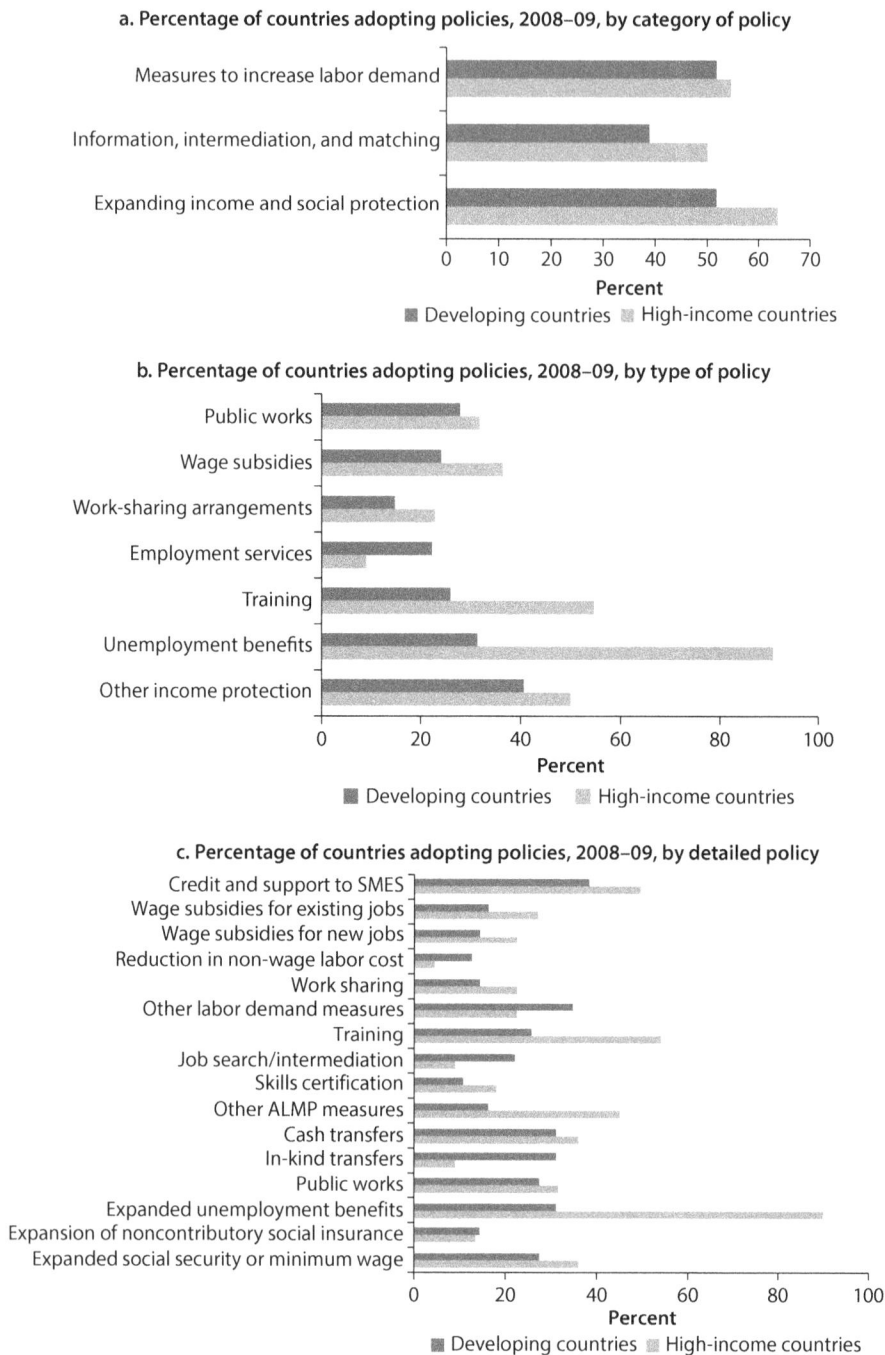

a. Percentage of countries adopting policies, 2008–09, by category of policy

b. Percentage of countries adopting policies, 2008–09, by type of policy

c. Percentage of countries adopting policies, 2008–09, by detailed policy

Source: Calculations based on ILO-WB Inventory of Policy Responses (see annex and International Labour Organization and World Bank 2012 for details).
Note: ALMP = active labor market program.

Figure 4.4 Percentage of Labor or Social Protection Interventions That Were New, 2008–09

a. Categories of policies

b. Types of policies

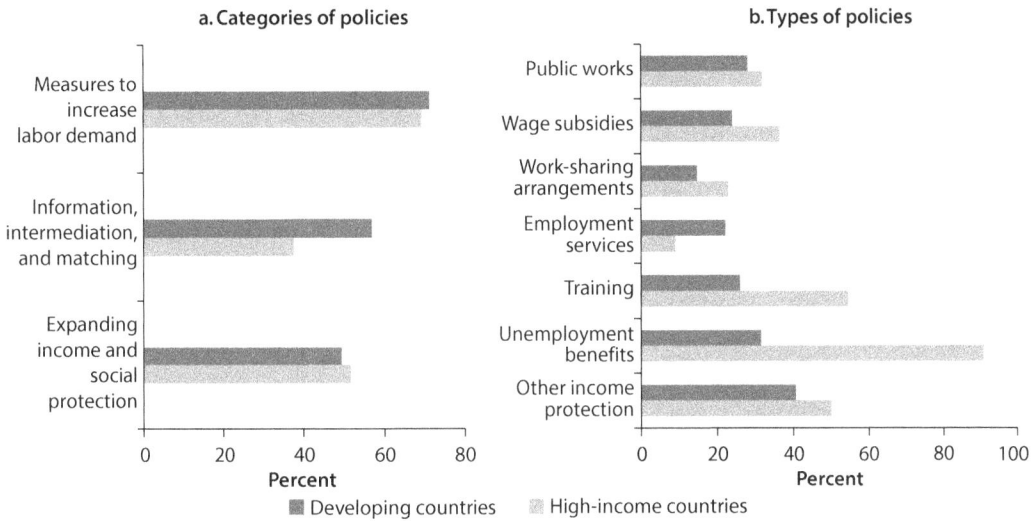

Developing countries   High-income countries

Source: Calculations based on ILO-WB Inventory of Policy Responses.

Figure 4.5 Average Total Country Expenditure as a Share of GDP, by Year and Program Type, 2008–09

a. Categories of policies

b. Specific policies

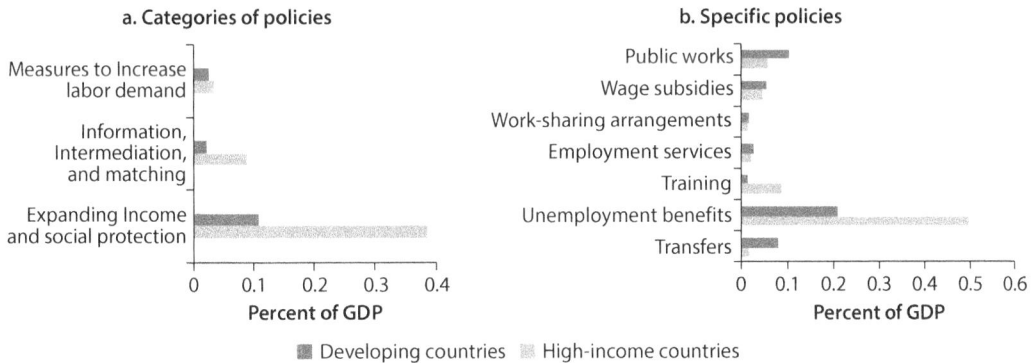

Developing countries   High-income countries

Source: Calculations based on ILO-WB Inventory of Policy Responses.
Note: GDP = gross domestic product.

of gross domestic product (GDP), on all programs of a particular type. Of the 16 countries that reported cost information for at least one labor demand program, median country expenditure was a paltry 0.02 percent of GDP. Expenditures were similarly low on intermediation programs, including training. This is consistent with the experience of the G-20, where only 2.5 percent of stimulus programs were devoted to ALMPs (ILO 2010). Expanding income and social protection was a bigger priority, as the median expenditure across 28 countries was 0.1 percent of GDP. Unemployment benefits were particularly expensive for many countries, comprising 0.2 percent of GDP in India and 0.4 percent in the former Yugoslav Republic of Macedonia. Expenditures on benefits in these three countries were comparable to those of most developed countries, which tended to spend 0.4 percent of GDP on unemployment benefits.

Figure 4.6 Median Number of Total Program Beneficiaries as a Share of the Labor Force, 2008–09

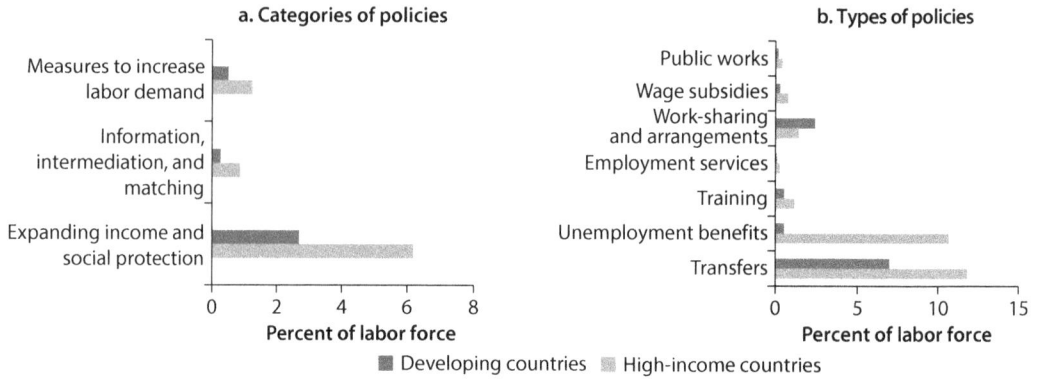

Source: Calculations based on ILO-WB Inventory of Policy Responses.

Because of low expenditures, coverage also tended to be low in developing countries, especially for public works, wage subsidies, and training programs (figure 4.6). Eleven countries reported the number of beneficiaries served by at least one public works program. The median number of beneficiaries was only 0.1 percent of the labor force. Wage subsidies, training programs, employment services, and unemployment benefits typically also served a tiny portion of the labor force. Work-sharing arrangements typically covered 1–2 percent of the labor force, but were implemented only in the Russian Federation and Turkey. Only other income protection programs—usually cash transfer—were able to reach more than 5 percent of the labor force. Examples of these programs include food subsidies in Bangladesh, the Bolsa Familia cash transfer program in Brazil, and the "families in action" conditional cash transfer (CCT) program in Colombia. In short, while many countries implemented programs, most of the effective response came in the form of preexisting transfer programs.

Did the Policy Response Match the Impacts of the Crisis?

In general, it does not appear that the more affected countries responded more aggressively. This finding can be seen in figure 4.7, panel a, which divides the 50 developing countries that implemented a policy in 2008 or 2009 into three terciles, based on the slowdown in their GDP growth in 2009 relative to the average growth rate in 2007 and 2008. On average, the growth rate of the most affected countries plummeted by 10 percentage points, while the corresponding drop was 5 percentage points for the middle tercile and 1.5 percentage points for the least affected countries. Despite these large differences in exposure to the crisis, however, the most affected countries were not more likely to implement policies. A larger share of the most affected countries did respond by establishing wage subsidies (for new or existing jobs) and work-sharing arrangements. In addition, training programs and unemployment benefit expansions were also less likely to be adopted by the least affected countries. But most policies—including support to enterprises, public works, and other labor demand measures—were not more prevalent in the most affected countries.

Similarly, the adoption of policies was not closely related to employment losses. Again, differences in changes in employment growth were substantial, reflecting the heterogeneity of labor market adjustments noted in chapter 1. The most affected countries suffered a slowdown of 7.5 percentage points on average, while the corresponding slowdowns for the middle and least affected countries were 3 and 1.5. As was the case for growth, however, there is little systematic difference between the policy response of countries that suffered steep employment drops and countries with more minor employment adjustments (figure 4.7).

The experience of a small subset of countries, in fact, suggests that the slowdown in employment growth and the level of expenditures on measures to support labor demand were not strongly correlated. Information on expenditures on labor demand policies and labor market adjustments is available for only 11 countries. Since the exact timing of the policies is in many cases unknown, it is impossible to disentangle whether the nature of the adjustment was influenced by the policy response (for example, were large policy responses associated with

Figure 4.7 Policy Responses and Slowdowns in Output and Employment Growth

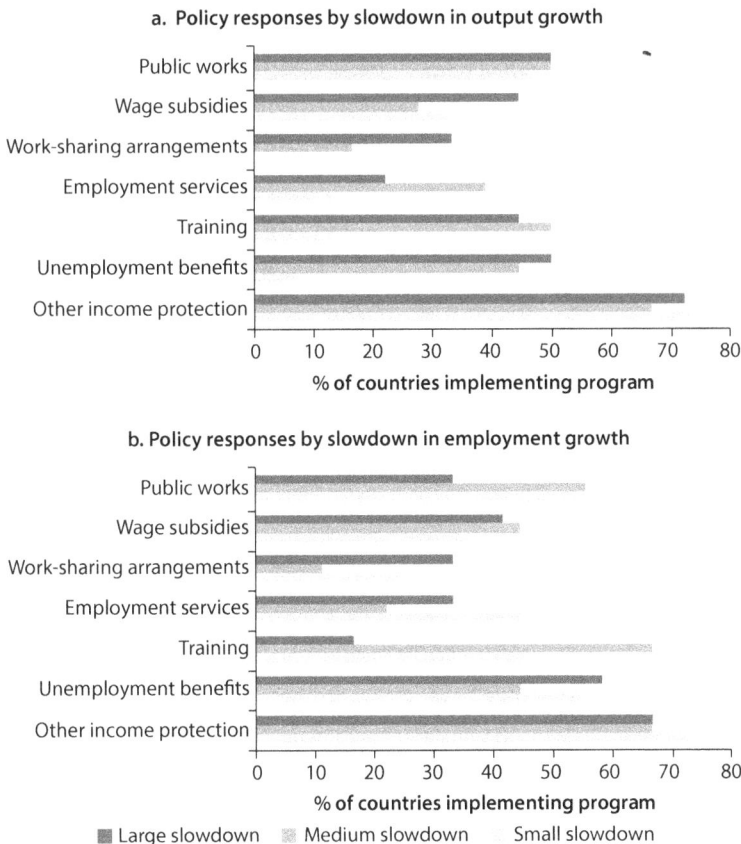

a. Policy responses by slowdown in output growth

b. Policy responses by slowdown in employment growth

■ Large slowdown   ▨ Medium slowdown   Small slowdown

Source: Calculations based on ILO-WB Inventory of Policy Responses.

small adjustments in employment?) or whether the reverse is true (for example, were large contractions in employment accompanied by large policy responses?). But what the data show is a weak relationship between changes in employment levels and the strength of the policy response to support labor demand. Two exceptions are Ecuador and Turkey, where aggressive policies to promote labor demand coincided with a limited fall in adjustment. The typical case, however, is more similar to Bulgaria or Latvia, where greater spending on labor demand programs did not appear to help maintain employment. Although Bulgaria spent more on these programs, their fall in net employment growth was significantly greater. Similarly, Latvia spent only 0.2 percent of GDP on public works, despite employment growth declining 20 percentage points.

Several low- and middle-income countries targeted programs to youth and women, but not necessarily when those were the most affected groups. A significant share of ALMPs, for instance, was targeted to youth and to a lesser extent women (see figure 4.8, panel a). But in only two countries, Costa Rica and Latvia, did the targeting coincide with a more severe slowdown in youth employment relative to adult employment (figure 4.8, panel b). On the contrary, in most countries where youth were more affected than adults, programs were not targeted to them.

Figure 4.8 Programs Targeting Youth and Women and Women in Selected Countries, 2008–09

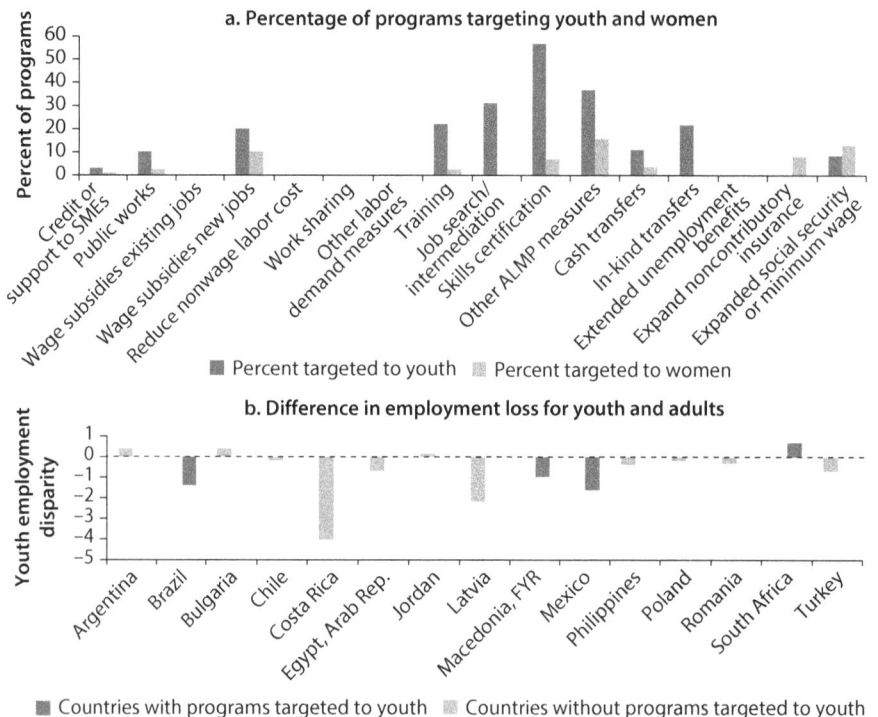

a. Percentage of programs targeting youth and women

■ Percent targeted to youth   ▨ Percent targeted to women

b. Difference in employment loss for youth and adults

■ Countries with programs targeted to youth   ▨ Countries without programs targeted to youth

Source: Calculations based on ILO-WB Policy Inventory.
Note: ALMP = active labor market program; SMEs = small and medium enterprises.

In general, the mix of policies implemented by countries did not correspond to the nature of the labor market adjustment. Surprisingly, given the large reductions in earnings growth observed in most countries, policy interventions were biased toward those that supported labor demand. Indeed, countries with larger falls in earnings growth, such as Serbia and Ukraine, tended to adopt a smaller share of income-support policies than countries with smaller falls in earnings. Conversely, countries with larger employment slowdowns reported that a smaller share of their programs targeted labor demand or promoted intermediation (see figure 4.9). Clearly, policies can differ greatly in their importance and budget. But overall, the evidence suggests that policies were often implemented with little understanding of the underlying labor market adjustments.

Review of Programs That Support Labor Demand

As discussed earlier, policies that support labor demand were the most prevalent and took many forms, including support to enterprises. Here, we focus on three types of social protection and labor policies: public works, wage subsidies, and work-sharing arrangements.

Public Works

These were important programs in the developing world and are likely to have made a difference among low-income workers and the poor. The existing empirical evidence suggests, in fact, that public works can play a significant role in absorbing excess labor during a downturn.[10] But there are still open questions about their design and cost-effectiveness.

Countries that were able to deploy public works during the crisis already had the systems in place. This was the case, for instance, for Mexico's Temporary Works Program, which was extended in 2009 to provide employment opportunities to an estimated 250,000 workers (0.5 percent of the labor force) for a period ranging between four and six months at a salary of twice the minimum wage. In Europe and Central Asia (ECA), two large-scale interventions were implemented in Kazakhstan and Turkey. In Kazakhstan, where the growth rates of output and employment contracted by 7.8 and 2.2 percentage points, respectively, public works focused on construction and maintenance of piped water, electricity and gas, sewage facilities, highways and local roads, schools, hospitals, and other socially important facilities.[11] The programs were also used in Africa. Kenya launched the Kazi Kwa Vijana program in April 2009, aiming to employ youth in rural and urban areas through labor-intensive public works implemented by different line ministries. Botswana introduced the Ipelegeng Program in July 2008 to create temporary employment on a rotational basis; it was subsequently expanded. Finally, South Africa responded to a severe contraction in employment growth (4.2 percentage points) by expanding its public works program.

Countries that tried to implement these programs from scratch could not do so in time. A good example is the Temporary Income-Support Program in El Salvador. The program's design is innovative in several respects. First, it guarantees a minimum income to poor urban families and provides labor market experience

Figure 4.9 Share of Policies That Support Income Protection, Labor Demand, and Labor Market Adjustment in Selected Developing Countries, 2009

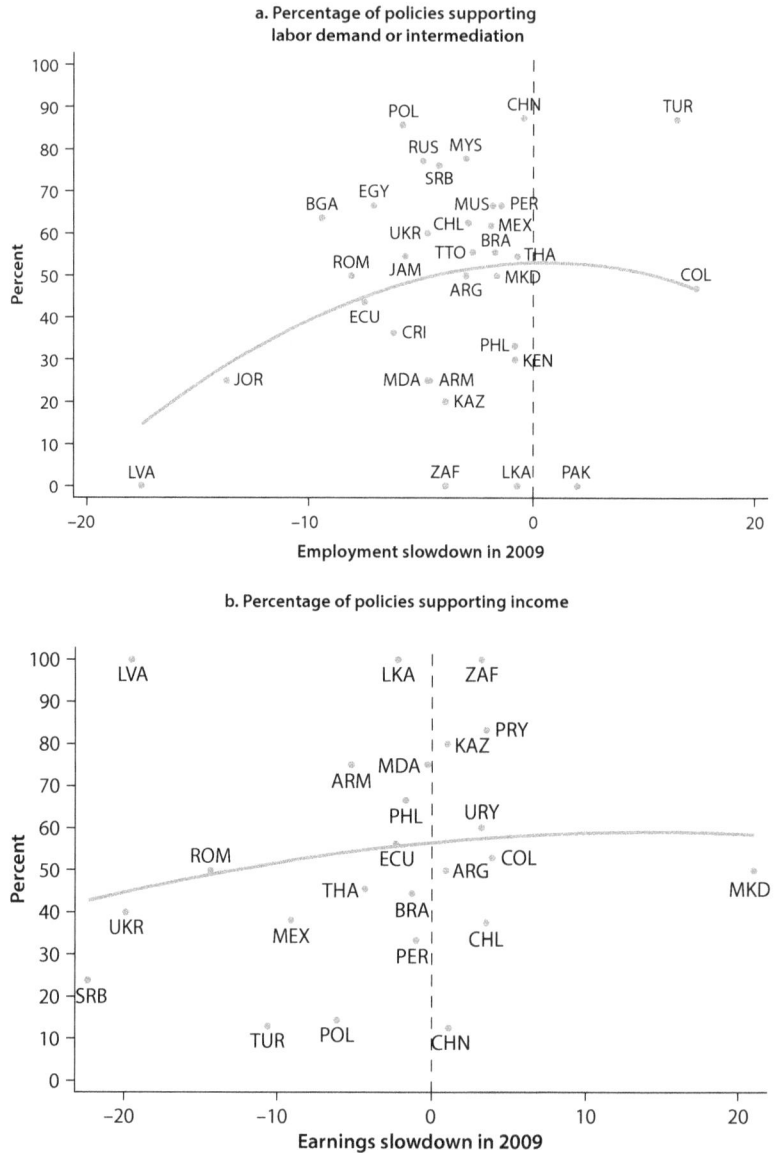

a. Percentage of policies supporting labor demand or intermediation

b. Percentage of policies supporting income

Source: ILO-WB Policy Inventory.

at the municipal level. Second, in contrast with traditional income-support programs, it pays individuals to work on projects submitted by municipalities, with emphasis on providing social services. And third, it also comprises an innovative training component that aims to enhance beneficiaries' technical skills as well as their soft skills for the labor market. The government expected to target urban youth between 16 and 24 years of age in addition to female household heads. Unfortunately, the program entered into operation only in March 2011, two years after the emergence of the crisis.

In the absence of unemployment insurance, public works may have provided an important alternative for low-income workers, particularly those in the agricultural or urban informal sector. If well designed, particularly regarding the length of the employment contract and the level of wages, programs can provide sufficient protection to unemployed low-income workers, without reducing incentives to work or search for jobs (see Ferreira and Robalino 2010).

Still, even the programs implemented before the crisis have not been evaluated for the most part, and questions about whether these are the best mechanisms for protecting the incomes of vulnerable workers remain. One important issue relates to the complexity of managing "construction" projects. If the goal is to protect incomes during periods of unemployment, why are public works superior to direct transfers? Questions about the efficiency of public works as a tool for building infrastructure also remain; since the goal is to create jobs, countries might end up choosing production technologies that are too costly for the projects at hand and give less attention to issues related to the quality and durability of the infrastructure created. An alternative model during a crisis would be to combine cash transfers to protect the most vulnerable with stimulus packages that, in part, are invested in infrastructure but through "normal" channels and procurement arrangements instead of public works (see Ribe, Robalino, and Walker 2012).

Wage Subsidies

Wage subsidies came in different forms, with different but related objectives. Subsidies were given to employers to stimulate demand or to employees to provide incentives for reemployment. They took the form of direct transfers or reductions in social security contributions. And they focused on those already employed or only on new hires.[12] This type of intervention remains controversial for several reasons. First, protecting jobs can incur efficiency losses and delay necessary structural adjustments and affect productivity growth over the medium term. Second, wage subsidies benefit mainly formal sector workers and can therefore be regressive (see Robalino and Banerji 2009).

Finally, wage subsidies may have small effects on total employment, if those with subsidies displace other workers (see Betcherman, Olivas, and Dar 2004; Dar and Tzannatos 1999). Between 2008 and 2009, the majority of OECD countries adopted wage subsidies, mainly through reductions in social security contributions, and often targeted small enterprises or disadvantaged groups. France, for instance, reduced employer social security contributions for firms with fewer than 10 employees that hired new low-wage workers in 2009. The reduction was the largest for workers hired at the minimum wage and declined as the wage increased up to 1.6 times the minimum wage. In Germany, employee and employer contributions to the unemployment insurance system were reduced. Spain reduced employer social contributions for the first two years of employment for unemployed people with children who transit to full-time permanent contracts. It also implemented a reduction in social security contributions for youth or disabled workers who start up a business as self-employed. A different approach was taken in the United Kingdom, where companies received £2,500 for hiring workers who had been unemployed for more than six months. Across the board, hiring subsidies were set to be phased out in early 2011 (see OECD 2010).

In middle-income countries, wage subsidies were used mainly in Eastern Europe and Latin America. Bulgaria, Estonia, Hungary, FYR Macedonia, and Serbia introduced or expanded these programs predominantly for youth. In Turkey, as part of the so-called Labor Package 2008, social security contributions for employers were reduced by five percentage points. In Latin America, Chile introduced a new Youth Employment Subsidy Law in January 2009. This program offered a subsidy equal to 30 percent of the annual salary of those individuals between 18 and 24 years of age who finished secondary education, were working in a formal position, and earned less than Ch$360,000 (US$600) per year.[13] In Colombia, wage subsidies were broader and took the form of a payroll tax holiday for new small and medium firms.

How efficient these policies were, particularly in middle-income countries, is a source of debate. Overall, the evidence on the effects of wage subsidies on employment is mixed. Some studies emphasize that subsidies often go to workers who would have been hired (or would not have been fired) in any circumstance or that they induce substitutions between subsidized and nonsubsidized workers (see Betcherman, Olivas, and Dar 2004; Dar and Tzannatos 1999). Others, however, show that at the macroeconomic level net effects are usually positive.[14] Moreover, some evidence shows positive (dynamic) effects on the ability of beneficiaries to improve their labor market opportunities over the medium term (see Cockx, Goebel, and Robin 2013; Gerfin, Lechner, and Steiger 2002).

During the crisis, reductions in social security contributions are likely to have helped maintain employment and preserve human capital. Indeed, most evaluations agree that a lower wedge between the total cost of labor and take-home pay can both reduce dismissals and stimulate hiring.[15] The costs of effective wage subsidies, however, should not be underestimated.[16] Meaningful effects may require sizable reductions in the contribution rate (for example, a four-percentage-point reduction in the contribution rate to avoid a two-percentage-point reduction in employment), which implies substantial budgetary transfers or an increase in the unfunded liabilities of the social security system.

As for design, subsidies targeted to vulnerable workers (and linked to the stock of employees) are likely to be a better option than across-the-board subsidies.[17] The latter are not only more expensive but also subject to larger dead-weight losses. An alternative is to focus instead on lower-paid workers (usually low-skilled and young workers), with subsidies declining as wages increase (as in the example of France cited above). It is also important to link the subsidies to changes in the stock of employment. Wage subsidies that are simply linked to the wage could give firms more room for "gaming the system."

Nonetheless, concerns persist that these programs are regressive. Indeed, employment-based wage subsidies benefit mainly formal sector workers at the expense of those in the informal sector. Alternatives that could have been considered are targeted employee-based subsidies linked to other ALMPs, such as training.[18] These programs focus on helping the already unemployed find jobs—particularly such vulnerable groups as youth or unskilled workers—by combining on-the-job training, employment assistance, and training stipends, which serve part of the same purpose as wage subsidies. This approach has been successfully implemented by the Jovenes programs in several Latin American countries, including Argentina, Colombia, and the Dominican Republic.[19]

Work Sharing

Like wage subsidies, work sharing was implemented in different ways. In general, workers were required to reduce working hours and accept a proportional reduction in wages. Work sharing was often accompanied by partial unemployment benefits, provision of paid holidays, or provision of short-term training stipends (see Abraham and Houseman 1993).

Leading the implementation of these programs were OECD countries. Take-up rates increased rapidly and were the highest in Belgium (5.6 percent), Italy (3.3 percent), Germany (3.2 percent), and Japan (2.7 percent).[20] The design of the programs—notably, eligibility conditions, type and level of support, financing mechanisms, and duration—varied considerably. In a few countries, support was available only for reductions in daily working time spread over the entire week (as in Austria) or for temporary lay-offs at zero hours per week (like Denmark). Most European countries offered financial support for both reduced weekly hours and temporary layoffs (as in Belgium, France, Portugal, and Spain). In Austria, Belgium, France, Germany, Italy, Luxembourg, and Portugal employees received payments through the employer (partly or fully subsidized by the government); while in other countries, such as Denmark, Finland, Ireland, Spain, and the United Kingdom, public compensation for nonworked hours was paid directly to employees by the unemployment insurance scheme. A small number of countries, including the Netherlands and Portugal, made it compulsory for workers on short-time work to participate in training. However, training was not compulsory in the majority of countries, such as Austria, Belgium, Finland, Germany, Japan, Norway, Portugal, and Switzerland.

Outside the OECD, the main work-sharing arrangements were implemented in Argentina, Colombia, Costa Rica, and Mexico. Argentina reactivated the Programa de Recuperacion Activa that was designed during the 2002 crisis. This was a monthly wage supplement provided to employees for up to 12 months with an agreement with employers not to dismiss workers and adjust work schedules. In Colombia and Mexico, shorter work schedules were complemented by subsidized training. A different approach was used in Costa Rica, where the reduction in the number of hours was not conditional on a reduction in hourly wages. In all cases, the focus was on formal firms, but little information about implementation arrangements and even the number of workers who benefited from the programs is available.

Overall, the effect of mandatory work sharing on employment is still under debate. Some evidence, in the case of France, for instance, suggests that aggregate employment was unaffected but that labor turnover increased as firms shed workers who became more expensive.[21] A review of programs in European countries shows mixed results, with impacts depending on the setting (Kapteyn, Kalwij, and Zaidi 2000).

Two important issues in program design involve training and compensation mechanisms for lower wages. A practice in industrialized countries worth considering is encouraging employees who are on work-sharing schemes to participate in training and retraining activities to upgrade their skills and improve their employability. As for compensation mechanisms, the unemployment insurance system is usually used to top off wages. When this option is unavailable (which is typically the case in most middle- and low-income countries), an alternative approach is to link reduced work schedules to pension systems. In this case, compensation for lower wages could be financed by borrowing from individuals' pension wealth (see Robalino, Vodopivec, and Bodor 2009).

In general, work-sharing arrangements entail substantial administrative costs for employers and heavy demands on public institutional capacity. Employers would need to introduce substantial changes in human resource management practices. Short-term costs also occur, due to changes in scheduling and work organization.[22] On the government side, implementation can be difficult when the social security administration does not have well-developed contribution, collection, and record-keeping systems that provide information about the earnings of various workers in a firm. Costs, as in the case of wage subsidies, should be considered carefully. Unless the unemployment system is well funded, reduced work schedules involve government subsidies that can be costly and regressive, since transfers are likely to benefit mainly formal sector workers. The administrative and budgetary demands from these programs suggest that they may be more suitable for upper-middle-income countries and should be established before a downturn.

Review of Job Search Assistance and Training Programs
Several ALMPs were used during the crisis to facilitate job search and to preserve or build skills. Here, the focus is on general employment services and training programs.

Employment Services
As discussed earlier, employment services programs can help address problems related to limited information in the labor market: workers with given skills may not know what types of job opportunities are out there for them or might need guidance in building the skills needed to apply to a given set of vacancies. Similarly, employers may have difficulties identifying the best matches for the vacancies they open. Questions about the effectiveness of such programs during the crisis—particularly in middle- and low-income countries where institutional capacity and the general performance of these programs are weak—persist.

Most OECD countries responded to the surge in the number of job seekers by increasing public employment services (PES). Over the past three years, the increase in Germany, Hungary, and Japan has been around 10 percent (see OECD 2010). Austria, Finland, and New Zealand have been allocating additional PES resources to provide job search assistance to youth. Finland has further deployed extra PES resources to immigrants. People with short-term contracts benefited from additional resources in Belgium and France. Several countries have also expanded the role of private employment services to provide supplementary capacity (France, Italy, and the Republic of Korea, for example). As a result of high caseloads, however, the number of job seekers placed in both 2008 and 2009 generally fell, with the largest percentage decline in placements in Finland (34.6 percent), Korea (33.1 percent), Belgium (20.5 percent), and Australia (20.4 percent).

In ECA, several countries significantly increased the funding of "traditional" employment programs provided through the public employment services (see table 4.1). Judging from the number of beneficiaries, the most popular programs tended to be career counseling and professional orientation, job search assistance, and training. Latvia, for example, increased the number of beneficiaries of job search assistance and counseling programs from 65,300 in 2008 to 171,800 in 2009; Kazakhstan, from 130,000 to 250,000; and Lithuania, from 1.1 million to 2.1 million. To serve more beneficiaries, several countries increased the number of staff in the PES relative to 2008.[23] Others, instead, reallocated functions, putting more staff to work on the front lines (Azerbaijan, Bulgaria, Latvia, and Moldova, for instance). In general, however, the estimated number of beneficiaries of employment services remained low. Among countries where data are available, the share of participants in employment services compared to the annual stock of registered unemployed was the highest in Kazakhstan, Montenegro, and Tajikistan, at around 25 percent. In the other countries, this share was less than 5 percent.[24]

In Latin America, at least six countries resorted to policies to support job search. In most cases, the intervention consisted of reinforcing the core functions of public employment offices, including counseling, intermediation, and job search. This was the case, for instance, in Argentina, Chile, Mexico, the Dominican

Table 4.1 Budgets for Employment Services as a Percentage of GDP in Selected Countries in Europe and Central Asia, 2008 and 2009

Country	2008	2009
Armenia	0.03	0.02
Bosnia and Herzegovina	0.02	0.03
Bulgaria	0.04	0.39
Croatia	0.04	0.04
Estonia	0.04	0.12
Latvia	0.06	0.24
Lithuania	0.15	0.16
Montenegro	0.39	0.50
Slovenia	0.09	0.33

Sources: National PES; GDP data are from the IMF World Economic Outlook Database April 2010.
Note: GDP estimates for Montenegro, Slovenia, Croatia, and Bosnia and Herzegovina are for 2009.

Republic, and Peru. As an example, Mexico allocated additional budget to the National Unemployment Service to extend hours and improve services. Nicaragua took a more narrow approach, focusing only on the intermediation function. Unfortunately, with the exception of Chile and probably Peru, employment services in the other countries are known to operate poorly (see Robalino and Sanchez-Puerta 2012).

Although job search programs can be cost-effective in industrialized countries during noncrisis periods, some have concerns about their performance in middle-income countries.[25] One issue is their heavy reliance on public offices with low coverage and limited human resources. Another is poor governance and financing arrangements, which can give staff in these offices weak incentives to respond to the needs of their clients.[26] The two issues combine to reduce the incentives of employers and job seekers to join the system and undermine the usefulness of such programs.

Even if they are well designed, public employment services may not be very effective during a downturn when firms are not hiring or are actively shedding jobs. Undoubtedly, employment services might have an important role to play when linked to the unemployment benefits systems. In this case, the increase in the number of applicants for such benefits might justify a temporary increase in the operational budget or at least a reorganization of staff and functions. But, otherwise, strengthening counseling, job search assistance, and intermediation functions might not be the most efficient use of limited public resources when the number of vacancies relative to the number of unemployed is falling.

Looking forward, countries need to consider structural reforms of public employment services. Some issues to consider in improving performance include providing incentives to both employees and employers to join, relying more on information technologies and working more with private providers through contract-and-payment systems that generate incentives to maximize placement rates (see Robalino and Sanchez-Puerta 2012).

Training

Countries intervened through different arrangements: technical and vocational education and training (TVET), on-the-job training, and training-related ALMPs. In principle, these programs ought to be an important intervention during a downturn when the opportunity cost of training is likely to fall. But it is not clear what the best intervention should be. As in the case of employment services, public training programs in middle- and low-income countries often suffer from poor performance. They are often supply driven, unresponsive to market demands, and focused on formal sector workers.[27] Programs to promote on-the-job training, in contrast, have tended to distort labor markets through higher payroll taxes without generating meaningful investments in training (see Almeida and Cho 2012). Questions about the effectiveness of the various interventions implemented during the crisis thus remain.

In OECD countries, training programs played a prominent role, focusing on the unemployed (often youth) and workers who would have been laid off. Some countries such as Finland, Germany, and Sweden have expanded existing training programs by up to 36 percent of the labor force. Training programs were often part of employment services in OECD countries and are offered by accredited providers as well as by the companies themselves. In such cases, the employment service pays full social security contributions and training costs. And, as discussed above, some of the work-sharing arrangements, like the one in Germany, are conditional on training.

In ECA, training was also one of the important programs provided by employment services. Training programs expanded in most countries. In Latvia, for instance, the number of participants in training programs increased from 8,600 in 2008 to 29,200 in 2009; in Slovenia, from 16,300 to 23,400; and in Russia, from 248,000 to 453,000. It is important to note that in some countries, the private sector was actively involved in the provision of labor market services, including training, as an integral part of PES reform. Private sector participation reduces the pressure on public budgets and provides a wider array of options for a diverse range of clients. By 2009, according to the national PES, over 2,800 private employment agencies were registered in Poland; 2,176 in the Czech Republic; 531 in Bulgaria; 63 in Latvia; 51 in Slovenia; and 41 in Lithuania.

Support to training programs was also very common in Latin America, although traditional services seem to have received priority relative to the more innovative programs. Colombia, for instance, doubled the number of training slots through employment offices and training institutes, targeting youth in the 16–26 age range. Chile, Costa Rica, and Mexico introduced training programs for workers in enterprises affected by the crisis, while providing incentives to preserve jobs. Chile's ambitious fiscal stimulus plan also included provisions of tax credits to firms that carried out training activities with their workers. But there is no evidence that the government attempted to expand some of the successful programs targeted to youth, which are demand driven and integrate other services such as counseling and job search assistance.

In Africa and Asia, programs more commonly operated outside traditional TVET, on-the-job training, and employment services. A good example can be found in Mauritius. In May 2010, the government announced that its National Employment Foundation would run a work-cum-training scheme. The program targeted companies in the manufacturing and tourism sectors that had been facing a reduction in their turnover and encouraged them to send their employees on training instead of laying them off. Training was provided for up to two days a week for a maximum period of 18 months. The authorities expected to prevent some 6,000 employees from being laid off, while at the same time improving their skills.[28]

Another relevant project was implemented in Thailand to train the unemployed. The so-called Tonkla Archeep (Career Sprout) intensive vocational training program aimed to train 500,000 unemployed, soon to be unemployed, and new graduates. The program offered one month of training and a cash allowance of three months for participants to start their businesses or find a job. As of September 2009, of the 550,000 applicants, 173,000 had already completed the training, while 134,000 were no longer in need of the training, having found a job in the meantime. According to government sources, Tonkla Archeep had already helped 150,000 trainees find jobs and another 20,000–30,000 to run their own business, which constitutes a substantial portion of the estimated 572,000 unemployed Thai workers in 2009.[29]

The main issue with public training programs such as TVET or training-related ALMPs, whether implemented during a crisis or not, is the government's ability to provide high-quality and relevant training (see Almeida, Behrman, and Robalino 2012). Indeed, most of the training subsidies in ECA and particularly in the Latin America and the Caribbean (LAC) region are likely to have gone to public providers that lack the right set of incentives and necessary margin of maneuver to respond to the needs of trainees and employers. It is common, for instance, for teachers' remuneration and career prospects to be unrelated to their performance and for budgets to be delinked from the demand for the center's services. Even when the right incentives are in place, managers tend to have their hands tied by excessive centralization or inappropriate regulations. Clearly, during a downturn, any training might be better than unemployment or pure inactivity. Still, it is important for governments to consider options for maximizing the impact that resources allocated to training can have on individuals' labor market opportunities.

Training within enterprises could be a more effective alternative if adequate attention is given to the distribution of subsidies. Simply subsidizing training within firms, à la Mauritius above, is likely to benefit mainly formal sector workers and not necessarily those most in need of upgrading their skills. Alternatives to consider include allocating subsidies directly to vulnerable individuals (such as the unemployed or youth transiting from school to work), perhaps in the form of vouchers, that they can use to finance internships or specific courses that can link them to jobs. Thailand seems to have followed this approach, although little is known about its effectiveness. The Jovenes programs in Latin America, which provide training and job placement services for youth, are another model to consider.[30]

Review of Income Protection Programs

Income protection interventions—including cash and in-kind transfers, noncontributory pensions and health insurance, early retirement programs, and unemployment benefits—were more common in developing countries. The various transfers (or social assistance programs) are likely to have been the most effective intervention for protecting the vulnerable, particularly where well targeted. The concern with early retirement and unemployment benefits programs, however, is their potential regressiveness, given low coverage rates. Early retirement programs, in particular, tend to increase the actuarial imbalance of pension funds that will need to be financed out of general revenues eventually. At the same time, these programs are not the appropriate response for workers in the informal sector and the nonpoor who saw their earnings decline as a result of lower wages or fewer working hours (see chapter 2).

Transfers

Given the characteristics of this crisis, with its sharp drop in earnings and the low coverage of the social insurance system, transfer programs are likely the most efficient way to distribute limited resources to vulnerable workers. As discussed below, the main design innovations have come from Latin America, where several countries have integrated safety nets into CCTs and gradually moved away from less efficient in-kind transfers. Unfortunately, the majority of countries still have yet to implement this type of program, and even among the leaders important design and implementation issues need to be resolved.

In many OECD countries, those without jobs who are not eligible for unemployment benefits are often able to access social assistance (welfare) and housing support payments. For example, in the United States, federal funding has been provided for social assistance payments to the unemployed who have exhausted their unemployment benefits (see Cazes, Verick, and Heuer 2009). Belgium has increased social assistance payments for job losers, while France has made one-off payments to social assistance recipients. Other new support measures include assistance for employers who continue to provide housing to laid-off workers in Japan. An interesting intervention took place in Canada, where, as part of the Economic Action Plan, the Wage Earner Protection Program (WEPP) was expanded in January 2009 to include coverage of termination and severance pay.[31] This expansion was essentially intended to protect workers in firms that could not afford to give severance pay. This type of program, of course, encourages risky behavior by firms by effectively providing public insurance for severance pay liabilities.

Cash transfers were most common in Latin America, where before the crisis CCTs had been implemented in 15 countries, covering an estimated 22 million households (over 90 million people, or 16 percent of the region's population) (see Ferreira and Robalino 2010). Most countries expanded these programs, thus protecting the incomes of the poorest. For example, in Brazil, the Bolsa Familia program quickly responded by expanding coverage to 12 million families and increasing the amount of transfers by 10 percent in 2009. Colombia's Familias en Acción, a program focusing on strengthening nutrition and education for children, expanded to an additional 1.5 million families. Honduras's Asignación Familiar doubled its expenditures from US$20 million to US$40 million, and Mexico's Oportunidades increased benefits by US$1.5 billion. Paraguay expanded the Tekepora program, reaching 120,000 poor families for a total coverage of 600,000 people (which is half of those living in extreme poverty).[32] Two countries that did not have CCTs in place, Barbados and Belize, implemented those programs in 2009.

Other types of transfers were also used during the crisis. Countries with noncontributory pensions (social pensions) or noncontributory health insurance expanded these programs. Examples include Argentina, the Dominican Republic, and El Salvador. Countries like Nicaragua and Panama relied instead on in-kind transfers (mainly food programs). At the other extreme, Argentina expanded the coverage of family allowances, a benefit typically offered to those covered by the social security system, to informal sector workers. Although there is no evidence about who benefited from the program, it is one of the few interventions that could have reached nonpoor informal sector workers. Chile also introduced an extraordinary payment of Ch$40,000 (US$67) to families and individuals who benefit from certain social programs (Subsidio Familiar, Asignación Familiar, Chile Solidario, and Asignación Maternal).

In Africa and Asia, cash or in-kind transfers were implemented in most of the countries surveyed. In-kind transfers seem to have been more prevalent than in other regions and continue to be an important mechanism for protecting workers. Nonetheless, more governments are introducing in-cash transfer schemes. In Africa, the government in Kenya invested considerable effort and funds to expand an existing cash transfer program to support households living with orphans and vulnerable children. The additional funds aimed to at least double the number of households covered under the program (from around 48,000 in June 2009 to approximately 115,000 households by end-June 2010).

Some of the evidence suggests that countries that were better able to protect the most vulnerable during the recent crisis already had well-functioning safety nets in place, in particular, CCT. When such systems are not in place, policy makers' options for responding effectively to a crisis are far more limited, and they are forced to turn to less efficient interventions such as general food subsidies or temporary workfare programs, which are costly and have a limited impact (see Ferreira and Robalino 2010).

Before the crisis, CCTs made important contributions to poverty reduction in at least some of the countries where they have been implemented. These reductions come about primarily because the CCT benefits have been unusually well targeted and are not substantively offset by labor supply disincentives.[33] Thus, the combination of geographical targeting and proxy means testing used by many CCTs to identify beneficiary households has proved to be one of the main reasons for their success. For instance, Mexico's Oportunidades delivers 45 percent of all benefits to the poorest 10 percent of its population, while programs in Chile and Jamaica cover 35–40 percent of the bottom decile.[34]

Although CCTs can be an important component of crisis response, it is challenging to implement them well; they are primarily a means of providing social assistance rather than social insurance. At a minimum, any program should include a well-established targeting mechanism, reliable databases of registered households, management information systems, payment and delivery mechanisms, and tools for basic monitoring, oversight, and control. Three challenges then need to be addressed:

- *First, improving the management of conditionalities and the quality of supply-side interventions.* In countries such as Ecuador, for instance, conditionalities exist but are not enforced. And, in all cases, the low quality of education and health services reduces the impact of the programs.

- *Second, adapting the programs to urban areas*, where issues related to incentives and targeting are likely to be different (see Ribe, Robalino, and Walker 2012).
- *Third, managing critical enrollment, registration, and recertification systems effectively, particularly during a crisis.* The long-term goal is to have more flexible arrangements for managing flows in and out of the system, so that poor families do not have to wait to receive benefits and those whose income has increased past a given threshold graduate from the programs. Because of the administrative demands this entails, CCTs by themselves are not an adequate substitute for social insurance programs.

Unemployment Benefits

For the majority of countries, protection against unemployment relies essentially on severance pay, which is known to be an ineffective system for providing income protection to workers, in part because employers do not finance these liabilities.[35] Even among the countries that have implemented unemployment benefits systems, however, coverage is very low. Across the board, less than 5 percent of the unemployed are receiving benefits, either because they were not in a formal sector job and are thus ineligible for benefits (which seems to be common among youth)[36] or because their unemployment benefits have expired. Extending the duration of unemployment benefits during a downturn, though, will most likely benefit only a minority of workers, and those they do benefit are generally not the most vulnerable. In addition, the subsidies involved can be regressive.

Outside the OECD, the rules for unemployment benefits changed in several ECA countries in both duration and level. In Poland, for example, the social unemployment subsidy was extended from 12 to 18 months in 2009 and in Romania from 6 to 9 months. In the Czech Republic, the duration of unemployment benefits was extended by 1 month, favoring adults relative to young workers (if the person was below 50, the benefit was paid for 6 months; if the age was between 50 and 55, for 9 months; and above 55, for 12 months). The Czech Republic, like Russia, also increased the level of benefits (for the first 2 months, from 65 to 80 percent of the average net monthly salary of the unemployed person; for the other 2 months, from 50 to 55 percent; and for the remaining months, from 45 to 55 percent).[37]

In LAC, most countries that had established unemployment benefits systems also expanded them during the crisis. This was the case for Argentina, Brazil, Chile, Colombia, and Uruguay. In these countries, the duration of unemployment benefits was extended either in specific sectors or across sectors, aiming to protect formal sector workers from longer spells of unemployment. Brazil, for instance, extended the duration of unemployment benefits by two months, but only for those sectors most affected by the crisis, such as mining and metalwork. In Chile, unemployment insurance was expanded to cover workers with fixed-term employment or service contracts for up to two months at replacement rates of 35 percent of income. Mexico does not have a proper unemployment benefits system, but during the crisis the government issued regulations to facilitate the withdrawal of savings from the mandatory individual pension accounts. No systematic information is available for determining the incidence of unemployment benefits, but as in the case of ECA, coverage rates are quite low.[38] For example, in Argentina it is estimated that only between 7 and 13 percent of the total unemployed population was covered by unemployment insurance in 2008. The extension of benefits in the case of Brazil reached only 216,500 workers out of an estimated 7–8 million total unemployed.[39]

The performance of the Chilean unemployment benefits system during the crisis shows its limited reach. Chile has established one of the best-designed of such systems in the world. Its coverage has been increasing rapidly over time, from around 10 percent of the unemployed in 2000 to over 20 percent. During the crisis period of 2007–09, however, while the unemployment rate increased, the coverage of the system fell (see figure 4.10). Less than 20 percent of the unemployed and less than 15 percent of those who lost their jobs between 2008 and 2009 had access to unemployment benefits. Most of Chile's large increase in expenditures on unemployment benefits (expenditures increased by 47 percent between 2008 and 2009) came from individual accounts and transfers that were more likely focused on low-income workers. In other countries, the coverage of the system fell, despite increases in expenditure financed out of the general revenues rather than individual contributions.

An ongoing question for unemployment benefits systems, irrespective of the crisis, is how best to expand coverage while maintaining incentives to work. The concern with classic unemployment insurance is "moral hazard," meaning that unemployment benefits can reduce the incentives workers have to keep or find jobs. This problem is particularly worrisome in the presence of large informal sectors and weak institutional capacity to control abuse.[40] An alternative is

Figure 4.10 The Percentage of Chilean Workers Covered by Unemployment Benefits and the Unemployment Rate, 2000–10

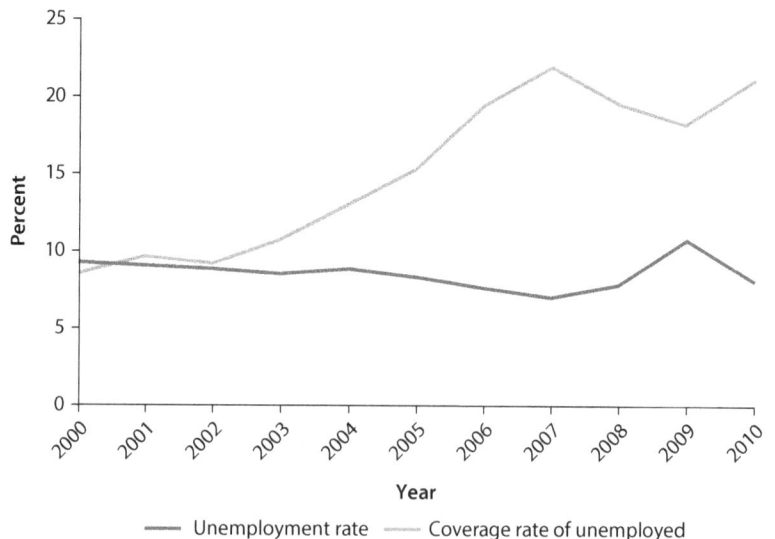

Source: Data derived by authors from country sources.

greater reliance on savings as opposed to risk pooling. Indeed, some evidence suggests that unemployment individual savings accounts (UISAs) implemented in countries like Brazil and Chile provide stronger incentives for job search. Administratively, UISAs can piggyback on the infrastructure of the pension system. And, because the system relies on savings, there is less need to police individuals' job search activities and employment status. UISAs can be complemented by explicit redistributive arrangements to protect the most vulnerable workers, which could be expanded during downturns. Countries can also consider more flexible approaches for allocating savings between short-term and long-term benefits. For instance, during a crisis, unemployment benefits systems could be expanded rapidly by allowing individuals to borrow from their pension wealth.[41] This measure is particularly appealing in countries with very large mandates for old-age pensions (see Robalino, Vodopivic, and Bodor 2009).

What Can Be Done to Be Better Prepared in the Future?

The discussion in the last two sections suggests four areas for engagement. The first involves building social protection systems that can better respond to economic downturns by expanding coverage and improving the functioning of individual programs. The second is to reform fiscal policy so that its effectiveness can be increased when aggregate demand falls. The third area is improving labor market information systems to better monitor labor market adjustments and their impact on different types of workers. Finally, a better grasp of how to sequence policies at different points during the cycle is important, which requires a more complete understanding of the impacts of individual programs. Below, we discuss in more detail these broad issues.

Social Protection Systems

Countries might consider moving toward a system that effectively combines social insurance, social assistance, and ALMPs that can be scaled up during a crisis. During normal times, this system could help address market failures that limit self-insurance and distort labor market decisions. During crises, social insurance and assistance programs would need to be expanded to protect workers who become unemployed or see their earnings decline, while ALMPs are used to bring willing nonparticipants back into the labor market, facilitate labor reallocations, or simply support job search.

The main challenge for social insurance programs is expanding coverage. Even in upper-middle-income countries such as Chile and Mexico, the social insurance system covers fewer than 60 percent of the labor force (see Holzmann, Robalino, and Takayama 2009). For workers in the informal sector who are not poor enough to benefit from assistance, social protection programs may not be available. In low-income countries, the situation is even worse. Social insurance coverage in Africa and most of Asia, for instance, is below 5 percent of the labor force. In South Asian and African countries, the share of those in self-employment or household enterprises is above 50 percent.[42] Social insurance programs thus cover mainly civil servants and workers in public enterprises. Only recently have public works and targeted transfer programs begun being adopted (see Grosh *et al.* 2008).

Various suggestions have been made about how to move forward (see Levy 2008; Ribe, Robalino, and Walker 2012). In general, however, it is clear that access to social insurance needs to be delinked from the labor contract, since only a minority of workers have these contracts. Expanding coverage also requires implementing effective redistributive arrangements to reach those with limited or no savings capacity, while minimizing labor market distortions. But more work is needed to identify the most efficient program designs and financing, governance, and administrative arrangements.

For social assistance programs, an important aim should be to consolidate dispersed programs and introduce institutional arrangements that allow them to expand and contract in response to economic cycles. Countries could consider setting up integrated cash transfer programs, for instance, that include requirements for investing in human capital, participating in public works, or establishing programs for improving individuals' employability. These transfers would be targeted to the most vulnerable individuals, while relying on well-designed administrative, monitoring, and evaluation systems.

ALMPs can play an important part in addressing information problems in labor and capital markets, but it is not clear that they should be used to protect jobs. Programs that protect jobs risk affecting productivity growth and the recovery by delaying necessary reallocations of labor and capital. Clearly, job protection can bestow social benefits, including the improved welfare of workers who keep their jobs, the maintenance of their marginal contribution to aggregate demand (that presumably supports other jobs), the preservation of their human capital (assuming that skills depreciate during unemployment), and the lowered costs of firms' dismissal and rehiring (see Messenger and Rodriguez 2010). The first two benefits, however, can be achieved by stimulating aggregate demand, without targeting particular firms and workers. Targeted interventions can also retrain or upgrade the skills of those who are in need. As for firms, those that are solvent and face only a temporary drop in sales as a result of a recession should be able to assess whether it pays to keep workers idle for a period, rather than firing and rehiring them. Government can help by ensuring that credit is available to these firms, particularly to SMEs, not by lending directly to them but by focusing on restoring credit in the financial system as a whole.

ALMPs designed to facilitate job reallocation can be helpful but might not be a priority during a crisis. Well-designed employment services, retraining programs, and strategically chosen individual wage subsidies for on-the-job training can contribute to labor reallocation during a period of rapid change. But these programs are typically too small to serve large numbers of workers effectively during a crisis, and there is little convincing evidence that they are cost-effective even during normal times. Reducing labor costs can, of course, also help stimulate labor demand. But instead of through ad hoc freezes or reductions in social security contribution rates, reduction of labor costs could be better achieved through structural reforms in the financing of the social security systems that permanently reduce the taxes that drive a wedge between wages and labor costs and by reforms to labor regulations.

Fiscal Constraints

Lessons from past financial crises show that fiscal impacts can be quite large; deficits increase and fewer resources are available for social protection and labor policies. Among a group of 13 countries that went through a financial crisis between 1985 and 2002, the fiscal deficit increased between 2.6 percentage points (Mexico, 1994) and 15.4 percentage points (Sweden, 1991) (Reinhart and Rogoff 2009). In Latin America, the increase was 9.5 percentage points in Argentina (2001), 8 in Chile (1980), and 3.8 in Colombia (1998). The 1997 crisis in Asia led to an increase in the fiscal deficit of 5.8 percentage points in Indonesia, 6.5 in Malaysia, and 5.8 in Thailand. These numbers are associated with financial crises, which are unusually long compared to normal recessions (the latter usually last less than a year, unless they occur in countries in need of major structural adjustments).[43] Still, they indicate that government budgets can be under considerable pressure during a downturn.

Data for the current crisis also show a strong correlation between the size of the contraction in economic growth and the increase in the fiscal deficit. In 2007, the relationship between growth and fiscal policy was weak, except in the few countries that experienced large growth slowdowns that year. In 2008, however, countries with a greater slowdown in growth began to run larger deficits, as indicated by a slight downward shift in the smoothed line in figure 4.11, panel b. This trend reflects the response of countries like Kazakhstan, Montenegro, and Pakistan, where deficits expanded by as much as four percentage points of GDP, despite moderate slowdowns in growth. In 2009, the relationship between GDP growth and the fiscal balance strengthened further, as most countries with a percentage point or greater decline in GDP growth expanded deficit spending by at least two percentage points of GDP. Finally, despite a rapid turnaround in growth in 2010, which boosted government revenue, improvements in the overall fiscal balance were generally limited. For a significant number of countries in the bottom right quadrant of figure 4.11, panel d, the fiscal balance continued to deteriorate despite improving growth rates.

Because countries affected by crisis tend to experience a rapid deterioration and a slow recovery in their fiscal stance, systems for managing labor market risk cannot count on financing from discretionary transfers during a downturn. Responding effectively to such a downturn, therefore, requires relying as much as possible on insurance and savings schemes, rethinking redistributive arrangements, and building appropriate reserves. Indeed, the larger the number of workers covered by insurance pools or savings schemes, the lower the demand for discretionary transfers. Moreover, considerable resources can be freed up if implicit subsidies are removed from current insurance programs.[44] These implicit subsidies can then be reallocated toward building reserves that finance the expansion of cash transfers during downturns.[45] Finally, it is necessary to restore the long-term balance of the social insurance programs

Figure 4.11 Changes in Fiscal Balance and GDP Growth during the Financial Crisis in Selected Countries, 2007–10

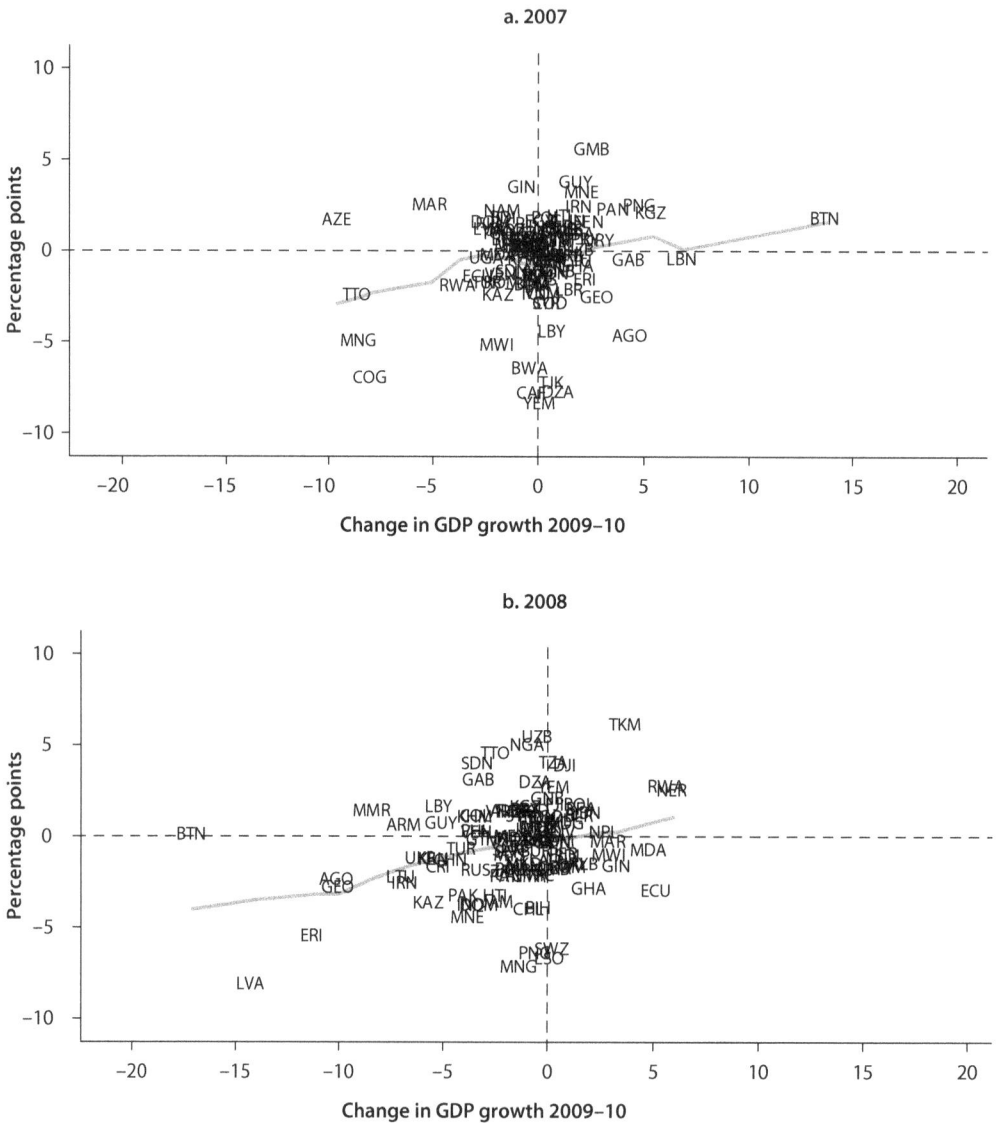

a. 2007

b. 2008

figure continues next page

Figure 4.11 Changes in Fiscal Balance and GDP Growth during the Financial Crisis in Selected Countries, 2007–10
(continued)

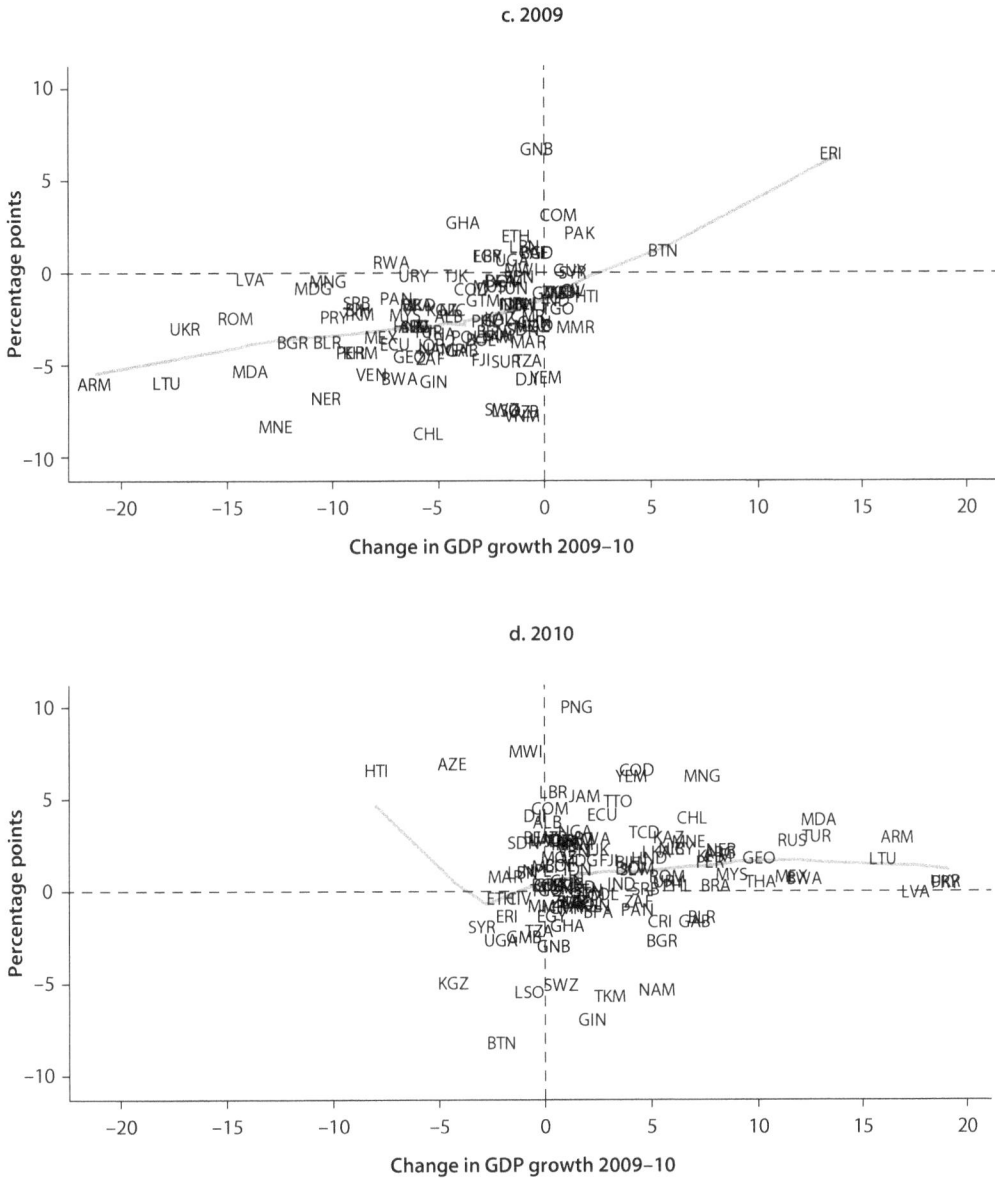

c. 2009

d. 2010

Source: World Economic Outlook April 2011 database, IMF 2011.

and build liquid financial assets to improve resilience to macroeconomic shocks (see Robalino 2010).

Statistics on Labor Markets

Labor market data are critical to policy makers' understanding of how labor markets adjust to a given shock, so that they can decide how best to intervene

Map 4.1 Years of Available Data on Country Labor Markets, 2000–08

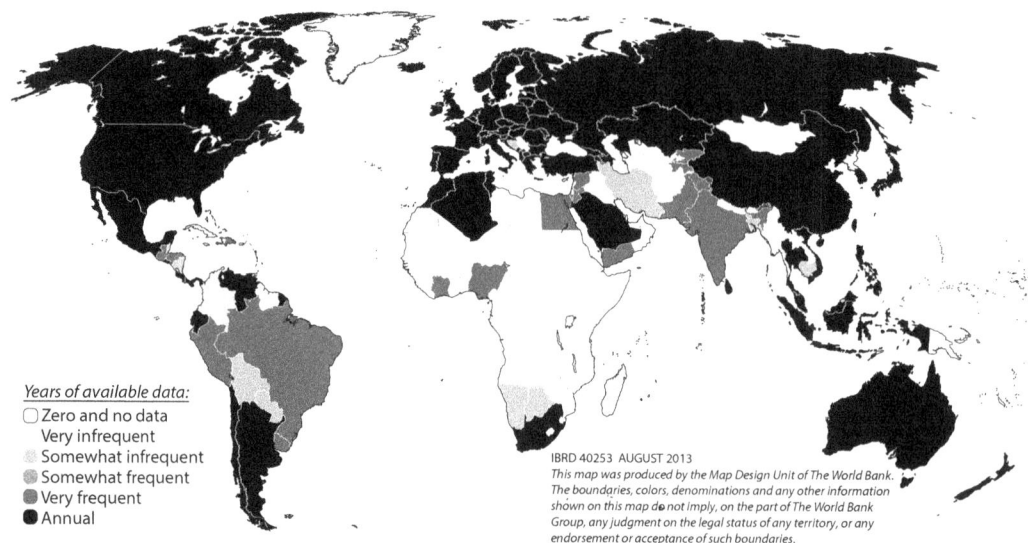

Years of available data:
○ Zero and no data
   Very infrequent
   Somewhat infrequent
   Somewhat frequent
● Very frequent
● Annual

IBRD 40253 AUGUST 2013
This map was produced by the Map Design Unit of The World Bank.
The boundaries, colors, denominations and any other information
shown on this map do not imply, on the part of The World Bank
Group, any judgment on the legal status of any territory, or any
endorsement or acceptance of such boundaries.

Source: Calculations from LABORSTA, CEIC and HAVER Analytics data.
Note: Data for Montenegro and Serbia could not be mapped due to coding issues.

and later evaluate the impact of these interventions. As shown in chapter 2, the
channels through which the downturn affected labor markets were numerous
and complex; effects depended on a number of factors, such as exposure to
foreign trade, dependence on remittances, the amount of debt or savings held
in foreign banks or countries, the importance of foreign-owned firms and foreign direct investment, and many others. Labor market adjustments varied
considerably from country to country. In addition, workers or employers may
behave in unexpected ways, or not react at all, when a policy is implemented
in a particular way in a given setting. Understanding these behavioral responses,
which requires impact evaluations and measurement of outcomes, is critical to
decision makers.

Unfortunately, many developing countries do not collect and disseminate the
data necessary to inform policy. Map 4.1 shows the world with the number of
years of employment data published by each country between 2000 and 2008.[46]
Although most OECD countries and some larger middle- and low-income
countries (Argentina, China, Indonesia, Mexico, Russia, and South Africa) published employment data in each of the eight years, data collection and
dissemination in some parts of the world, especially Africa, are lagging. On the
whole, of the 200 countries shown in the figure, only 110 have published labor
market data of any sort since 2000.[47] But even among those publishing, the frequency is too low. For instance, data on employment for 2008 were missing for
57 percent of the 200 countries covered. In some cases (Bangladesh, Colombia,
India, Kenya, and Paraguay, for instance), no data were available for the entire
interval 2006–08, while in others (Brazil, the Arab Republic of Egypt, the Islamic

Republic of Iran, Nigeria, and Pakistan) the issue was more of timeliness, as countries had still not published data on the labor market situation in 2008 by the middle of 2010.

Better data collection and dissemination will require that governments make improving data availability a priority, build institutional capacity, and adopt open-access policies. The obvious first step is for governments to consider the collection of labor market data a precondition of efficient policy making and, just as important, devote sufficient resources to it. In general, the cost of the surveys needed for collecting labor market data represents a small amount when compared to total government spending. In addition, the potential improvements in program design that such data allow can lead to savings that compensate for the costs. Once resources have been allocated, implementation requires significant institutional capacity, which is often lacking.[48] However, it is possible to invest in this capacity, and international organizations have an important role in supporting these efforts. Once the data have been collected, decisions about how to disseminate the information become critical.[49] Often, statistical institutes can be extremely protective of the data, sometimes not even providing the information to important line ministries so that they can craft better policy responses. Government needs to ensure that data on the state of the labor market are available to the public at large inside and outside the country.

Sequencing Policies

More research and policy analysis are needed to provide an understanding of the impact of various programs during the downturn. In this chapter, we have argued that the focus should be on protecting workers who are most at risk of becoming unemployed or of seeing their incomes fall. Unemployment benefits systems (ideally, also covering workers in the informal sector), cash transfers, and public works are the programs that should receive the most attention. Policy makers should also try to ensure that credit is available, including for small enterprises and the self-employed in the informal sector. Policies that facilitate job search, however, are less likely to be effective if the formal sector is not hiring. But firm conclusions on these issues require a better understanding of the impact of labor and social protection programs. For instance, training programs for the unemployed, particularly for those needing to switch sectors or careers, also have a role to play (see table 4.2).

Policy makers also need to understand what works better during a recovery. Indeed, past crises show that, following a downturn, it takes considerable time for labor markets to return to the precrisis situation. During a recession, unemployment rates typically increase for almost five years, and the fall to precrisis levels can take equally as long. For instance, when the U.S. economy contracted in 2001, the recession officially lasted for eight months—March 2001 to November 2001. But employment started contracting at the beginning of 2001 and continued shrinking until July 2006; it reached precrisis levels only in January–February 2005. The impacts of the recent financial crisis have been even more severe.

Working through the Crisis • http://dx.doi.org/10.1596/978-0-8213-8967-6

Table 4.2 Adjusting Labor and Social Protection Policies as Countries Move from an Economic Downturn to Recovery

Policies	During the downturn	During the recovery
Labor demand		
Wage subsidies stock	+	
Wage subsidies new		++
Public works	+++	−
Credit	+++	+++
Job search		
Employment services	+	+++
Training	+++	+++
Skills recertification	+	++
Income support		
Unemployment benefits	+++	−
Transfers	+++	−
Workfare	+++	−
Labor regulations		
Hiring and dismissal		+++
Severance pay		+++
Tax wedge		+++

Note: The number of pluses and minuses provide a rough indication of how policies become more or less desirable during downturns and recoveries. Empty cells indicate neutrality.

As the economy starts to recover and hiring rates increase in the formal sector—and presumably unemployment risks fall—policy makers will need to switch gears, focusing on policies that activate the jobless into employment and facilitate employment creation. To start with, it will be necessary to provide incentives for job search to those receiving unemployment benefits or welfare transfers, which implies cutting down on subsidies. Well-designed intermediation and counseling programs can then have a role to play and could be linked to training programs with targeted wage subsidies to finance internships. Clearly, policies that increase access to credit should continue. We speculate that the start of a recovery could also be a politically attractive period for reviewing labor legislation. At that point, there will be more room and optimism for dealing with difficult issues, and the fact that job creation will remain a priority may provide incentives to reach compromises between employers and workers' organizations.

Annex 4A: Description of the Policy Inventory

The policy inventory provides an overview of the most important employment and social policy responses to the labor market impacts of the severe economic downturn of 2008–09. Information was collected both on policies that were already implemented and on those in the process of being implemented.

The inventory questionnaire consists of two main sections. The first section collects information on policies designed to accelerate employment creation, while the second is devoted to policies designed to expand income protections. In the first section, information is separately collected on four subsections: macroeconomic policy, policies to support specific sectors, policies to support labor demand, and ALMPs to support information, intermediation, and matching. The first two of these subsections are excluded from the analysis presented in this chapter, leaving three main sets of policies: support for labor demand, ALMPs, and the income-support programs from the second main section of the survey. All income-support programs are included, except that only one indicator is used for the implementation of expanded unemployment benefits: whether a country's spending on unemployment benefits increased. Within these three sets of categories, the questionnaire contains information on 35 distinct types of policies. Across the 52 developing countries and 22 high-income countries surveyed (a list of countries is provided in figure 4A.1), 2,858 policies were reported. However, many of the policies are duplicates, defined as two policies that are reported by the same country and that contain identical titles, target populations, and starting dates. After removing these duplicates, 1,763 policies remain.

The 35 types of policies in the original survey were consolidated into the 16 categories to make the analysis more manageable and in some cases to improve its accuracy. Table 4A.1 describes the classification scheme. In some cases, information was taken from the presence of key words in the title of the policy to distinguish between categories. Finally, additional keywords such as *accredit*, *employment service*, and *SMEs* were used to reclassify policies in categories such as "other labor demand support policies" to more appropriate categories. Not every type of policy in the original data is classified into one of these 16 categories.[50] As a result, after the classification, 786 policies remain in developing countries, and 429 remain in developed countries (see table 4A.1).

All the analysis reported in the chapter is based on programs that were listed as beginning in 2008 or 2009, because many of the policies enumerated in the survey were "in the process of being implemented" and may never have been enacted. Therefore, the analysis in this chapter includes only the subset of policies that listed a starting date of 2008 or 2009. This approach limits the analysis to policies that were actually enacted or passed in the first two years after the crisis, which we consider to be a more accurate measure of the policy response than the full inventory. As table 4A.2 indicates, 493 policies in developing countries and 327 in developed countries remain. Finally, a portion of the analysis examines the extent to which policies targeted youth or women. Targeted policies were identified by whether the title or the description of the policy contained the word *women*, *youth*, or several of their synonyms. Casual inspection of these policies suggests that this classification scheme captured programs designed to target those groups.

Figure 4A.1 Number of Countries in the Policy Inventory and Number of Unique Programs, 2008–09

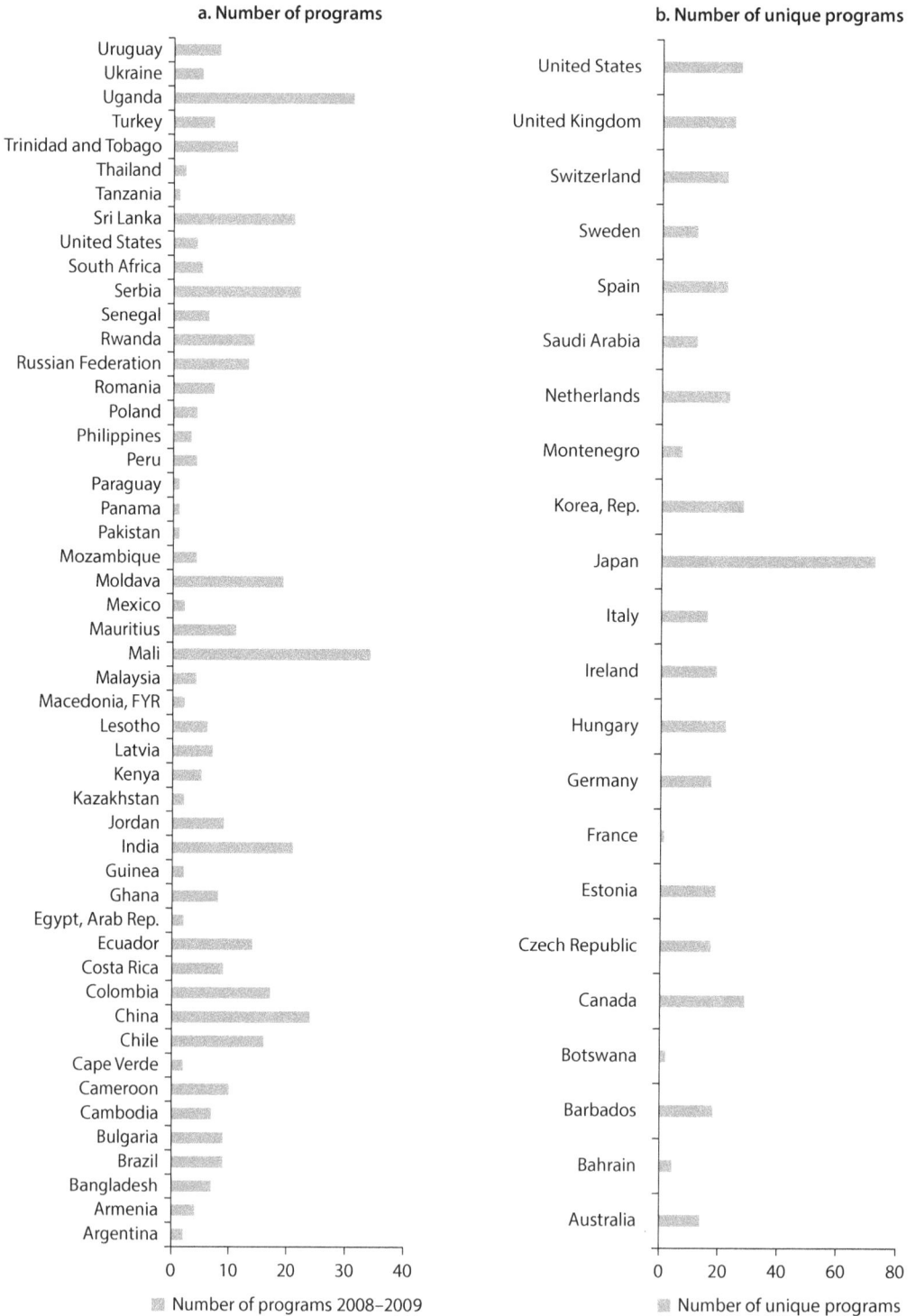

a. Number of programs

b. Number of unique programs

Number of programs 2008–2009

Number of unique programs

Source: World Bank Staff.

Table 4A.1 Classification Scheme for Policies

Question	Keywords in title	Category name
Section 1		
1. Lowering nonwage labor cost (that is, across-the-board reduction in employer social security contributions)		Reduction of nonwage labor cost
2. Subsidies to employers who maintain existing jobs		Wage subsidies for existing jobs
3. Credit facilities, access to credit guarantees		Credit and support to SMEs
4. Payment facilities		Credit and support to SMEs
5. Access to public tenders		Credit and support to SMEs
6. Subsidies of various sorts (nonwage labor cost, export credit facilities)		Reduction of nonwage labor cost
7. Facilities for training programs, skills development, upgrading and reskilling (for example, through institutionalized sector-specific skills development)		Training
8. Tax reductions		Other labor demand
9. Supportive regulatory environment for sustainable enterprises		
10. Other special measures for SMEs, microenterprises, and cooperatives		Credit and support to SMEs
11. Subsidies for job creation targeted on newly created jobs		Wage subsidies for new jobs
12. Subsidies or tax exonerations for hiring individuals from certain groups (for example, reductions in employer social security contributions for newly hired workers who were previously long-term unemployed)		Wage subsidies for new jobs
13. Public sector job creation programs, including employment guarantee schemes, emergency public works, other direct job creation schemes, public spending on infrastructure and on green jobs		Public works
14. Employment-retention measures, including working time reductions, wage subsidies. and others		Work sharing
15. Wage reductions (nonwage cost, for example, social security contributions or wage)		Reduction of nonwage labor cost
16. Training measures (such as "certification measures,""qualification measures,""external validation of workers' skills")		Skills certification

table continues next page

Table 4A.1 Classification Scheme for Policies (*continued*)

Question	Keywords in title	Category name
Section 2		
1. Did funding for ALMPs increase in 2009?	Train	Training
	Public employment services	Job search; intermediation
2. Were there any budget reallocations of ALMPs?		
3. Did public employment services recruit additional case managers?		Job search; intermediation
4. Did private placement agencies expand?		
5. Was there an expansion (or contraction) of the number of training slots available to unemployment benefit recipients or changes in the mix of training offered (for example, the mix between short-term and long-term training courses)?	Expand	Training
6. Were other ALMP measures taken to assist workers? (training, job orientation measures, skills certification, youth programs, programs for disabled, programs for vulnerable workers)	Train	Training
7. Were other ALMP measures taken to assist workers? (training, job orientation measures, skills certification, youth programs, programs for disabled, programs for vulnerable workers)	Certific	Skills certification
8. Were other ALMP measures taken to assist workers? (training, job orientation measures, skills certification, youth programs, programs for disabled, programs for vulnerable workers)	Not train; not certific	Other ALMP measures
9. Were other measures taken in the field of Information, Intermediation, and matching?		Job search; intermediation
Section 3		
1. Was there an increase in spending on unemployment benefits (UB)?		Extended level or duration of UB
2. Was there an increase in spending on UB as a percentage of GDP?		Extended level or duration of UB

table continues next page

Table 4A.1 Classification Scheme for Policies *(continued)*

Question	Keywords in title	Category name
Section 4		
	Train	Training
1. Did social spending increase as a percentage of GDP?		Extended level or duration of UB
2. Were measures adopted to protect purchasing power of low-wage earners, for example, avoiding deflationary wage spirals including minimum wage policies?	Minimum or wage	Other income-support programs
3. Were there any measures adopted to reduce the gender wage gap?		
4. Was there an expansion of cash transfer programs, including for vulnerable groups?		Cash transfer
5. Was there an expansion of in-kind programs?		
6. Was there an expansion of noncontributory social insurance? (social pension, health insurance, unemployment assistance)		In-kind transfer
7. Was social security coverage for temporary and nonregular workers expanded?		Expanded social insurance
8. Were there any measures adopted such as those for domestic migrant workers and international migrant workers, protection and support in receiving countries, measures to encourage return migration or other measures affecting the protection of migrant workers?		Other income-support programs
9. Were prospective changes in financing of the social security system adopted, including contribution requirements and future benefits?		Other income-support programs
10. Were there any other measures adopted to expand social protection?		Other income-support programs

Source: World Bank Staff.

Note: This table describes how different programs in the policy inventory were classified. Classifications are based both on the questions based on the survey, as well as the presence of text key words in the program's title.

125

Table 4A.2 Construction of the Policy Inventory

	Low- and middle-income countries		High-income countries	
	Programs	Countries	Programs	Countries
Total	1,206	52	652	22
Nonduplicates	1,129	52	634	22
Categorized	786	52	429	22
% that support labor demand	58	96	56	91
% that support information, intermediation, and matching	15	71	16	77
% that support expanding income and social protection	27	87	28	95
Number implemented in 2008–09	443	50	307	20
% that support labor demand	60	81	56	82
% that support information, intermediation, and matching	13	50	14	55
% that support expanding income and social protection	27	79	29	91

Notes

1. The main arguments are that the multiplier effect of public spending is not as high as one would expect, suggesting considerable crowding out of private consumption and investment; that, on the contrary, tax multipliers are high; and that, in any case, designing and implementing an efficient and timely stimulus package is difficult. For discussions, see Becker, Davis, and Murphy (2010), Fama (2009), and Kirchner *et al.* (2009). See also the IMF 2008 *World Economic Outlook* finds that discretionary fiscal policy can have moderately countercyclical effects in advanced economies but that stimulus packages are typically less successful in emerging economies. On average, for all economies, a discretionary stimulus package equivalent to 1 percent of a country's GDP is associated with GDP increases of about 0.1–0.2 percent.

2. In their view, the largest share of a fiscal stimulus package is spent (through consumption and investment) instead of saved, and this increases production (or at least reduces inventories so that production restarts faster) and employment. And if fiscal policy is well managed, governments have ample room to refinance and repay their debt as economic growth resumes and government revenues increase—without having to raise taxes. For example, see Spillembergo *et al.* (2009) and Delong and Summers (2012).

3. In technical terms, there is adverse selection.

4. See Freeman (2010) for a review. For example, Kugler (1999) finds that reducing severance pay by 70 percent in Colombia reduced unemployment by only 0.3 percentage points. Heckman and Pages (2004) and Montenegro and Pages (2004) find mixed effects in Latin America, while OECD (2003) and Addison and Grosso (1996) find mixed or small effects in OECD countries. While Ahsan and Pages (2009) find that state employment protection legislation regulations are associated with

employment reductions in Indian states, the results are not robust to controlling for state-specific time trends.

5. See Kugler (1999), Gonzaga (2003), and Saavedra and Torero (2004) for evidence that labor regulations reduce aggregate mobility.

6. Boeri, Helppie, and Macis (2008) review evidence on the negative impacts of employment protection legislation on output, investment, productivity, and firms' ability to adjust to shocks. Davis and Haltiwanger (1999) review the significant role that job reallocation plays in promoting aggregate productivity growth.

7. This is the classic unemployment "insurance" program where employers and workers contribute to a common pool or fund that pays benefits to those who become unemployed for a given period of time based on the number of past contributions.

8. See Manning (2000) for a discussion of the case of Indonesia in 1997.

9. The analysis presented here is based on a unique survey of government policy responses to the crisis prepared by the ILO and World Bank (2012). The policy inventory currently covers 52 middle- and low-income countries and 22 high-income countries and provides information about over 1,800 interventions. Of these, primary attention is given to the 443 policies that were implemented in developing countries as the crisis was unfolding in 2008 and 2009. For a more detailed description of the policy inventory, see the annex.

10. See the analysis of the Argentinian program Jefes y Jefas by Galasso and Ravallion (2004). Other studies of public works programs include Almeida and Galasso (2010) and Jalan and Ravallion (2003).

11. The strategy also includes creating up to 63,100 "social jobs" (up to six months, with a wage subsidy of 50 percent of wage costs) plus 34,400 fully subsidized jobs for six months for graduates.

12. See Lee (2005) for a typology.

13. This law also includes extensions to maternity benefits and additional leave associated with training activities.

14. See Bell, Blundell, and Van Reenan (1999) and Richardson (1997) for a discussion.

15. See Robalino, Vodopivec, and Bodor (2009) and OECD (2003) for a review.

16. Studies suggest that overall a 10-percentage-point reduction in the tax wedge (the difference between the cost of labor and take-home pay) could increase employment between one and five percentage points (see Betcherman and Pages 2007; Kugler and Kugler 2003; Nikell 2003; Rutkowski 2007).

17. See Phelps (1994) for a discussion of the rationale and OECD (2003) for a discussion of the evidence.

18. For evidence on the positive impact of this combined program, see Katz (1996) and Cockx, Van der Lindern, and Karaa (1998).

19. See Robalino and Sanchez-Puerta (2012) for a review.

20. Numbers are for 2009.

21. See Estevão and Sá (2008). The authors also show based on survey responses that the effects vary by gender, with women benefiting more from the implementation of a shorter work week.

22. See Estevão and Sá (2008) for evidence of these costs in the case of France.

23. For example, in Estonia the number of staff increased from 352 to 455 in 2009 and in the Russian Federation from 36,400 to 42,300.

24. *Annual stock of registered unemployed* refers to the number of registered by the PES unemployed at the beginning of the year plus inflow of the newly registered unemployed during the year.

25. Meta-analysis of job search assistance programs in industrialized countries reveals that besides being relatively cheap, they have positive short-term effects with regard to employment outcomes (Kluve 2010). However, during economic downturns, expanding these programs requires increases in human and financial resources for public employment services. Moreover, assistance with job search is likely to be less effective in the short run during periods when labor demand is low.

26. For a review of employment services in Latin America, see Ribe, Robalino, and Walker (2010); in South Asia, World Bank (2012); and in the Middle East and North Africa, region, Angel-Urdinola and Kuddo (2010). For a comparison of staffing levels in employment offices across countries, see Kuddo (2012).

27. For a review of problems with training programs and a typology of market and government failures that need to receive attention, see Almedia, Berhman, and Robalino (2012).

28. For more details, see ILO 2009.

29. See http://www.nationmultimedia.com/worldhotnews/30111997/Tonkla-Archeep -target-to-be-lowered-amid-recovery; http://www.thailandoutlook.tv/toc/ViewData .aspx?DataID=1018038.

30. See chapter 5 in Almeida, Behrman, and Robalino (2012).

31. The Wage Earner Protection Program (WEPP) is a targeted federal program that came into effect on July 7, 2008. Employees who have lost their employment as a result of the bankruptcy or receivership of their employer are provided with financial assistance through the WEPP.

32. According to ECLAC (2009), "The reactions of Governments of the Americas to the International Crisis: An Overview of Policy Measures up to 31 May 2009." United Nations, Chile.

33. See assessments for Mexico (Skoufias and di Maro 2006), Ecuador (Edmonds and Schady 2008), and Cambodia (Filmer and Schady 2009). Only in Nicaragua did Maluccio and Flores (2005) find that the Red de Protección Social appears to have resulted in a significant decline in the number of hours worked by adult men (but not women). Bourguignon, Ferreira, and Leite (2003) find little effect of (the older) Bolsa Escola program on child work, but Edmonds and Schady (2008) find a bigger impact in Ecuador.

34. See chapter 3 in Fiszbein and Schady (2009).

35. See Holzmann and Vodopivec (2012) and chapter 5 in Ribe, Robalino, and Walker (2012).

36. See Robalino and Zylberstajn (2009) and chapter 2 in Ribe, Robalino, and Walker (2012).

37. As the recovery takes place, a few countries are tightening the regulations on unemployment benefits. In Hungary, the government is implementing a program called the Way to Work, which restricts the eligibility criteria of welfare provisions for the long-term unemployed who have already exhausted the duration of their benefits. The rationale behind this measure is to encourage more effective training and job-seeking activities.

38. A recent study shows that the coverage of unemployment benefits is even lower than that of old-age pensions. Less than 20 percent of the labor force in countries that have implemented the systems are likely to be covered. This is, in part, because eligibility also depends on the number of months of continuous contributions to the social security system (see Ribe, Robalino, and Walker (2012).

39. In other regions, the prevalence of unemployment benefits is much lower. In Africa, only Algeria, the Arab Republic of Egypt, Jordan, Mauritius, Morocco, South Africa, and Tunisia have some form of unemployment benefits program. In Asia, only Indonesia, Thailand, and Vietnam do (see ILO 2009; Pham 2009).

40. For a discussion and references to the literature, see Robalino, Vodopivec, and Bodor (2009).

41. The pension wealth is the presented value of future pension payments.

42. For South Asia, see World Bank (2012) and for Africa, see Fox and Gaal (2009).

43. Two examples cited in Reinhart and Rogoff (2009) are Britain in 1970, before the reforms of Margaret Thatcher, and Japan in 1992, when the economy had to be restructured in response to China's rise.

44. The reason is that contributions are not linked to benefits; some workers can pay more than their expected benefits (a tax) while others pay less (a subsidy). But it is not clear ex ante who is eligible for taxes or subsidies, and ex post transfers can go from low- to high-income workers (see Ribe, Robalino, and Walker [2012] for a discussion).

45. Several countries still maintain explicit subsidies on commodities, which are also regressive, and a plethora of poorly targeted or untargeted social assistance programs. Reforming these systems can also create fiscal space to increase spending on social assistance programs.

46. The data referred to in this section were drawn from the LABORSTA database in December 2009, from the CEIC database in May 2010, and from the HAVER analytics database in June 2010.

47. Annual publication is defined here as having a series of at least three consecutive annual observations over the 2000–08 interval.

48. Some of the key activities in which expertise needs to be developed include: (1) management and logistics, (2) questionnaire development, (3) sampling, (4) staffing and training, (5) data management, (6) field work, and (7) data analysis and documentation.

49. The Statistical Data and Metadata Exchange Initiative (http://sdmx.org) provides guidelines for countries on how to present and disseminate data to the broader community in a common framework to improve their understanding and comparability.

50. For example, income support programs to reduce the gender gap are excluded. While this may appear to underestimate the percentage of programs targeted to women, in fact many of these gender gap programs are either unspecified or of questionable relevance, such as the adoption of a new labor code in Rwanda, a nondiscriminatory increase in wages in Sri Lanka, or proclamation of a national equal pay day and establishment of an equal pay enforcement task force in the United States.

References

Abraham, K., and S. Houseman. 1993. "Does Employment Protection Inhibit Labor Market Flexibility? Lessons from Germany, France, and Belgium." NBER Working Paper W4390, National Bureau of Economic Research, Cambridge, MA.

Addison, J. T., and J-L. Grosso. 1996. "Job Security Provisions and Employment: Revised Estimates." *Industrial Relations* 35 (4): 585–603.

Ahsan, A., and C. Pages. 2009. "Are All Labor Market Regulations Equal? Evidence from Indian Manufacturing." *Journal of Comparative Economics* 37 (1): 62–75.

Almeida, R., J. Behrman, and D. Robalino. 2012. *The Right Skills for the Job? Rethinking Training Policies in Developing Countries*. Washington, DC: World Bank.

Almeida, R., and Y. Cho. 2012. "On the Job Training: Stylized Facts and Policies around the Developing World." In *The Right Skills for the Job? Rethinking Training Policies in Developing Countries*, edited by R. Almeida, J. Berhman, and D. Robalino. Washington, DC: World Bank.

Almeida, R., and E. Galasso. 2010. "Jump-Starting Self-Employment? Evidence among Welfare Participants in Argentina." *World Development* 38 (5): 742–55.

Angel-Urdinola, D., and A. Kuddo. 2010. "Key Characteristics of Employment Regulation in the Middle East and North Africa." Social Protection Discussion Paper 1006, World Bank, Washington, DC.

Auerbach, A., W. Gale, and B. Harris. 2010. "Activist Fiscal Policy." *Journal of Economic Perspectives* 24 (4): 141–64.

Baily, M., C. Hulten, and D. Campbell. 1992. "Productivity Dynamics in Manufacturing Plants." *Brookings Papers on Economic Activity. Microeconomics* 187–249.

Barlevy, G. 2002. "The Sullying Effect of Recessions." *Review of Economic Studies* 69 (1): 65–96.

———. 2003. "Credit Market Frictions and the Allocation of Resources over the Business Cycle." *Journal of Monetary Economics* 50 (8): 1795–818.

Beck, T., and A. Demirguc-Kunt. 2011. "Is Small Beautiful? Financial Structure, Size, and Access to Finance." Policy Research Working Paper 5806, World Bank, Washington, DC.

Becker, G., S. Davis, and K. Murphy. 2010. "Uncertainty and the Slow Recovery." *Wall Street Journal*, January 4.

Bell, B., R. Blundell, and J. Van Reenen. 1999. "Getting the Unemployed Back to Work: The Role of Targeted Wage Subsidies." Working Paper Series W99/12, Institution for Fiscal Studies, London.

Betcherman, G., K. Olivas, and A. Dar. 2004. "Impact of Active Labor Market Programs: New Evidence from Evaluations with Particular Attention to Developing and Transition Countries." Social Protection Discussion Paper Series 0402, World Bank, Washington, DC.

Betcherman, G., and C. Pages. 2007. *Estimating the Impact of Labor Taxes on Employment and the Balances of the Social Insurance Funds in Turkey: Synthesis Report*. Washington, DC: World Bank.

Boeri, T., B. Helppie, and M. Macis. 2008. "Labor Regulations in Developing Countries: A Review of the Evidence and Directions for Further Research." Social Protection Discussion Paper 833, World Bank, Washington, DC.

Bourguignon, F., F. Ferreira, and P. Leite. 2003. "Conditional Cash Transfers, Schooling, and Child Labor: Micro-Simulating Brazil's Bolsa Escola Program." *World Bank Economic Review* 17 (2): 229–54.

Caballero, R., and M. Hammour. 1994. "The Cleansing Effect of Recessions." *American Economic Review* 84 (5): 1350–68.

———. 1996. "On the Timing and Efficiency of Creative Destruction." *Quarterly Journal of Economics* 446 (3): 805–52.

Cazes, S., S. Verick, and C. Heuer. 2009. "Labor Market Policies in Time of Crisis." Employment Working Paper 35, International Labour Office, Geneva, Switzerland.

Cockx, B., C. Goebel, and S. Robin. 2013. "Can Income Support for Part-Time Workers Serve as a Stepping Stone to Regular Jobs? An Application to Young Long-Term Unemployed Women." *Empirical Economics* 44(1): 1–41.

Cockx, B., B. Van der Lindern, and A. Karaa. 1998. "Active Labor Market Policies and Job Tenure." *Oxford Economic Papers* 50: 685–708.

Cunningham, W., M. L. Sanchez-Puerta, and A. Wuermli. 2010. "Active Labor Market Programs for Youth: A Framework to Guide Youth Employment Interventions." *World Bank Employment Policy Primer* 16 (November).

Dar, A., and Z. Tzannatos. 1999. "Active Labor Market Programs: A Review of the Evidence from Evaluations." World Bank, Washington, DC.

Davis, S., and J. Haltiwanger. 1999. "Gross Job Flows." In *Handbook of Labor Economics*, vol. 3, part B, 2711–805. Amsterdam: Elsevier.

Delong, J. B., and L. Summers. 2012. "Fiscal Policy in a Depressed Economy." *Brookings Papers on Economic Activity* 1.

ECLAC (Economic Commission for Latin America and the Caribbean). 2009. "The Reactions of Governments of the Americas to the International Crisis: An Overview of Policy Measures up to 31 May 2009." United Nations, Chile.

Edmonds, E., and N. Schady. 2008. "Poverty Alleviation and Child Labor." NBER Working Paper 15345, National Bureau of Economic Research, Cambridge, MA.

Estevão M., and F. Sá. 2008. "The 35 Hour Workweek in France: Straightjacket or Welfare Improvement?" *Economic Policy* 23 (July): 417–63.

Fallon, P., and R. Lucas. 2002. "The Impact of Financial Crises on Labor Markets, Household Incomes, and Poverty: A Review of Evidence." *World Bank Research Observer* 17 (1): 21–45.

Fama, E., 2009. "Bailouts and Stimulus Plans." The Fama-French Forum blog. http://investorsolutions.com/blog/the-fama-french-forum.

Ferreira, F., and D. Robalino. 2010. "Social Protection in Latin America: Achievements and Limitations." Policy Research Working Paper 5305, World Bank, Washington, DC.

Filmer, D., and N. Schady. 2009. "Are There Diminishing Returns to Transfer Size in Conditional Cash Transfers?" Policy Research Working Paper 4999, World Bank, Washington, DC.

Fiszbein, A., and N. Schady. 2009. *Conditional Cash Transfers: Reducing Present and Future Poverty*. Policy Research Report, Washington, DC: World Bank.

Fox, L., and M. Gaal. 2009. *Working Out of Poverty: Job Creation and the Quality of Growth in Africa*. Washington, DC: World Bank.

Freeman, R. B. 2010. "Labor Regulations, Unions, and Social Protection in Developing Countries: Market Distortions or Efficient Institutions?" In *Handbook of Development Economics*, vol. 5, 4657–702. Amsterdam: North Holland.

Galasso, E., and M. Ravallion. 2004. "Social Protection in a Crisis: Argentina's Plan Jefes y Jefas." *World Bank Economic Review* 18 (3): 367–99.

Gerfin, M., M. Lechner, and H. Steiger. 2002. "Does Subsidized Temporary Employment Get the Unemployed Back to Work? An Econometric Analysis of Two Different Schemes." CEPR Discussion Paper 3669, Center for Economic Policy Research, Washington, DC.

Gonzaga, G. 2003. "Labor Turnover and Labor Legislation in Brazil." *Economia* 4 (1): 165–222.

Grosh, M., C. del Ninno, E. Tesliuc, and A. Ouerghi. 2008. *For Protection and Promotion.* Washington, DC: World Bank.

Heckman, J., and C. Pages, eds. 2004. *Law and Employment: Lessons from Latin America and the Caribbean.* Chicago, IL: University of Chicago Press.

Holzmann, R., D. A. Robalino, and N. Takayama. 2009. *Closing the Coverage Gap: The Role of Social Pensions and Other Retirement Income Transfers.* Washington, DC: World Bank.

Holzmann, R., and M. Vodopivec. 2012. "Severance Pay under Review: Key Issues, Policy Conclusions, and Research Agenda." In *Reforming Severance Pay: An International Perspective*, edited by R. Holzmann and M. Vodopivec, 1–16. Washington, DC: World Bank.

ILO (International Labour Organization). 2009. "Labour Market Policies in Times of Crisis." Employment Working Paper 35, International Labour Office, Geneva, Switzerland.

———. 2010. "Employment and Social Protection Policies: From Crisis to Recovery and Beyond: A Review of Experience." Report to G-20 Labour and Employment Ministers' Meeting, Washington, DC, April 20–21.

———. 2011. *World of Work Report 2011.* Geneva, Switzerland: International Labour Office.

ILO and World Bank. 2012. *Joint Synthesis Report: ILO and World Bank Joint Inventory of Policy Responses to the Financial and Economic Crisis.* Washington, DC: ILO, World Bank.

IMF (International Monetary Fund). 2011. *World Economic Outlook.* Washington, DC: IMF.

Jalan, J., and M. Ravallion. 2003. "Estimating the Benefit Incidence of an Antipoverty Program by Propensity-Score Matching." *Journal of Business and Economics Statistics* 21 (1): 19–30.

Kahn, L. 2010. "Labor Market Policy: A Comparative View of the Costs and Benefits of Labor Market Flexibility." *Journal of Policy Analysis and Management* 31 (1).

Kapteyn, A., A. S. Kalwij, and A. Zaidi. 2000. "The Myth of Worksharing." IZA Discussion Paper 188, Institute for the Study of Labor (IZA), Bonn, Germany.

Katz, L. 1996. "Wage Subsidies for the Disadvantaged." NBER Working Paper 5679, National Bureau of Economic Research, Cambridge, MA.

Kirchner, S., J. Taylor, T. Makin, and R. Carling. 2009. *Fiscal Fallacies: The Failure of Activist Fiscal Policy.* Crisis Commentary Series 1. St. Leonards, Australia: Centre for Independent Studies.

Kluve, J. 2010. "The Effectiveness of European Active Labor Market Programs." *Labour Economics* 17 (6): 904–18.

Kuddo, A. 2012. "Public Employment Services and Activation Policies." Social Protection Discussion Paper 1215, World Bank, Washington, DC.

Kugler, A. 1999. "The Impact of Firing Costs on Turnover and Unemployment: Evidence from the Colombian Labor Market Reform." *International Tax and Public Finance Journal* 6 (3): 389–410.

Kugler, A., and M. Kugler. 2003. "The Labor Market Effects of Payroll Taxes in a Middle-Income Country: Evidence from Colombia." CEPR Discussion Paper 4046, Center for Economic and Policy Research, Washington, DC.

Lee, J-K. 2005. "Evaluation of and Lessons from Wage Subsidy Programmes in OECD Countries." Directorate of Employment, Labour and Social Affairs, Organisation for Economic Co-operation and Development, Paris.

Levy, S. 2008. *Good Intentions, Bad Outcomes: Social Policy, Informality, and Economic Growth in Mexico.* Washington, DC: Brookings Institution.

Maluccio, J. A., and R. Flores, 2005. *Impact Evaluation of a Conditional Cash Transfer Program: The Nicaraguan Red de Protección Social.* Research Report 141. Washington, DC: International Food Policy Research Institute.

Manning, C. 2000. "Labour Market Adjustment to Indonesia's Economic Crisis: Context, Trends and Implications." *Bulletin of Indonesian Economic Studies* 36 (1):105–36.

Mckenzie, D. 2004. "Aggregate Shocks and Urban Labor Market Responses." *Economic Development and Cultural Change* 52 (4): 719–58.

Messenger, J., and S. Rodriguez. 2010. "New Developments in Work Sharing in Middle-Income Countries." Travail Policy Brief 2, International Labour Office, Geneva, Switzerland.

Montenegro, C., and C. Pages. 2004. "Who Benefits from Labor Market Regulations? Chile, 1968–1988." In *Law and Employment: Lessons from Latin America and the Caribbean,* edited by. J. Heckman and C. Pages. Cambridge, MA: National Bureau of Economic Research.

Nikell, S. 2003. "Employment and Taxes." CESifo working paper no. 1009. Munich, Germany.

OECD (Organisation for Economic Co-operation and Development). *Employment Outlook. 2003.* Paris: OECD.

———. 2010. *Employment Outlook 2010: Moving beyond the Jobs Crisis.* Paris: OECD.

Paci, P., A. Revenga, and B. Rijkers. 2009. "Coping with Crises: How and Why to Protect Earnings." Policy Research Paper 5094, World Bank, Washington, DC.

Pham, N. Q. 2009. "Impact of the Global Financial and Economic Crisis on Vietnam: A Rapid Assessment." ILO Regional Office for Asia and Pacific, Bangkok, and Policy Integration and Statistics Department, Geneva, Switzerland.

Phelps, E. 1994. "Low-Wage Employment Subsidies vs. the Welfare State." *American Economic Review* 84 (2): 45–58.

Reinhart, C. M., and K. S. Rogoff. 2009. "The Aftermath of Financial Crises." *American Economic Review* 99 (2): 466–72.

Ribe, H., D. Robalino, and I. Walker. 2012. *From Right to Reality: Incentives, Labor Markets, and the Challenged of Universal Social Protection in Latin America and the Caribbean.* Washington, DC: World Bank.

Richardson, J. 1997. "Wage Subsidies for the Long-Term Unemployed: A Search Theoretical Analysis." Discussion Paper 347, Centre for Economic Performance, London.

Robalino, D., and A. Banerji. 2009. "Addressing the Employment Effects of the Financial Crisis: The Role of Wage Subsidies and Reduced Work Schedules." Employment Policy Primer, World Bank, Washington, DC.

Robalino, D., and L. Sanchez-Puerta. 2012. "Managing Labor Market Risks." In *From Right to Reality: Incentives, Labor Markets, and the Challenge of Universal Social Protection in Latin America and the Caribbean.* Washington, DC: World Bank.

Robalino, D., M. Vodopivec, and A. Bodor. 2009. "Savings for Good and Bad Times: Introducing Unemployment Insurance to Developing Countries." Social Protection Discussion Paper, World Bank, Washington, DC.

Robalino, D., and H. Zylberstajn. 2009. "Ex-Ante Methods to Assess the Impact of Social Insurance Policies on Labor Supply with an Application to Brazil." Policy Research Paper 5027, World Bank, Washington, DC.

Rutkowski, J. 2007. "Labor Taxes and Employment in ECA." Manuscript, World Bank, Washington, DC.

Saavedra, J., and M. Torero. 2004. "Labor Market Reforms and Their Impact over Formal Labor Demand and Job Market Turnover." In *Law and Employment: Lessons from Latin America and the Caribbean*, edited by J. J. Heckman and Carmen, 131–82. Chicago, IL: University of Chicago Press.

Skoufias, E., and V. di Maro. 2006. "Conditional Cash Transfers, Adult Work Incentives, and Poverty." Policy Research Working Paper 3973, World Bank, Washington, DC.

Spillembergo, A., S. Symansky, O. Blanchard, and C. Cottarelli. 2009. "Fiscal Policy for the Crisis." Staff Position Note, International Monetary Fund, Washington, DC.

Verho, J. 2008. "Scars of Recession: The Long-Term Costs of the Finnish Economic Crisis." Working Paper Series 2008:9, Institute for Labour Market Policy Evaluation, Uppsala, Finland.

World Bank. 2012. *More and Better Jobs in South Asia.* Washington, DC: World Bank.

———. 2013. *Jobs for Shared Prosperity: Time for Action in the Middle East and North Africa.* Washington, DC : World Bank.

CHAPTER 5

The Labor Market Impact of the 2009 Financial Crisis in Indonesia

Neil McCulloch, Amit Grover, and Asep Suryahadi

While several studies explored the impact of the global financial crisis on developing countries (Griffith-Jones and Ocampo 2009; IMF 2009a; Mendoza 2009; Naudé 2009; ODI 2009; World Bank 2009a), most of them focused on the macroeconomic impact of the crisis, elaborating the effect of the crisis on the growth of gross domestic product (GDP), current and capital account balances, debt, and inflation. However, policy makers have also been keen to understand the microeconomic impact of the crisis, most notably on poverty and employment. In previous crises, researchers have attempted to estimate such impacts by simulating impact based on precrisis data, along with macroeconomic data on the shocks and some assumptions about the pathways through which households are likely to have been affected (Friedman and Levinsohn 2002, for example). Such approaches can be extremely valuable in helping policy makers identify the groups likely to be most affected so that they can put in place suitable policy responses. But, inevitably, policy makers depend on possibly inaccurate assumptions about the channels of transmission.

An alternative way of obtaining timely information about the impact of the crisis on households is to undertake rapid qualitative evaluations in selected locations. These have been done in several countries (see IDS [2009] for syntheses of qualitative country case studies). These give detailed accounts of what has actually happened in the selected communities. They also help uncover the pathways through which impacts have been felt and provide preliminary indications about the effectiveness of various assistance programs. However, because budget and time constraints mean that such studies can usually be conducted in only a small

Neil McCulloch and Amit Grover did the work on this chapter while at the Institute of Development Studies, University of Sussex, United Kingdom. Asep Suryahadi is at SMERU, Jakarta, Indonesia. Neil McCulloch (N.McCulloch@ids.ac.uk) is the corresponding author.

number of locations in a country, the extent to which the results are typical of those that might be found elsewhere is unclear.

Fortunately, national survey data for a few countries were collected from both before and after the crisis. Indonesia is one such country. The availability of such data provides an opportunity to draw on the strengths of both qualitative and quantitative analysis: qualitative case studies can be used to derive hypotheses about which groups are likely to be most affected and through which channels; the nationally representative quantitative data can then be used to test these hypotheses. Conversely, quantitative data may provide interesting results that can then be explored in more depth through subsequent qualitative work (Kanbur 2002).

Previewing the main results of this chapter, the authors find that, despite being done in only a handful of locations, the qualitative studies paint a reasonably accurate picture of how the crisis has (or has not) affected households throughout Indonesia. The macroeconomic shocks experienced by Indonesia have, relative to many other countries, been quite mild. For Indonesia, this crisis is only a shadow of the Asian financial crisis of 1997–98. However, growth did slow sharply at the end of 2008, trade contracted rapidly, and prices of commodities important to Indonesia fell significantly. Despite these shocks, the authors see little evidence for changes in school dropout or attendance, except for younger students where dropout and attendance improved. Similarly, labor participation was unchanged for most but fell for younger workers. Unemployment declined on average but increased for the young, while the sectoral distribution of employment did not shift dramatically. Perhaps the most surprising finding was the significant *increases* in real wages for employees, even after accounting for changes in the composition of the workforce over the crisis. However, incomes for those outside the formal sector fell during the crisis, although they subsequently recovered.

This chapter proceeds as follows: the next section describes Indonesia's macroeconomic performance before and during the crisis period. The following section summarizes the response of the Indonesian government to the crisis. The chapter then describes the data and its limitations. The next section presents the results, focusing on changes the labor market, notably in employment, hours worked, and wages and incomes, using cross-sectional data from February 2008, August 2008, February 2009, and August 2009. The final section offers some conclusions.

Indonesian Macroeconomic Context

Indonesia's economy was performing reasonably well before the onset of the current crisis in the last quarter of 2008. GDP growth averaged more than 5 percent a year from 2001 to 2008 and was on an increasing trend: in 2008 up to the third quarter, GDP growth was 6.4 percent (Yudo, Titiheruw, and Soeastro 2009).[1] Unemployment was falling, as were poverty numbers, albeit slowly. Inflation, which peaked at 11 percent in mid-2008 due to the global food price crisis and reductions in government fuel subsidies, was falling steadily. Investment had been growing at 12 percent year on year, with large increases in capital goods imports. This investment, along with the higher price of imported fuel, resulted in import growth of 65 percent in 2008, up to the third quarter. But exports had also been performing well in the preceding years, driven by the boom in commodity prices. Total exports reached US$136 billion in 2008, 20 percent above 2007's exports, which in turn were 13 percent above 2006 levels. Agricultural and natural resource goods contributed most to export growth—notably, crude palm oil, rubber, ores, minerals, petroleum, and natural gas. Exports of certain manufactured products such as clothing, footwear, and automotive parts also increased considerably (World Bank 2009b). Indonesia's strong merchandise trade surplus, particularly in 2006 and 2007, gave rise to surpluses on the current account, which, when added to inflows of foreign capital, resulted in a balance of payments of more than 3 percent of GDP. Although the collapse in commodity prices in 2008 pushed the balance of payments into deficit, Indonesia's foreign reserves were still almost US$58 billion by mid-2008.

The macroeconomic shock experienced by Indonesia did not start with the global financial crisis. Commodity prices collapsed in the latter half of 2008, stabilizing in early 2009 at around 40 percent of their mid-2008 peaks. The price decreases particularly affected the sectors that had contributed most to export growth in the preceding years. The financial crisis compounded those price declines. As a result, export values dropped sharply: by January 2009 export values were 36.1 percent below the level of a year earlier, with the fall in oil prices by more than two-thirds driving much of this drop. But export volumes also fell along with reduced demand from key markets and by the first quarter of 2009 were almost a fifth lower than a year previously. Imports also fell at least as fast as exports. Total import values in the first quarter of 2009 were down one-third relative to the previous year. Again, these decreases were driven by the sharp falls in the price of oil. Import volume was also down by 28 percent, however, because of drops in intermediate goods as well as in capital and transport goods.

On the capital account, sharp reversals of portfolio flows in the last quarter of 2008 contributed to a major fall in the value of shares on the Indonesian stock exchange. At the end of 2008, domestic equity market capitalization was down 51 percent. The exchange rate also came under significant pressure and fell from around Rp 9,200 to the U.S. dollar to Rp 11,325 by the end of the final quarter of 2008 (Yudo, Titiheruw, and Soeastro 2009). Real investment dropped in the first quarter of 2009 because of lower spending on machinery, appliances, and transport equipment, in contrast to growth rates of around 12 percent in much of 2007 and 2008. Credit also fell sharply: approvals for new loans were down by 50–60 percent in March 2009, year on year.

Taken on its own, therefore, Indonesia experienced a significant macroeconomic shock at the end of 2008. However, Indonesia was one of the least affected countries in Southeast Asia. Although GDP growth slowed markedly to 4.4 percent in the first quarter of 2009, it did not experience the collapse in growth

Table 5.1 Selected Macroeconomic Variables for Indonesia before, during, and after the Crisis, 2008 and 2009

Year-on-year change	3rd quarter 2008	1st quarter 2009	3rd quarter 2009
GDP (%)	6.4	4.40	4.20
Inflation[a] (%)	13.5	8.48	2.83
Exports (%)	10.6	−19.10	−22.30[b]
Imports (%)	11	−24.10	−30.80[b]
Exchange rate (Rp/U.S. dollar)	9,331	11,517	9,633
Investment (%)	12.2	3.50	4

Sources: BPS 1996; World Bank 2009b.
Note: GDP = gross domestic product.
a. Inflation figures are year-on-year figures for the end of the last month of each quarter.
b. January–October 2009 over January–October 2008.

experienced by countries such as the Republic of Korea, Malaysia, and Thailand. In part, Indonesia fared better because the major impact of the crisis was on exports, and the share of Indonesia's output that is exported is the smallest of all the major Southeast Asian economies (World Bank 2009b). In recent years, growth has been driven predominantly by nontradables rather than tradables, and, although the crisis reduced growth across the board, sectors such as transport and communications and utilities have continued to grow in double digits. At the same time, the best-performing tradable sector is agriculture, which, at 4.8 percent, has experienced its strongest growth since the East Asian crisis, helping to compensate for the effects of the 2008–09 crisis.

Moreover, Indonesia's economic performance in 2009 was remarkably good, with full-year GDP growth of 4.5 percent. The stock market restored all the substantial losses associated with the crisis, and inflation declined to 2.78 percent by the end of 2009 because of the drops in international commodity and fuel prices. Food inflation fell particularly fast, helping poor households. Domestic credit growth was still much lower than in 2008, but this trend may reflect declining demand for loans as well as more stringent lending conditions. Table 5.1 shows the key macroeconomic variables for Indonesia before the crisis, during the last quarter of 2008, and for the first and third quarters of 2009.

The Response of the Indonesian Government to the Crisis

Indonesia's relatively good performance in the crisis may also be due to strong responses on the part of the government. Interest rates, while initially high to counter the inflation caused by high food prices and booming bank credit, were brought down from 9.5 percent in June 2008 to 6.5 percent by September 2009. Careful management by the central bank—including the arrangement of foreign exchange swaps and the establishment, with donors, of a large public expenditure support facility of US$4 billion—helped restore confidence in the markets, bringing the exchange rate down to precrisis levels. Steps like increasing deposit insurance were also taken to bolster confidence in the banks, along with a series of measures to provide greater liquidity.

More broadly, the government approved a fiscal stimulus program (FSP) with the aim of sustaining public purchasing power, helping businesses through the crisis, maintaining export competitiveness, and creating jobs, as well as reducing job losses (Ministry of Finance 2008). The FSP consisted of three components:

- Tax cuts amounting to Rp 43 trillion
- Subsidies on import duties of Rp 13.3 trillion
- Subsidies and government expenditure of Rp 15 trillion

In total, the Indonesian FSP was worth Rp 71.3 trillion, equal to 1.4 percent of GDP (Marbun 2010).[2] This percentage was large by international standards. For example, the United Kingdom and the United Sates had FSPs of 1.2 percent and 1.1 percent of GDP, respectively, while those of China and India were even lower at 0.6 percent and 0.9 percent of GDP.

The first objective of the FSP was to sustain public purchasing power to maintain consumption growth at 4–4.7 percent. The FSP provisions aimed at this objective included cuts in personal income tax rates, increases in the tax-free income band, and provision of a number of price subsidies for generic medicines and cooking oil, as well as value-added tax (VAT) subsidies for downstream cooking-oil products and biofuels.

The second objective of the FSP was to sustain business resilience and export competitiveness. Provisions included tax measures (for example, cuts in a single corporate tax rate), subsidies (subsidies for import duty relief, VAT support, payroll tax incentives, cuts in electricity billing rates for industrial users, cuts in the prices for automotive diesel, for instance), and financing (equity injections for microfinance credits and export guarantees, for example).

Tax measures were also an important part of the Indonesian FSP. The country was fortunate, because long before the onset of the crisis, it had started to amend its income tax law. A new law was passed in 2008, which included reductions in various tax rates. The government therefore incorporated these tax rate reductions into the tax component of the FSP (Marbun 2010). Moreover, the tax measures were considered the most effective components of the FSP because they applied immediately and benefited a broad spectrum of taxpayers, both corporate and individual.[3]

The third objective of the FSP was to create jobs and reduce the effects of job losses. Measures included government expenditures for various labor-intensive infrastructure projects across the country and additional block grants to support the National Community Empowerment Program. Funds from the FSP were allocated to sectoral ministries and then channeled to various infrastructure projects proposed by regional (provincial, district, and city) governments. The implementation of the infrastructure projects funded through the FSP commenced with an open tender process in May–June 2009 in each district or city; the actual work started in July–August 2009, and all projects were completed by the end of the 2009 fiscal year in December.

Although all provinces received an allocation of the FSP fund, not all districts and cities within a province received an allocation; the amount allocated varied greatly among those that did. Moreover, because the central government did not target regional governments, the severity of the crisis across regions was not correlated with the regional allocation of the FSP fund (Hastuti, Mawardi, and Marbun 2010). Similarly, the National Community Empowerment Program and other social protection programs were implemented as normal, without adjustments for the differing regional impacts (Hastuti, Mawardi, Sodo, Marbun, and Ruhmaniyati 2010).

The number of employment opportunities created by the program was significant. The government's official report states that 1,072,612 workers were employed by FSP projects (National Development Planning Agency 2010). Workers were paid local market wage rates. However, most of the workers employed in these projects were not the unemployed or those who were recently laid off, and project implementers were not required to hire them. Indeed, implementers reported that it was not easy to recruit unemployed or laid-off workers (Hastuti, Mawardi, and Marbun 2010). Conversely, it was not easy for laid-off workers to find new employment, mainly because of a mismatch between their skills and those demanded by the market (Hastuti, Mawardi, Marbun, and Arief 2010).

Separate from the fiscal stimulus package, a significant unconditional cash transfer program was implemented during the crisis. Although this program was a response to fuel price increases in May 2008 rather than the financial crisis, delays in implementation meant that the program was implemented approximately when the crisis emerged. The program served 19 million beneficiary households with Rp 100,000 per month for nine months and cost approximately Rp 14 trillion (0.3 percent of GDP) in 2008 and Rp 4 trillion in 2009. Moreover, regular social protection programs were also implemented during the crisis period, which included free health care provided at community health centers and selected wards of public hospitals for 76 million poor or near-poor beneficiaries, an operational support fund for schools for all students in primary and junior high schools, and community empowerment block grants for all subdistricts in the country. Finally, although not an explicit support program, the nationwide elections in April 2009 and the subsequent presidential election in July gave rise to large local expenditures by the competing parties from early 2009 onward.

Data

The statistics for employment, working status, schooling, income, and hours worked presented in this chapter have been compiled from the 2008 and 2009 Indonesian Labor Force Survey (known by its Indonesian acronym Sakernas).[4] Data from four waves of this survey are used: February 2008, August 2008, February 2009, and August 2009. Having data for the same months for two years allows differentiation between seasonal and crisis-related changes. The period between the first two waves marks the run up to the financial crisis during the midst of the global food crisis; the immediate impact of the financial crisis was felt between the second and third waves of the survey and is likely to have continued at least until August 2009, the fourth wave of the survey.

The main annual Sakernas survey is conducted by the Indonesian Central Bureau of Statistics (BPS) every August. In August 2008, 931,890 individuals were sampled from 291,689 households across all of Indonesia. Similarly, in August 2009, 926,538 individuals were sampled from 298,428 households. The February Sakernas surveys cover a random subset of the August sample. In 2008 and 2009, it sampled 218,833 individuals (69,114 households) and 291,689 individuals (68,535 households), respectively. The Sakernas surveys are stratified into rural and urban samples. Samples are clustered at the household level. All estimators take into account stratification and clustering and use sample weights to calculate population estimates.

The Sakernas questionnaire is designed to collect data for individuals aged 10 and over. However, households are sampled only if they live in a physical building and are either a family living together, an individual renting a room independently, or a group of lodgers of fewer than 10 people. Lodgings with more than 10 people and those whose daily needs are provided for by a foundation or organization, such as a prison or dormitory, are not sampled. This approach to data collection may have implications for the analysis, since the qualitative study suggested that many of those affected by the crisis in industrial areas could be migrant workers. Many young migrant workers tend to live in rented blocks of one- or two-person rooms in boarding houses, known as *kos*. Whether these are included in the sample will depend on whether the rooms are individually rented or whether they are rented collectively, for example, by a contract labor supply company. If migrant workers are only partly sampled, depending on their living arrangements, indicators may not capture the full impact of the crisis on some groups of migrant workers and some sections of the poor who do not live in physical buildings.

The chapter relies on the national definitions of *employment* and *unemployment*. A person is employed if he or she is of working age (15 years or older in Indonesia) and has had paid work in the past week or is temporarily not working but usually has a job. A person is unemployed if he or she is not working and is either looking for work, establishing a new business or firm, or not looking for work out of discouragement or is waiting to start a new job (see Cuevas *et al.* 2009).[5]

Net monthly wages from the main work activity are defined as "the income received by a worker/employee which [are]…paid in cash or in goods (in local price) by the establishment/employer after deductions for discounts, obligatory contributions, and income taxes" (BPS 1996). In addition, the net monthly income from the main work activity is reported for employees, single-person enterprises, and casual agricultural and nonagricultural workers. However, the survey does not ask about the income of individuals who are owners of businesses that employ temporary, family, or paid workers, since it would be difficult to distinguish between the income of the business and their personal income.

Thus, the Sakernas survey provides evidence about the wages of employees and the income levels for roughly half the self-employed who are casual workers or operate single-person enterprises but cannot make any statements about the impact of the financial crisis on a large portion of the informal sector.

Wages and income may be underestimated since the questionnaire asks only for wages and income from the main activity; respondents' incomes will be higher if they have more than one job or if they are employed and simultaneously run a business. Thus, if the financial crisis has reduced income from a secondary activity, the wages or income figures reported will not reflect that drop. Conversely, if the crisis forces people to increase hours in a secondary job to compensate for reduced income in their primary job, the data will not capture that increase. Qualitative work gives some support to the idea that livelihood diversification increased during the crisis (Hastuti, Mawardi, Sodo, Marbun, and Ruhmaniyati 2010). The analysis is therefore significantly limited in its ability to assess changes in average wages and average incomes since around 14 percent of working individuals have a secondary job and individuals with a secondary job typically spend just over a quarter of their working hours on this job. Nominal income and wages are adjusted for inflation using consumer price index deflators for each province. In calculating provincial deflators, the authors follow Friedman and Levinsohn (2002) in mapping the 66 cities in which the BPS collects price data for the 33 provinces using population-weighted averages.

Results

This section presents results of the study, including information on participation in the labor force, employment, and hours worked; changes in wages and income; and the flow into and out of employment. This section also compares qualitative and quantitative results.

Labor Force Participation, Unemployment, and Hours Worked

In 1997–98, women's participation in the labor force sharply increased, in addition to a small increase in overall participation (Manning 2000). Frankenberg, Thomas, and Beegle (1999) also report little evidence of overall change, in aggregate, in participation or hours of work, although they also find considerably higher proportions of women working in 1998 than in 1997. Similarly, Levine and Ames (2003) find an increase in the labor force participation of female heads of household of over 10 percent between 1997 and 1999. It is therefore interesting to see that, in the current crisis, there is no statistically significant change in labor force participation for men and only a temporary increase in female participation between August 2008 and February 2009—an increase that disappears six months later (table 5.2). Breaking down the results by age shows a slightly higher share of older workers ages 46–55 in the labor force in August 2009 than a year earlier, but the main finding is the large decline in the share of children in the labor force. Participation among children aged 10–14 dropped by 18 percent between February 2008 and February 2009 and has

Table 5.2 Participation, Unemployment, and Hours of Work by Age and Gender in Indonesia, February 2008–August 2009

Percent

Age group and gender	Participation (%)							Unemployment (%)							Hours of work						
	Feb. 2008	Aug. 2008	Feb. 2008– Aug. 2008	Feb. 2009	Feb. 2008– Feb. 2009	Aug. 2009	Aug. 2008– Aug. 2009	Feb. 2008	Aug. 2008	Feb. 2008– Aug. 2008	Feb. 2009	Feb. 2008– Feb. 2009	Aug. 2009	Aug. 2008– Aug. 2009	Feb. 2008	Aug. 2008	Feb. 2008– Aug. 2008	Feb. 2009	Feb. 2008– Feb. 2009	Aug. 2009	Aug. 2008– Aug. 2009
10–14	6.5	5.0	***	5.3	***	5.2		9.6	13.9	***	10.1	***	13.3		20.5	22.8	***	20.9		20.8	***
15–17	26.3	24.2	***	23.8	***	24.0		21.1	24.9	***	22.3	***	23.5	*	33.3	35.7	***	33.8		34.1	***
18–25	64.3	65.9	***	64.8		65.6		19.8	21.6	***	21.4	***	20.4	***	41.1	41.9	***	41.3		41.7	
26–35	75.4	75.3		75.7		75.2		8.7	8.2	**	8.2	*	6.9	***	42.6	42.8	*	42.6		42.6	*
36–45	79.8	79.3	*	79.6		79.3		5.2	3.6	***	4.3	***	3.5		42.2	42.3		42.2		42.2	
46–55	77.7	79.0	***	80.1	***	79.4		2.3	1.7	***	1.6	***	2.8	***	40.4	40.5		40.4		40.3	*
56+	54.3	53.0	***	54.9		54.0	***	0.8	1.3	***	0.8		1.4		34.8	35.2	**	35.1		35.1	
Male	83.6	83.5		83.6		83.6		7.9	7.6	***	7.7		7.5		42.1	42.6	***	42.1		42.5	*
Female	51.3	51.1		51.8	**	51.0		9.3	9.7	**	8.8	**	8.5	***	37.6	38.0	***	38.1	***	37.6	***
Total	67.3	67.2		67.6		67.2		8.5	8.4		8.1	**	7.9	***	40.4	40.9	***	40.5		40.6	***

Source: World Bank staff, based on Indonesian Labor Force Survey (Sakernas).

Significance level: * = 10 percent, ** = 5 percent, *** = 1 percent.

remained lower since; similarly, participation for 15–17-year-olds had declined by almost 10 percent by August 2009.

Data on school enrollment and attendance bear out the drop in labor market participation rates of the young. In the Asian crisis of 1997–98, Frankenberg, Thomas, and Beegle (1999) found an increase in the percentage of 13–19-year-olds not currently enrolled in school between 1997 and 1998, although Cameron (2000) found only a slight drop in school enrollment, and Levine and Ames (2003) found that enrollments overall were stable or increasing. The authors used the Sakernas data for the recent crisis to calculate the share of children of each age from 10 to 17 who are no longer in school, as well as the share in school last week.[6] For most age cohorts, school dropout rates fell, and the cohort that was in school the previous week increased. Of particular note is the fact that more 15–17-year-olds were in school in August 2009 than a year earlier (and attendance was also higher). This finding suggests that parents may have decided to keep children in school when faced with a potentially worse labor market for young school leavers.

Breaking down the results by gender shows that the decline in school dropouts from August 2008 to August 2009 applied to both boys and girls. The share of girls no longer in school increased between February 2008 and August 2008, but, by February 2009, the share was little different from that of a year previously. Perhaps households badly affected by the strong rises in food prices during 2008 temporarily withdrew their girls from school to help with household management, but, as food price inflation fell markedly toward the end of 2008, the girls had gone back to school by February 2009.

The changes in unemployment are also revealing. In the 1997–98 crisis, unemployment increased only slightly, with the increase greatest among female workers ages 15–24 and younger rural males (Manning 2000). The recent financial crisis has led to higher unemployment in most countries in Southeast Asia. The results discussed in this chapter suggest that Indonesia has proved to be an exception to this trend, as national unemployment actually fell by 0.6 percent over the 18-month period spanning the food and financial crisis. However, the authors find a sharp contrast between younger and older workers. Unemployment rates rose for workers younger than 25 (table 5.2). The rise between February 2008 and August 2008 undoubtedly reflects the influence of recent school leavers, but for workers 18–25 the increase in unemployment persisted in February 2009, starting to decline only by August 2009. This finding may help explain falling school dropout and rising enrollment: there is no point in students' leaving school if they are unlikely to get a job. By contrast, unemployment rates have been falling for workers 25–55, although most of this fall occurred before the onset of the crisis. Unemployment among female workers has declined significantly since August 2008. However, between February 2009 and August 2009 the unemployment rate for 44–55-year-olds increased, which may suggest that firms are adjusting their cost structure in light of the crisis.

In keeping with the findings from the previous crisis, hours of work changed very little. The small seasonal increase between February 2008 and August 2008 had been reversed by February 2009 (except for female workers who continued to work longer hours), but there was no clear evidence of major reductions in working hours caused by falling labor demand due to the crisis or, conversely, of people increasing their working hours to compensate for lost income. However, the February 2009 level of working hours appears to have persisted through August 2009, suggesting that firms have been cautious about increasing output during the recovery.

During the 1997–98 crisis, agriculture acted as an employment option of last resort, with a significant increase in the share of employment in this sector (Manning 2000), unlike in the most recent crisis (table 5.3). The share of employment in agriculture fell between February 2008 and 2009 (ignoring seasonal changes between February and August), and the changes in hours worked in the sector have been small. The construction sector saw a temporary fall in its employment share in the year between February 2008 and February 2009 but no change in hours worked; the mining sector, surprisingly, did not see any change in its employment share as the crisis hit, although hours worked fell significantly. More surprising still, given the strong decline in exports, is the lack of any reduction in the employment share or hours worked in this industry. The only sectors experiencing an increase in their share of employment were the trade and restaurant sector and the social and personal services sector, both of which also saw small reductions in hours of work. Since these sectors accommodate a large number of nonagricultural informal workers, this finding may suggest that the number of casual workers grew as a result of the crisis.

To shed further light on whether workers were pushed into the informal sector, table 5.4 shows the share of employment by category of work over time. Consistent with the story of increasing informality, the share of workers that own a single-person business has increased, as well as the share of workers doing casual nonagricultural work. However, both of these changes happen between February and August 2008; over the year February 2008 to February 2009, the increase in the share of workers in the informal sector is quite small. The share of people running businesses with nonpermanent or unpaid workers also declined slightly, suggesting that small businesses may have shed nonpermanent or unpaid workers and therefore changed classification into single-person businesses as a result of the crisis. The changes in hours worked are also small and mostly seasonal, although hours spent by unpaid workers and owners of businesses with nonpermanent or unpaid workers increased slightly over the year (see McCulloch and Grover 2010).

Wage and Income Change

The overriding story of the 1997–98 crisis in Indonesia was the collapse in real wages. Manning (2000) shows that the evidence strongly supports a neoclassical view of the labor market, with little change in employment but large reductions in real wages. This phenomenon is not unique to Indonesia; McKenzie (2004) shows that Argentina suffered from large drops in real wages across all sectors in the wake of the 2002 financial crisis.

Table 5.3 Hours of Work and Share of Employment by Sector in Indonesia, February 2008–August 2009

Percent

Sector	Hours of work							Share of employment (%)						
	Feb. 2008	Aug. 2008	Feb. 2008–Aug. 2009	Feb. 2009	Feb. 2008–Feb. 2009	Aug. 2009	Aug. 2008–Aug. 2009	Feb. 2008	Aug. 2008	Feb. 2008–Aug. 2009	Feb. 2009	Feb. 2008–Feb. 2009	Aug. 2009	Aug. 2008–Aug. 2009
Agriculture	32.4	33.2	***	32.6	*	33.0	***	42.1	40.5	***	41.1	***	39.9	***
Mining and quarrying	45.2	44.2	*	44.0	*	44.4		1.0	1.0		1.1		1.1	**
Industry	43.8	43.7		43.6		43.8		12.2	12.2		12.1		12.2	
Electricity, gas, and water	42.6	44.0		42.8		44.3		0.2	0.2		0.2		0.2	
Construction	46.0	47.0	***	45.8		46.8		4.6	5.3		4.4	*	5.2	
Trade, restaurant, and accommodations	49.3	49.3		48.8	**	48.6	***	20.3	20.7		21.0	***	20.9	
Transport and communications	48.4	49.1	**	49.0		48.8		5.8	6.0		5.7		5.8	***
Financial institutions, real estate	44.1	42.9	**	43.0	*	43.1		1.4	1.4		1.4		1.4	
Social services, social and personal services	43.0	42.0	***	43.3		41.5	***	12.4	12.6		13.0	***	13.3	***

Source: World Bank staff, based on Indonesian Labor Force Survey (Sakernas).

Significance level: * = 10 percent, ** = 5 percent, *** = 1 percent.

Table 5.4 Share of Employment by Category of Work in Indonesia, February 2008–August 2009

Percent

Category	February 2008	August 2008	February 2009	August 2009
Own business	19.5	20.3***	19.9*	19.9***
Business owners with nonpermanent or unpaid workers	20.9	21.0	20.3***	20.7**
Business owners with permanent or paid workers	2.9	2.9	2.8	2.9
Employee	27.7	27.3*	27.7	27.6
Casual work, agriculture	6.0	5.8	6.1	5.6***
Casual work, nonagriculture	4.7	5.1***	4.9**	5.4***
Unpaid work	18.3	17.5***	18.3	17.9**

Source: World Bank staff, based on Indonesian Labor Force Survey (Sakernas).
Significance level: * = 10 percent, ** = 5 percent, *** = 1 percent.

In contrast to the past crisis, wages increased during this episode. Table 5.5 shows the real and nominal wages for employees by age group and gender; table 5.6 gives breakdowns by sector. The data suggest that the average real wage increased by 6 percent between February 2008 and February 2009 and by 11 percent between August 2008 and August 2009. This increase occurred predominately during the financial crisis period. When wages are disaggregated by age, the table shows that workers below the age of 25 did not see an increase in real wages in February 2009 but did benefit from real increases by August 2009, once output had begun to recover. These workers are precisely those indentified in the qualitative study as being hit hardest, both by contract termination and by reduction in overtime and other benefits. The data suggest, however, that the remaining workers did not see, on average, significant declines in real wages.

Wage increases were not uniformly distributed across sectors (see table 5.6). In mining and quarrying, the sudden drops in world commodity prices triggered by the financial crisis led to a 13 percent drop in the average real wage.[7] However, by August 2009, once commodity prices had rebounded, the average real wage in mining had risen above its level a year earlier. Agriculture is the only sector that has continued to suffer a decline in real wages since the start of the financial crisis, with real wages 7 percent lower in August 2009 than at the same point in the previous year. Most other sectors saw a real wage increase even before the recovery in the rest of Asia had begun: by February 2009, real wages had risen year-on-year by 4 percent in industry, by 7 percent in construction, and by a remarkable 17 percent in the transport and communications sector. In most sectors, the increase in real wages between August 2008 and August 2009 was even larger, although this rise mostly reflects the fact that real wages were lower in August 2008 due to the rapid inflation immediately before the crisis.

A large increase in the real wage of employees does not necessarily mean increases in income for all categories of employment. Table 5.7 shows that

Table 5.5 Real and Nominal Wages by Age Category and Gender, Indonesia, February 2008–August 2009

Age and gender	Real wages (Rp per month)				Percent change		
	Feb. 2008	Aug. 2008	Feb. 2009	Aug. 2009	Feb. 2008–Aug. 2008	Feb. 2008–Feb. 2009	Aug. 2008–Aug. 2009
15–17	493,976	470,892*	487,492	499,488**	−5	−1	2
18–25	761,080	700,371***	766,301	784,041***	−8	1	12
26–35	1,056,669	998,353***	1,079,121	1,101,300***	−6	2	10
36–45	1,377,236	1,332,889*	1,467,072***	1,440,310***	−3	7	8
46–55	1,689,170	1,641,481	1,791,450**	1,836,680***	−3	6	12
56+	1,305,101	1,216,640	1,497,851*	1,358,490***	−7	15	12
Male	1,221,163	1,173,385***	1,293,418***	1,316,450***	−4	6	12
Female	930,151	909,449	985,406***	997,948***	−2	6	10
Total	1,124,099	1,082,360***	1,191,543***	1,201,670***	−4	6	11
	Nominal wages (Rp per month)				Percent change		
15–17	493,976	502,855	529,973**	549,537***	2	7	9
18–25	761,080	747,424	832,087***	861,382***	−2	9	15
26–35	1,056,670	1,065,430	1,171,340***	1,209,390***	1	11	14
36–45	1,377,240	1,423,380*	1,592,900***	1,582,400***	3	16	11
46–55	1,689,170	1,752,970	1,945,860***	2,017,680***	4	15	15
56+	1,305,100	1,298,750	1,624,610***	1,491,640***	0	24	15
Male	1,221,160	1,252,980**	1,404,670***	1,446,490***	3	15	15
Female	930,151	970,307***	1,069,190***	1,095,480***	4	15	13
Total	1,124,099	1,155,490***	1,293,710***	1,320,000***	3	15	14

Source: World Bank staff, based on Indonesian Labor Force Survey (Sakernas).
Note: Real wages are for wage employees only and are given in February 2008 constant prices.
Significance level: * = 10 percent, ** = 5 percent, *** = 1 percent.

single-person businesses saw their income fall by 12 percent between August 2008 and February 2009, following a previous rise in income, leaving business owners slightly worse off than they were in February 2008. But it was casual workers who saw the largest fall: their real monthly incomes fell by 6–9 percent between February 2008 and February 2009. Disaggregating incomes for single-person businesses by sector (table 5.8) reveals significant increases in real income for many sectors before the crisis, followed by a sharp fall. For most sectors, this fall left them no worse off in February 2009 than in the previous year, and by August 2009 all sectors had recovered the gains achieved during 2008. However, for those self-employed in both the finance and the social and personal services sectors, the fall in real income resulting from the crisis was particularly severe, leaving them significantly worse off in February 2009 relative to the previous year.[8] Similarly, real income fell between February 2008 and February 2009 for casual nonagricultural workers in nearly every sector (with mining being a surprising exception). However, by August 2009, the average real income of casual nonagricultural workers in every sector had recovered to at least the level of the previous year.

Since results at the mean can be driven by outliers when the sample population is small, the authors also calculated the real wage results at the median and

Table 5.6 Real and Nominal Wages by Sector, Indonesia, February 2008–August 2009

	Real wages (Rp per month)				Percent change		
	Feb. 2008	Aug. 2008	Feb. 2009	Aug. 2009	Feb. 2008–Aug. 2008	Feb. 2008–Feb. 2009	Aug. 2008–Aug. 2009
Agriculture	756,034	795,119*	724,079*	738,844***	5	−4	−7
Mining and quarrying	2,125,965	2,102,264	1,840,817*	2,233,380	−1	−13	6
Industry	966,614	869,769***	1,002,452	1,020,330***	−10	4	17
Electricity, gas, and water	1,941,746	1,767,199	1,806,329	1,871,280	−9	−7	6
Construction	1,138,929	1,024,250***	1,218,567	1,121,310***	−10	7	9
Trade, restaurant, and accommodations	946,907	914,102	955,459	1,003,950***	−3	1	10
Transport and communications	1,337,079	1,277,662	1,570,727***	1,379,040**	−4	17	8
Financial institutions, real estate	1,830,455	1,652,934**	1,831,938	1,911,000***	−10	0	16
Social services, social and personal services	1,241,538	1,246,432	1,345,569***	1,366,020***	0	8	10

	Nominal wages (Rp per month)				Percent change		
	Feb. 2008	Aug. 2008	Feb. 2009	Aug. 2009	Feb. 2008–Aug. 2008	Feb. 2008–Feb. 2009	Aug. 2008–Aug. 2009
Agriculture	756,034	851,767***	788,761*	814,191*	13	4	−4
Mining and quarrying	2,125,965	2,258,565	2,015,870	2,471,590	6	−5	9
Industry	966,614	927,115**	1,086,060***	1,118,400***	−4	12	21
Electricity, gas ,and water	1,941,746	1,888,439	1,959,080	2,054,160	−3	1	9
Construction	1,138,929	1,093,257	1,324,360***	1,232,430***	−4	16	13
Trade, restaurant, and accommodations	946,907	974,677	1,035,480***	1,101,480***	3	9	13
Transport and communications	1,337,079	1,362,912	1,705,150***	1,513,460***	2	28	11
Financial institutions, real estate	1,830,455	1,761,249	1,984,690	2,092,790***	−4	8	19
Social services, social and personal services	1,241,538	1,331,335***	1,462,290***	1,501,860***	7	18	13

Source: World Bank staff, calculations based on Indonesian Labor Force Survey (Sakernas).
Note: Wages are for wage employees only.
Significance level: * = 10 percent, ** = 5 percent, *** = 1 percent.

upper and lower quartiles.[9] Those results hold when analyzing the median incomes of casual workers, while for single-person businesses the gap between the middle and the upper end of the income distribution narrowed at the start of 2009, as median income increased and the upper quartile fell. But the data suggest that even for those workers adversely affected by the downturn at the start of 2009, incomes by August 2009 had returned to levels similar to those prevailing in the previous year. Nonetheless, the contrast with the substantial real wage growth of employees suggests that the divide in income between formal and informal workers may be growing.

Working through the Crisis • http://dx.doi.org/10.1596/978-0-8213-8967-6

Table 5.7 Real Income and Real Wages by Category of Worker, Indonesia, February 2008–August 2009

Category of work	Feb. 2008 (Rp per month)	Aug. 2008 (Rp per month)	Feb. 2009 (Rp per month)	Aug. 2009 (Rp per month)	Feb. 2008– Aug. 2008 (%)	Feb. 2008– Feb. 2009 (%)	Aug. 2008– Aug. 2009 (%)
Own business	742,468	825,304***	722,942**	810,527*	11	−3	−2
Employee	1,124,099	1,082,360***	1,191,543***	1,201,670***	−4	6	11
Casual work, agriculture	380,977	385,016	358,317**	391,515	1	−6	2
Casual work, nonagriculture	617,941	607,836	562,338***	613,171	−2	−9	1

Source: World Bank staff, based on Indonesian Labor Force Survey (Sakernas).
Note: The Sakernas survey does not provide income data for business owners, either with nonpermanent or unpaid workers, or with permanent or paid workers. Data on the incomes of unpaid workers are unavailable, and these categories are omitted above.
Significance level: * = 10 percent, ** = 5 percent, *** = 1 percent.

Table 5.8 Real Income for Single-Person Businesses and Casual Nonagricultural Workers Disaggregated by Sector, Indonesia, February 2008–August 2009
Rupiah per month

Sector	Real income			
	Feb. 2008	Aug. 2008	Feb. 2009	Aug. 2009
Single-person business				
Agriculture	569,955	724,131***	549,691	642,139
Mining and quarrying	778,444	1,107,550**	865,881	1,145,200
Industry	575,083	653,558***	584,431	559,155
Electricity, gas, and water[a]	1,247,290	1,175,630	630,071***	2,585,560
Construction	960,049	1,071,630**	949,460	1,206,870
Trade, restaurant, and accommodation	828,114	858,907**	842,729	879,500
Transport and communications	751,152	857,446***	757,577	882,539
Financial institutions and real estate	1,612,460	1,709,740	1,211,310**	1,535,010
Social services, social and personal services	865,239	900,915	678,600***	771,034
Casual nonagricultural worker				
Mining and quarrying	635,517	599,467	816,385***	657,640*
Industry	420,633	402,866	331,649***	435,990***
Electricity, gas, and water	608,260	732,463	470,014	631,920
Construction	736,969	706,306**	703,245**	697,101
Trade, restaurant, and accommodation	501,555	568,482*	467,623	595,537
Transport and communications	697,277	700,822	632,615**	676,183
Financial institutions and real estate	765,769	570,000	437,108*	784,922***
Social services, social and personal services	463,185	484,061	408,376**	502,368

Source: World Bank staff, based on Indonesian Labor Force Survey (Sakernas).
a. The large changes in this sector reflect the very small sample size in this sector.
Significance level: * = 10 percent, ** = 5 percent, *** = 1 percent.

Overall, such large increases in real wages are surprising, given the collapse in exports and commodity prices. These results are not driven by outliers: a 1 percent trimmed sample produces much the same pattern of results. Moreover, wages appeared to increase throughout the distribution, as the same pattern emerges in median wages and income or in the lower or upper quartile.[10]

The higher inflation of mid-2008 possibly led to demands for higher nominal wages. If formal sector employment contracts were decided after August but before the onset of the crisis in October, then employers may have agreed to relatively large nominal wage increases. But, as noted above, the collapse in commodity and world food prices led to a rapid reduction in domestic inflation, greatly increasing the value of any nominal wage gains.

Another possible explanation for the increase in average wages may be that compositional changes are taking place in the workforce. Specifically, employers may have used the crisis as an opportunity to release lower-paid workers, thereby increasing the average wage. Table 5.2 indicated that unemployment rose most among young workers, who earn around two-thirds of the national average wage. Moreover, employers may have removed the less skilled workers in each age class. To explore this idea further, the authors drew on a set of weights constructed by the World Bank (forthcoming) that gives the proportion of wage workers in different education, age, gender, and rural-urban categories. The authors calculated the nominal and real wages for each of the 16 different combinations of the four characteristics[11] and then used fixed precrisis (August 2006) proportions of people in each of the 16 cells to calculate what the average wage would have been had there been no compositional change over the crisis period. The results are shown in table 5.9.

Although compositional change has clearly played a role, the main trends remain the same:

- Real income from owner-operated businesses increased before the crisis, fell sharply over the crisis, but has since recovered most of its original gains.
- Real wages for employees fell before the crisis but increased from August 2008 to February 2009.[12]
- Real wages for both agricultural and nonagricultural casual workers fell sharply over the crisis but recovered subsequently.

Flow into and Out of Employment

From August 2008 onward, participants in the survey were asked if they had changed jobs or stopped working in the past year. Table 5.10 shows the number of people ending employment or changing jobs as a share of those who worked before. The share of people changing jobs or work status is typically much higher for younger workers and higher for men than for women. In the immediate aftermath of the financial crisis, the exit rate increased for every age group and for both men and women, with a larger increase in the share of men leaving jobs than women. The average exit rate increased to just over 13 percent in February 2009 before returning to 11 percent six months later, suggesting that this finding may have been a short-run effect of the crisis. Again, the increased share of workers leaving jobs was more pronounced for those 25 and under.

A focus just on those who stopped working (table 5.11) shows that this change is driven by a substantial increase—between 20 and 25 percent—in the share of people who were laid off or who were employed in a business that failed.

Working through the Crisis • http://dx.doi.org/10.1596/978-0-8213-8967-6

Table 5.9 Nominal and Real Wages by Category of Work Controlling for Compositional Change, Indonesia, February 2008–August 2009

Rupiah per month

Category of work	Real wages and real income				Nominal wages and nominal income			
	Feb. 2008	*Aug. 2008*	*Feb. 2009*	*Aug. 2009*	*Feb. 2008*	*Aug. 2008*	*Feb. 2009*	*Aug. 2009*
Own business	751,534	807,012***	718,878***	806,828	751,534	862,749***	781,682***	886,655***
Employee	1,184,760	1,106,270***	1,186,630	1,212,160***	1,184,760	1,180,780	1,287,940***	1,330,850***
Casual work, agriculture	355,301	373,833***	345,089	380,637	355,301	399,440***	374,337**	417,546***
Casual work, nonagriculture	603,787	615,271	564,483***	614,678	603,787	656,348***	611,830	673,705*

Source: World Bank staff, based on Indonesian Labor Force Survey (Sakernas).

Note: Sakernas does not provide income data for business owners, either with nonpermanent or unpaid workers, or with permanent or paid workers. Similarly, the authors do not have data on the incomes of unpaid workers and so these categories are omitted above. Estimated for workers aged 15+.

Significance level: * = 10 percent, ** = 5 percent, *** = 1 percent.

Table 5.10 Total Share of Workers Ending Employment or Changing Jobs by Age and Gender, Indonesia, August 2008–August 2009

Percent

Age and gender	Aug. 2008	Feb. 2009	Aug. 2009
10–14	30.0	36.4	27.9
15–17	36.6	38.1	37.5
18–25	27.4	30.5***	26.6
26–35	13.5	14.7***	13.0**
36–45	9.1	10.2***	9.0
46–55	7.8	8.5*	7.6
56+	4.5	4.8	4.3
Male	12.8	14.5***	12.4*
Female	10.7	11.7***	10.3*
Total	11.9	13.2***	11.5**

Source: World Bank staff, based on Indonesian Labor Force Survey (Sakernas).
Significance level relative to August 2008: * = 10 percent, ** = 5 percent, *** = 1 percent.

Table 5.11 Share of Workers Ending Employment or Changing Jobs, Indonesia, August 2008–August 2009

Percent

Indicator	Aug. 2008	Feb. 2009	Aug. 2009
Laid off	5.0	6.0***	5.8***
Business collapse	14.1	17.5***	16.7***
Insufficient income	20.5	19.5*	19.9
Unsuitable working conditions	9.3	9.5	9.3
Work contract finished	15.7	16.6	16.4
Other	35.3	31.0***	31.9***

Source: World Bank staff, based on Indonesian Labor Force Survey (Sakernas).
Significance level relative to August 2008: * = 10 percent, ** = 5 percent, *** = 1 percent.

Most sectors report a rise in the share of workers whose employment was terminated for these two reasons (table 5.12), with an average increase of 30 percent in this share across sectors. Perhaps not surprisingly, the share of terminated workers increased most in mining and quarrying, rising by more than 100 percent between August 2008 and February 2009. The increase in the share of exits due to layoffs or business failure has also been persistent: although this share has shown modest declines across most sectors, the share of exits due to layoffs and business failure was still significantly higher in August 2009 than a year previously for almost all sectors.

Table 5.13 compares entrance and exit rates by age and gender. A large increase in the share of people that stopped working occurred between August 2008 and February 2009, particularly for younger workers. However, this exit rate fell rapidly during 2009; by August 2009, the share of people who had stopped working during the previous year was lower for all age groups than in August 2008, suggesting that workers, facing a tighter job market, were less inclined to leave employment if they could avoid it. Further evidence for this

Table 5.12 Share of Workers Who Ended Employment Either because They Were Laid Off or Their Business Collapsed Due to Falling Demand by Previous Employment Sector, Indonesia, August 2008–August 2009

Percent

Indicator	Aug. 2008	Feb. 2009	Aug. 2009
Agriculture	23.0	27.2***	29.0***
Mining and quarrying	11.6	23.3***	17.5**
Industry	24.7	30.7***	28.3***
Electricity, gas, and water	13.1	14.5	10.9
Construction	25.8	34.0***	30.4***
Trade, restaurant, and accommodations	16.8	15.9	14.8**
Transport and communications	13.9	18.4**	15.0
Financial institutions, real estate	9.8	11.9	13.2
Social services, social and personal services	7.9	11.8***	11.1***

Source: World Bank staff, based on Indonesian Labor Force Survey (Sakernas).
Note: Shares of workers that were laid off or whose business failed are relative to the total number of people whose employment status changed.
Significance level relative to August 2008: * = 10 percent, ** = 5 percent, *** = 1 percent.

Table 5.13 Share of People Who Worked Before but Stopped Working and Share of New Entrants as a Percentage of Those Currently Employed, by Age and Gender, Indonesia, August 2008–August 2009

Percent

Age and gender	Those who stopped working			New entrants		
	Aug. 2008	Feb. 2009	Aug. 2009	Aug. 2008	Feb. 2009	Aug. 2009
10–14	21.9	22.0	15.7*	9.9	8.9	9.5
15–17	22.6	22.5	20.5	9.8	9.6	9.6
18–25	13.8	16.0***	12.9**	6.4	6.3	5.7***
26–35	5.3	6.1***	4.7***	1.6	1.5	1.3***
36–45	3.1	3.5**	2.8**	0.7	0.8	0.6***
46–55	3.1	3.2	2.9	0.0	0.0	0.0
56+	2.5	2.8*	2.3	0.3	0.3	0.2***
Male	4.2	5.0***	3.8***	1.7	1.6*	1.4***
Female	6.5	7.2***	6.0***	2.6	2.5	2.3***
Total	5.2	6.0***	4.8***	2.0	1.9	1.8***

Source: World Bank staff, based on Indonesian Labor Force Survey (Sakernas).
Note: New entrants are given as shares of the total number of people currently employed, whereas the share of people who have stopped working is relative to those who have worked before.
Significance level relative to August 2008: * = 10 percent, ** = 5 percent, *** = 1 percent.

finding comes from the data on new entrants. While there was no difference in the share of new entrants into the labor market between August 2008 and February 2009, by August 2009 the entry rate had declined significantly for all age groups and for men and women, suggesting that it was more difficult to enter employment than before.

Movements into and out of sectors give some indication of job availability both for new entrants and for workers changing sectors. Table 5.14 shows the share of workers joining and leaving a sector as a percentage of the total number

Table 5.14 Share of Workers Joining and Leaving a Sector as a Percentage of the Total Number of People Employed in That Sector, by Age and Gender, Indonesia, August 2008–August 2009

Percent

Age and gender	Workers joining the sector			Workers leaving the sector		
	Aug. 2008	Feb. 2009	Aug. 2009	Aug. 2008	Feb. 2009	Aug. 2009
Agriculture	2.2	2.2	2.8**	2.6	2.8***	3.0**
Mining and quarrying	9.1	10.7**	14.8*	6.9	6.7	10.9*
Industry	5.9	5.9	5.9*	7.6	8.1*	10.9*
Electricity, gas, and water	4.2	5.8	3.6**	6.7	4.5	8.4*
Construction	7.7	7.7	7.5*	8.8	9.7**	16.8*
Trade, restaurant, and accommodation	5.3	4.9**	5.9*	4.6	4.4	5.9**
Transport and communications	5.4	5.8	6.7*	5.1	4.8	6.4*
Financial institutions, real estate	6.5	7.2	7.7*	9.6	9.1	11.7*
Social services, social and personal services	4.4	4.1**	4.9**	5.7	5.5	6.6*

Source: World Bank staff, based on Indonesian Labor Force Survey (Sakernas).

Note: The total number of people flowing into a sector is defined as the sum of new entrants into the sector plus those who moved jobs from other sectors. Conversely, the total number of people leaving a sector is defined as the sum of the people who stopped working in the sector plus the people who shifted to a job out of the sector.

Significance level relative to August 2008: * = 10 percent, ** = 5 percent, *** = 1 percent.

of people employed. The rates of joining and leaving vary substantially across sectors: the mining and quarrying sector and the construction sector tend to have high shares of people moving in and out as employment is more intermittant in these sectors. Conversely, the flows into and out of agriculture make up a smaller share of the total sector's employment, given the traditional nature of the sector. Most sectors have experienced an increase in the share of people joining and leaving since the financial crisis. For example, by August 2009 there were large net flows out of industry, construction, and finance. By contrast, mining, despite the fall in commodity prices and the initial fall in real wages, saw an increase of 20 percent in the share of workers who had joined the sector by February 2009 and a further 40 percent increase in this share by August 2009, explaining the slight increase in employment in the sector. The trade and restaurant sector and the transport and communications sector also experienced modest net increases in employment.

Table 5.15 shows the average number of months spent searching for employment by gender and age group. Two features are apparent. First, job seekers under 18 experienced a large increase in the number of months spent searching, consistent with earlier evidence of a much more difficult job market for the youngest workers. Second, for job seekers between 18 and 35 the number of months spent searching declined sharply. Most of this decline predates the crisis, probably reflecting seasonal changes in the job market. But the fact that shorter search times persist through August 2009 could also reflect a response of workers to a tighter job market with greater churning of jobs, as they are more inclined to accept any job they can get rather than wait for one better matched to their skills.

Table 5.15 Average Number of Months Spent Looking for Work by Age and Gender, Indonesia, February 2008–August 2009

Percent

Age and gender	Feb. 2008	Aug. 2008	Feb. 2009	Aug. 2009
10–14	1.8	3.1	3.3***	2.5**
15–17	2.7	2.9	3.7***	2.8*
18–25	4.1	3.0	3.4***	3.0
26–35	3.7	3.0	2.9***	3.1
36–45	3.0	3.0	3.1	3.0
46–55	2.8	2.9	2.6	3.0
56+	1.6	2.7	2.5	3.0
Male	3.9	3.0	3.2***	3.0
Female	3.2	3.0	3.2	3.0
Total	3.5	3.0	3.2***	3.0

Source: World Bank staff, based on Indonesian Labor Force Survey (Sakernas).
Note: The sample consists of those who are actively seeking employment.
Significance level relative to August 2008: * = 10 percent, ** = 5 percent, *** = 1 percent.

Comparing Qualitative and Quantitative Results

Finally, it is instructive to briefly compare the quantitative results in this chapter with the results of a rapid qualitative study undertaken in February 2009 (Fillaili *et al.* 2009). That study used participatory methods for exploring the impact of the crisis, the pathways through which the effects had been felt, and both government and household responses. The work was done over two weeks in February 2009 in two villages chosen to illustrate the impact of the crisis. One urban and one rural village were selected.

The urban village, Gandasari, is in the district of Bekasi, just outside the capital city Jakarta. It is the site of a major industrial park and therefore houses a large number of migrant workers from other parts of Indonesia who work in the park. The rural village—Simpang Empat, in the district of Banjar, in South Kalimantan[13]—is heavily dependent on local rubber plantations as well as on employment in nearby coal stockpiles. Both coal and rubber prices dropped dramatically during the crisis.

Three features are particularly striking when the qualitative and quantitative studies are compared. First, despite the small, purposively selected sample for the qualitative study, the overall conclusions that Fillaili *et al.* draw (that there is little change in either schooling or participation in the labor force) are broadly similar to those obtained from the national data.

Second, the qualitative study highlighted the specific vulnerability of younger workers in an urban setting. This finding corresponds closely with the results given in this chapter, which show increasing unemployment and no initial increase in real wages for workers under age 25. The qualitative study also points to potential weaknesses in the way in which the labor force survey deals with migrant workers, which may explain why the results given here do not show a stronger negative impact for this group.

Finally, none of the interviews and discussions carried out in the two selected villages gave any indication of real wage increases for employees, in stark contrast to the increases in average real wages in the national data. This finding reflects the importance of caution in interpreting results from purposively sampled locations likely to have been hit most severely by the crisis.

Summary and Conclusions

Indonesia weathered the financial crisis of 2008–09 reasonably well. The macroeconomic shock it suffered was much less than those of neighboring countries and merely served to slow its already respectable growth rate. Nonetheless, the nature of the shock—acting through dramatically reduced exports and large declines in commodity prices—led to an expectation of some strong localized effects. In fact, the authors find little evidence of subgroups that were particularly badly affected, although the impact of the crisis on migrant workers may be understated by the data The share of children dropping out of school stayed the same, or continued to improve, with only small differences by gender, age, and rural-urban location. Labor force participation fell, particularly for children: it would seem that parents kept children in school as the labor market deteriorated for younger workers. In keeping with the findings from chapter 3 of this volume, the authors find that young workers bore the brunt of the crisis, with unemployment rising for workers between ages 18 and 25. However, unemployment continued to fall for workers above this age, average hours worked remained roughly the same, and no evidence for significant sectoral shifts in employment has emerged. While it is clear that reduced demand for labor became a much more important reason for ending or changing jobs, the continued fall in aggregate unemployment suggests that these workers have been absorbed within normal labor turnover, and the crisis does not seem to have altered the share of workers in the informal sector. Indeed, intersectoral churning in the labor market appears to have increased, while at the same time the rate of new entrants and permanent exits has fallen.

The big surprise from the analysis is what happened to real wages for employees. In a reversal of the experience of the 1997–98 crisis, where adjustment was achieved through a substantial fall in real wages, the period between August 2008 and February 2009 saw substantial increases in average real wages for employees over 35. Although real wages in mining, agriculture, and public utilities fell—reflecting the collapse in commodity prices—wages in industry, construction, transport and communications, and social and personal services increased quickly. However, it was primarily employees who gained, with informal sector businesses and casual workers seeing a significant initial fall in their incomes.

A number of reasons may explain why Indonesia has come out of this financial crisis reasonably well. The first is structural: Indonesia, as a large country, is much less dependent on international trade than most other countries in the region. The large drop in exports and imports therefore had a commensurately smaller effect on the domestic economy. In addition, the government's management of this crisis appears to have been good: rapid arrangements provided confidence to the market, limiting the fall in the value of the currency and hastening its early recovery. This action minimized the impact on import-dependent firms and avoided major shifts in resources between the tradable and nontradable sectors. Moreover, the large FSP and its raft of tax cuts, subsidies, and additional expenditures may have contributed, in part, to rising real wages in the formal sector and to the continued fall in unemployment for older workers (see Hastuti, Mawardi, Sodo, Marbun, and Ruhmaniyati 2010; World Bank 2010a).

The Indonesian experience may offer some useful broader lessons on the impact of the crisis. First, the nature of the shock was relatively narrowly focused on export sectors, particularly commodities and manufacturing. This focus poses a policy challenge, since it was engagement with the world market in these sectors that was driving growth for many countries before the crisis. Countries with large domestic markets, such as Indonesia, may be able to reduce their vulnerability to such shocks through boosting domestic demand, an option not available to smaller developing countries. Second, Indonesia's policy environment and responses to the crisis appear to provide a positive example of how to deal with such shocks. Careful monetary management prevented a long-lasting shock to the exchange rate, while a long period of prudential budget management had created the fiscal space for Indonesia to respond. At the same time, relatively flexible labor markets meant that affected firms could shed temporary labor rapidly, preventing widespread corporate failures as occurred during the East Asian crisis.

Third, Indonesia's experience suggests some priorities emerging from studies of the impact of the crisis on other countries (for example, Green, King, and Miller-Dawkins 2010). These include the importance of food prices, the impact on migrant workers, and the need to understand the informal sector better. The qualitative work strongly suggests that the persistence of high food prices is the single most important influence on the welfare of the poor and that therefore the run up in food prices during 2008 may have had a much stronger impact than the financial crisis itself. The disconnect between the qualitative findings of strong negative impacts on migrant workers and the lack of major negative impacts on employees in the dataset used in this chapter highlight the fact that labor force surveys often omit precisely the group that may be most negatively affected. Similarly, the disparity between the fortunes of formal sector workers and those in the informal sector points to the need for a better understanding of the ways in which the informal sector is affected by such crises. Developing the tools to improve the understanding of these issues could enable governments to provide better responses to future crises.

Notes

1. This section draws heavily on World Bank (2009a) and Yudo, Titiheruw, and Soesastro (2009); the regional context section draws on IMF (2009b and 2009c) and World Bank (2010b).

2. Later, the parliament included an additional fund of Rp 2 trillion proposed by its budget committee earmarked to finance infrastructure projects.

3. The payroll tax incentive was not effective because very few firms responded. Under this scheme, payroll taxes for workers in certain labor-intensive industries could be temporarily reduced. Not many firms applied for this incentive because they feared that, once the temporary reduction in the payroll tax ended, the take-home pay of workers would fall back to its previous level, creating the potential for worker unrest (Suhendra 2009).

4. See BPS (1996) for further information on the data.

5. The BPS definition of unemployment is broader than the International Labour Organization (ILO) definition because it includes people who are not working and not looking for work because they feel discouraged (Suryadarma, Suryhadi, and Sumarto 2005). The authors report measures using the BPS definitions; results using the ILO definitions are available on request.

6. See McCulloch and Grover (2010) for full results.

7. The median wage fell by 5 percent.

8. The collapse and subsequent recovery in real income for those self-employed in the electricity, gas, and water sector are driven by the very small sample size for this category.

9. Results are available on request.

10. With the exception, noted above, that income from single-person businesses increased by 14 percent from February 2008 to February 2009 at the median but barely changed for the lower and upper quartile suggests a narrowing of the distribution.

11. *Education* is defined as "better educated" if it is junior secondary or above; otherwise, it is classified as "less well educated"; age is defined as young (ages 15–24) or adult (ages 25–64).

12. Although the composition-adjusted results do not show a statistically significant increase between February 2008 and February 2009, this finding comes about primarily because the composition-adjusted real wage in February 2008 is higher. Both sets of results show real wages rising significantly from August 2008 to August 2009.

13. Kalimantan is the Indonesian part of the island of Borneo.

References

BPS (Bureau Pusat Statistik). 1996. *National Labor Force Survey: Enumerators Manual.* Jakarta: BPS.

Cameron, L. 2000. "The Impact of the Indonesian Financial Crisis on Children: An Analysis Using the 100 Villages Data." *Bulletin of Indonesian Economic Statistics* 37 (1): 43–64.

Cuevas, S., C. Mina, M. Barcenas, and A. Rosario. 2009. "Informal Employment in Indonesia." Economics Working Paper Series 156, Asian Development Bank, Manila.

Fillaili, R., W. I. Suharyo, B. Sulaksono, S. Hastuti, H. Widjanarko, S. Budiyati, S. Usman, N. Aini, and F. F. Seiff. 2009. *IDS Pilot Qualitative Study: Crisis Impact and Response. Indonesia—Country Report.* Jakarta: Social Monitoring and Early Response Unit.

Frankenberg, E., D. Thomas, and K. Beegle. 1999. "The Real Cost of Indonesia's Economic Crisis: Preliminary Findings from the Indonesian Family Life Surveys." Working Paper 99–04, Rand Corporation, Santa Monica, CA.

Friedman, J., and J. Levinsohn. 2002. "The Distributional Impact of Indonesia's Financial Crisis on Household Welfare: A 'Rapid Response' Methodology." *World Bank Economic Review* 16 (3): 397–423.

Green, D., R. King, and M. Miller-Dawkins. 2010. *The Global Economic Crisis and Developing Countries: Impact and Response*. Draft report, Oxfam, Oxford, U.K.

Griffith-Jones, S., and J. A. Ocampo. 2009. "The Financial Crisis and Its Impact on Developing Countries." Working Paper 53, International Policy Centre for Inclusive Growth, UNDP, Brasilia.

Hastuti, S. U., M. S Mawardi, and D. Marbun. 2010. "Peran Program Stimulus Fiskal untuk Peningkatan Infrastruktur Padat Karya dalam Merespon Dampak Krisis Keuangan Global 2008/09" [The Role of the Fiscal Stimulus Program through Labor Intensive Infrastructure Provision on Mitigating the Impact of Global Financial Crisis 2008/09]. Research report, SMERU Research Institute, Jakarta.

Hastuti, S. U., M. S. Mawardi, D. Marbun, and A. Arief. 2010. *Kondisi Tenaga Kerja Muda Sektor Industri di Perkotaan Terkait Dampak Krisis Keuangan Global 2008/09* [The Condition of Young Workers in the Urban Industrial Sector in Relation to the Impact of the Global Financial Crisis 2008/09]. Research report, SMERU Research Institute, Jakarta.

Hastuti, S. U., M. S. Mawardi, J. Sodo, D. Marbun, and Ruhmaniyati. 2010. "The Role of Social Protection in Reducing the Impact of the Global Financial Crisis 2008/09." Research report, SMERU Research Institute, Jakarta.

IDS (Institute of Development Studies). 2009. *Accounts of Crisis: Poor People's Experiences of the Food, Fuel and Financial Crises in Five Countries*. Brighton, U.K.: IDS.

IMF (International Monetary Fund). 2009a. *The Implications of the Global Financial Crisis for Low-Income Countries*. Washington, DC: IMF.

———. 2009b. *World Economic Outlook April 2009: Crisis and Recovery*. Washington, DC: IMF.

———. 2009c. *World Economic Outlook October 2009: Sustaining the Recovery*. Washington, DC: IMF.

Kanbur, R. 2002. *Q-squared: Combining Qualitative and Quantitative Methods in Poverty Appraisal*. New Delhi: Permanent Black.

Levine, D., and M. Ames. 2003. "Gender Bias and the Indonesian Financial Crisis: Were Girls Hit Hardest?" Working Paper Series C03-130, Center for International and Development Economics Research, Berkeley, CA.

Manning, C. 2000. "Labour Market Adjustment to Indonesia's Economic Crisis: Context, Trends and Implications." *Bulletin of Indonesian Economic Studies* 36 (1): 105–36.

Marbun, D. 2010. *Indonesia's Fiscal Stimulus Program: Understanding the Policy Making Process Using RAPID Framework*. Research report, SMERU Research Institute, Jakarta.

McCulloch, N., and A. Grover. 2010. "Estimating the National Impact of the Financial Crisis in Indonesia by Combining a Rapid Qualitative Study with Nationally Representative Survey." Working Paper 346, Institute of Development Studies, Brighton, U.K.

McKenzie, D. 2004. "Aggregate Shocks and Labour Market Responses: Evidence from Argentina's Financial Crisis." *Economic Development and Cultural Change* 52 (4): 719–58.

Mendoza, R. U. 2009. "Aggregate Shocks, Poor Households and Children." *Global Social Policy* 9 (55): 55–78.

Ministry of Finance. 2008. "Managing Impacts of Global Crisis through Fiscal Stimulus in the 2009 State Budget." Ministry of Finance of the Republic of Indonesia, Jakarta.

National Development Planning Agency. 2010. *Laporan Status Pelaksanaan Program Stimulus Fiskal 2009* [Report of the Implementation Status of the 2009 Fiscal Stimulus Program]. National Development Planning Agency, Jakarta.

Naudé, W. 2009. "The Financial Crisis of 2008 and the Developing Countries." WIDER Discussion Paper, United Nations University, World Institute for Development Economics Research, Helsinki.

ODI (Overseas Development Institute). 2009. *The Global Financial Crisis and Developing Countries: Preliminary Synthesis of Ten Draft Country Reports*. Overseas Development Institute, London.

Suhendra. 2009. "Perusahaan Takut Ambil Insentif PPh 21, Karyawan Gigit Jari" [Firms Are Afraid to Take the Payroll Tax Incentive, Workers are at Lost]. detikFinance, October 9. http://www.detikfinance.com/read/2009/10/09/182146/1218859/4/perusahaan-takut-ambil-insentif-pph-21-karyawan-gigit-jari.

Suryadarma, D., A. Suryahadi, and S. Sumarto. 2005. "The Measurement and Trends of Unemployment in Indonesia: The Issue of Discouraged Workers." Working paper, SMERU, Jakarta.

World Bank. 2009a. "Swimming against the Tide: How Developing Countries Are Coping with the Global Financial Crisis." Background paper prepared for the G-20 Finance Ministers' and Central Bank Governors' Meeting, Horsham, U.K., March 13–14.

———. 2009b. *Indonesia Economic Quarterly Update: Weathering the Storm*. Jakarta.

———. 2010a. "Indonesia's Crisis Monitoring and Response System (CMRS)." World Bank, Jakarta.

———. 2010b. *Global Economic Prospects 2010: Crisis Finance and Growth*. Washington, DC: World Bank.

———. Forthcoming. Indonesia Jobs Report. Washington, DC: World Bank.

Yudo, T., I. S. Titiheruw, and H. Soesastro. 2009. *Impacts of Global Financial Crisis on Indonesian Economy*. Jakarta: Centre for Strategic and International Studies.

Weathering a Storm: Survey-Based Perspectives on Employment in China in the Aftermath of the Global Financial Crisis

John Giles, Albert Park, Fang Cai, and Yang Du

The global financial crisis, well under way by the third quarter of 2008, did not originate in the developing world. It sparked immediate concerns, however, that its effects would be felt widely, particularly in those economies in which a substantial share of the workforce was engaged in export-oriented activities. China met the onset of the crisis with a strong fiscal stimulus program, coupled with active labor market policies, aimed both at providing training to laid-off migrant workers and at supporting the medium- and small-scale enterprises that were more exposed to shocks from the crisis. This chapter reviews evidence on the incidence of shocks related to the financial crisis in China, documents employment effects, and presents evidence of the recovery in 2009.

Analyzing the Effects of the Crisis

The lack of publicly available and nationally representative firm, labor force, and household surveys complicates an analysis of the precise effects of the financial crisis on China. Incidental surveys—such as a firm survey carried out by the People's Bank of China, a rural household survey conducted by China Center for Agricultural Policy at the Chinese Academy of Sciences, and the China Urban

The authors gratefully acknowledge support for this chapter and underlying research from the Gender Action Program and Knowledge for Change Trust Fund. John Giles is senior labor economist in the Development Research Group at the World Bank; Albert Park is professor of economics at Hong Kong University of Science and Technology; Fang Cai is professor and director of the Institute for Population and Labor Economics at the Chinese Academy of Social Sciences (CASS-IPLE); and Yang Du is a professor at CASS-IPLE.

Labor Survey conducted by the Chinese Academy of Social Sciences—may nonetheless be used in conjunction with information from national surveys and published research to tease out the employment effects of the crisis and recovery. This chapter reviews critically the evidence from these sources, with an eye toward highlighting data and measurement issues, while documenting a consistent narrative of crisis and recovery in China.

According to evidence from multiple sources, migrant workers were exposed more than other workers to the financial crisis. Given that migrant workers typically lack the formal employment contracts enjoyed by urban workers, they were easier for firms to lay off, providing flexibility to employers who needed to reduce costs in the face of crisis-related shocks. As migrants also typically lack the benefits that urban workers have, they were in a much more precarious position with little access to formal safety nets protecting them against unemployment. The recognition of this vulnerability provided an extra sense of urgency for development of a macroeconomic stimulus package that would facilitate reemployment of laid-off workers. The widespread reductions in employment that were evident by January 2009 could have placed existing institutions under considerable stress.

By the end of 2009, data from both firm and household surveys show that China had weathered the storm quite well. In spite of the ongoing slowdown elsewhere in the world, the labor market was tightening in China. Real wages of migrant workers continued to increase through the crisis, even as a significant percentage had suffered layoffs, and by late 2009 laid-off migrants looking for jobs were finding them.

The chapter proceeds as follows. The next section locates the shock of the financial crisis in the context of other adjustments already under way in the Chinese economy and documents the effects of the shock on the export sector. The following section reviews evidence on the employment effects of the crisis from firm and household surveys. The chapter then discusses the government's fiscal stimulus and active labor market programs and reviews evidence of the effect of the crisis and subsequent recovery on wages and incomes. The final section offers some conclusions.

The Trajectory of China's Economic Growth and the Global Financial Crisis

Between 2001 and 2007, the world economy experienced steady growth (figure 6.1, panel a). China and India consistently displayed growth rates of 4–12 percent, while other major economies registered healthy annual growth rates of 2 percent or more. China's growth rate was in fact so high by 2007 that in early 2008 the government was in the process of trying to cool off the economy and make growth more equitable. The government and the central bank had introduced contractionary macroeconomic policies in 2007, aiming to slow growth, and in January 2008 the new Labor Contract Law was put in place to provide employment protection to workers along with mandated social

Figure 6.1 Annual and Quarterly GDP Percentage Growth Rates for China and Other Major Economies, 2000–09

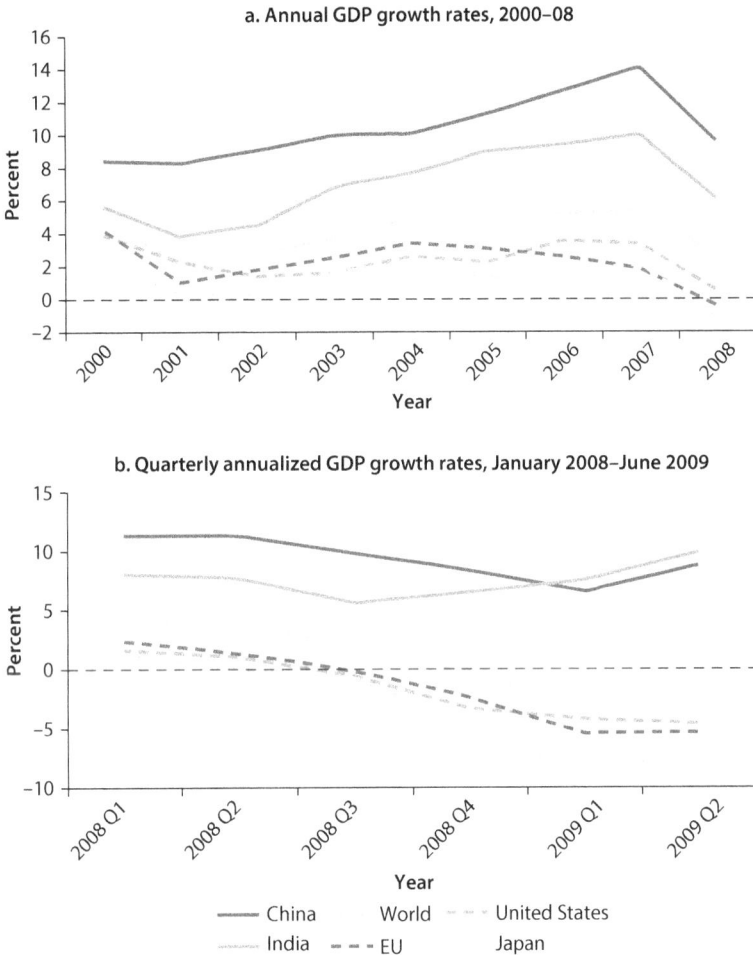

a. Annual GDP growth rates, 2000–08

b. Quarterly annualized GDP growth rates, January 2008–June 2009

China   World   United States
India   EU   Japan

Sources: IMF 2009; OECD.
Note: EU = European Union; GDP = gross domestic product.

insurance contributions from employers.[1] The timing of these two events nearly overlapped with the subsequent crisis and thus complicates efforts to link layoffs directly to the financial crisis. Nonetheless, evidence from quarterly data suggests that shocks associated with the crisis, which hit in the third quarter of 2008, may have had a stronger effect on gross domestic product (GDP) and employment than earlier policy shocks.

The events of September 2008 raised concerns that China would face a sharp drop in GDP. The global financial crisis changed the growth trajectories of all major world economies and plunged Japan, the United Kingdom, and the United States into deep recession (figure 6.1, panel b). By the first quarter of 2009, annual growth rates were negative in major developed economies; while the growth rates of China and India were still positive, they dropped steeply in both countries. In comparison to other major economies of the world, China experienced one of the largest changes in annual growth rates from 2007 to 2008. From the first and second quarter of 2008 to the fourth quarter of 2008 and the first quarter of 2009, China's annualized quarterly growth rate fell from more than 10 percent to 6 percent (figure 6.1, panel b).

Responsibility for the slowdown in China's GDP lies squarely with the global financial crisis, given that GDP growth declined well *after* contractionary domestic monetary and employment policies were implemented and that the timing was consistent with a sharp drop in export demand: the negative export demand shock contributed more to the contraction in aggregate demand that slowed China's economy. Customs data on China provide useful evidence on the scale of the shock to its exports. The aggregate decline in trade volume shown in figure 6.2 is driven by decreased exports to the European Union and the United States of 22.1 and 17.1 percent, respectively, over the same periods in the previous year. Given these sharp declines, it was apparent that China's economy would be hit hard by the decline in exports if no alternative sources of demand for goods and services emerged.

As shown in figure 6.3, the sharpest shock to China's economy occurred in the manufacturing sector, which is in the secondary sector in China's industry classification system (the primary sector comprises agriculture and mining, and the tertiary sector includes services and trade). While all three sectors experienced declines in their high rates of growth after mid-2007, manufacturing,

Figure 6.2 Monthly Changes in the Total Value of Imports and Exports, January 2006–November 2009

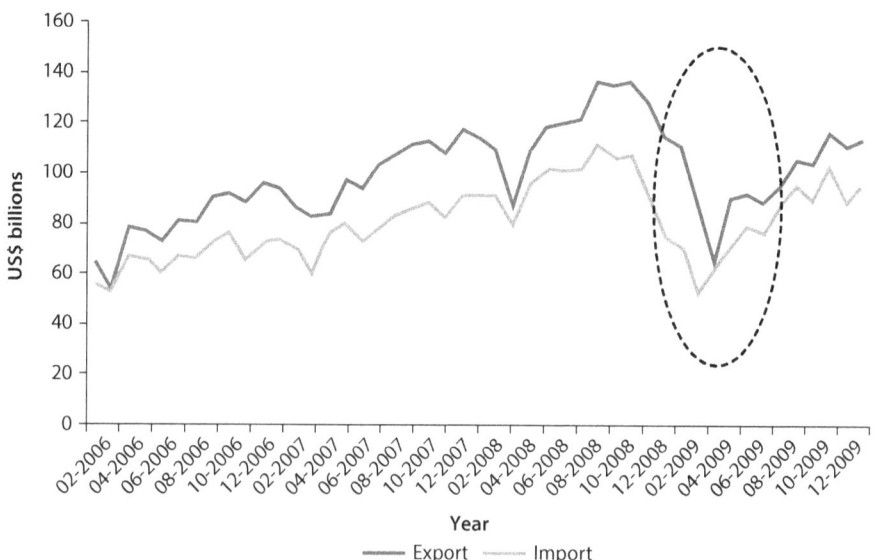

Source: China Customs 2010.
Note: The circle highlights the period of the global financial crisis.

Figure 6.3 China's Quarterly Growth Rates by Sector, 2004–09

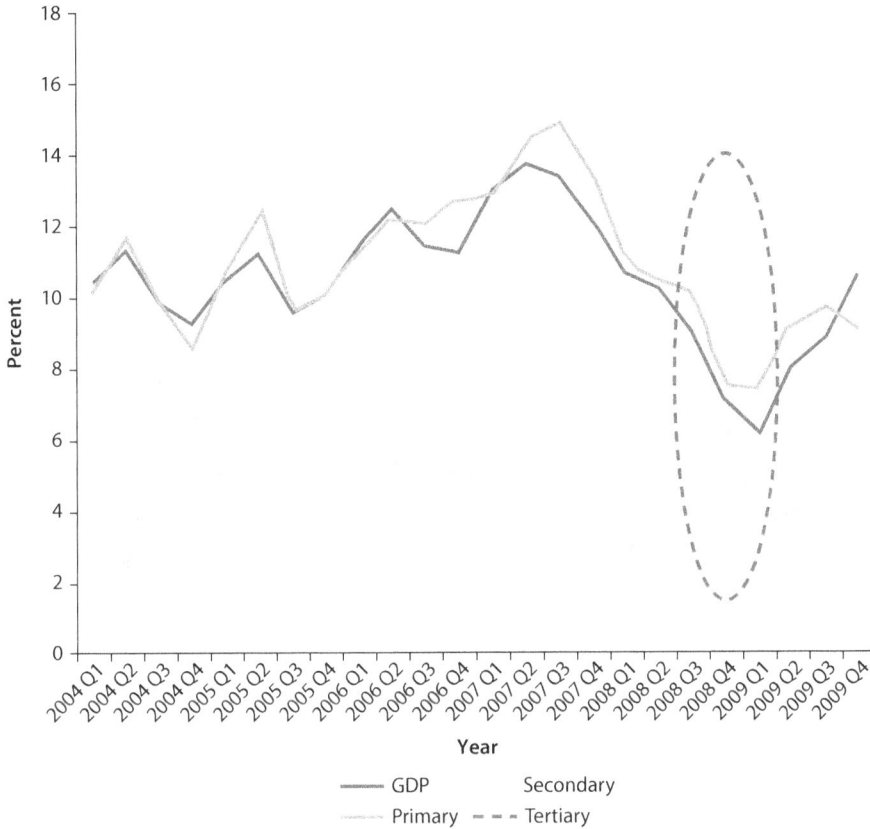

Source: NBS 2010b.
Note: GDP = gross domestic product. The circle highlights the period of the global financial crisis.

where exports are concentrated, experienced a sharp drop at the time of the crisis, and some of the effects of this shock likely spilled over into the services sector as well.

The Financial Crisis and Shocks to Employment

Anecdotal reports started showing up in both the Chinese and the international press that sparked early concern that the global financial crisis would have a serious impact on employment. For example, in October 2008, the owner of a textile factory in Shaoxing, a city 100 miles from Shanghai, fled in the middle of the night and left 4,000 workers unemployed and US$200 million in unpaid bills. When employees showed up to work in the morning and found the factory gates bolted, they erupted in protest (Xiao 2008). In addition, there was frequent documentation of laid-off migrant workers returning home to villages early for the spring festival in 2009 (see, for example, Johnson and Batson 2009) and in some cases creating conflict with those renting their land (Yang 2008).

Surveying firms, households, or individuals yields some perspectives on the employment impact of the crisis. Surveys at each level have both advantages and disadvantages. A firm survey that enumerates employment and vacancies is more likely to capture changes in demand for labor at the firm level. Since firms in export sectors can then be separated from other types of firms, this approach promises to provide a direct link to export shocks. At the same time, however, firm surveys typically oversample larger firms and may thus miss the effect of shocks on smaller firms, which are less likely to be in the formal sector. In addition, firm surveys—especially if they are repeated cross-sectional surveys—may understate the effects of labor market shocks because they do not capture shocks to employment resulting from firm bankruptcies. Alternatively, firm surveys may overstate labor market shocks if all firm attrition from a panel survey is attributed to bankruptcy or restructuring as a result of the crisis.

Evidence from Firm Surveys

Since 2001, the Ministry of Human Resources and Social Security (formerly Ministry of Labor) has maintained a labor force observation network, which compiles information from both firm and labor force surveys conducted in 159 cities.[2] From this data source, information on vacancies and job seekers may be combined to provide an indication of changing demand for labor. As the data presented in figure 6.4 show, the demand for labor dropped sharply, falling from 0.97 to 0.85 from the third to the fourth quarter of 2008. This finding is consistent with information from an Internet-based recruitment company, which reported that the growth in vacancies fell off significantly between the third quarter of 2008 and the first quarter of 2009 (Zeng, Yuxue, and Dajian 2009).

Figure 6.4 Quarterly Ratio of Vacancies to Job Seekers in China, 2001–09

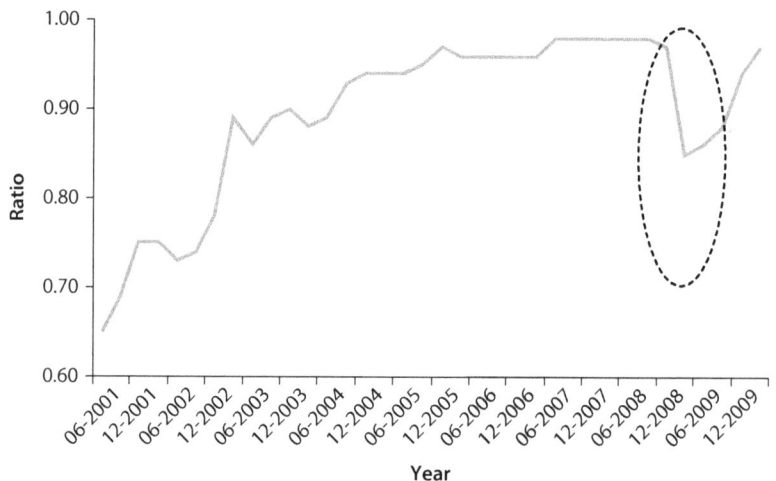

Source: China Labor Market Information Center 2010.
Note: The circle highlights the period of the global financial crisis.

Figure 6.5 Quarterly Ratio of Vacancies to Job Seekers in China, by Gender, 2001–09

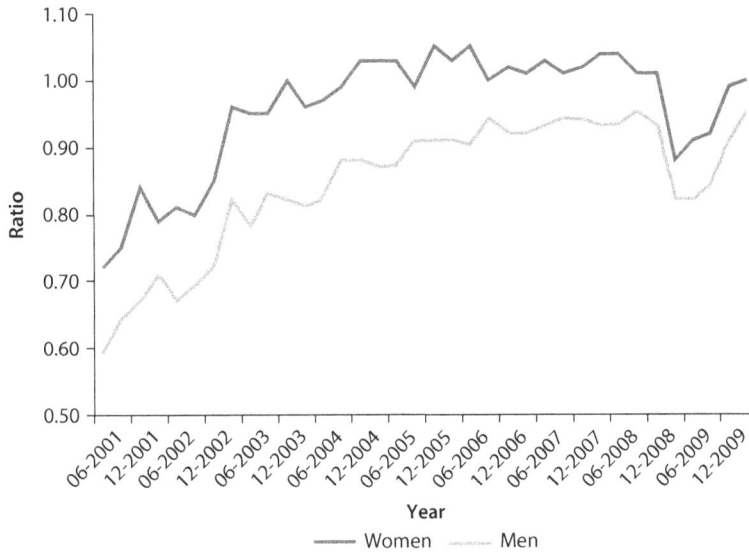

Source: China Labor Market Information Center 2010.

The ministry also reports this statistic by gender, based on assumptions about the gender composition of occupations and jobs typically held by men and women. According to variation in this statistic, fewer men than women are typically available for each vacancy: the ratio of vacancies to job seekers is always higher in male-dominated occupations than in female-dominated occupations. With the onset of the financial crisis, however, the percentage drop in vacancies per job seeker was steeper for men than for women (figure 6.5), suggesting that the shock hit the demand for male labor harder.

The labor market observation data have two shortcomings: first, the firm survey oversamples firms and vacancies in the formal sector, and the associated labor force survey oversamples long-term urban residents. Second, because the firm surveys are representative of enterprises operating at each period of time, they miss those shocks to employment that result from firm bankruptcy.

Interesting insights on the relationship among firm survival, migrant employment, and the financial crisis are provided by Kong, Meng, and Zhang (2009). This study makes use of a household sampling frame of migrants that was constructed by first sampling enterprises where migrants work and then randomly sampling migrants.[3] A first census of 489 blocks in 15 cities was conducted in 2007, and then the first wave of the survey was conducted in the spring of 2008. In October 2008, December 2008, and February 2009, tracking protocols required the team to recontact all respondents ahead of the spring 2009 follow-up survey. In the process of tracking migrants through firms, the team found that 9 percent of workplaces had closed in the 14 months following the November–December 2007 census; by matching workplaces to migrants they had employed, the team estimated that 13 percent of migrants in the 15 cities surveyed were affected by postcrisis shutdowns. If this lay-off rate were applied to an estimated 142 million long-term migrant workers in 2008, perhaps some 18.5 million migrant workers could have lost their jobs as a result of enterprise closings during the crisis period.

Not all cities were affected equally. Kong, Meng, and Zhang (2009) found that 34 percent of migrants in the export-oriented city of Dongguan (in Guangdong province) would have lost employment through enterprise closings. Across industry sectors, the study found that manufacturing (which is export oriented) was hit hard, but so too were construction and services. With large-scale layoffs in export-oriented sectors, however, it would not be surprising to find that sectors specializing in nontraded goods (construction, real estate, and services, for example) would be affected as well.

However, the Kong, Meng, and Zhang (2009) study has limitations that should lead to a healthy skepticism toward the results. First, the authors are unable to account for layoffs from firms that did not close. Second, the study makes a strong counterfactual assumption that no firms would close in the absence of the financial crisis (as a result of adjustments associated with the 2008 Labor Contract Law, for example, or the credit tightening associated with macroeconomic policies initiated in 2007). In practice, even a booming economy will have some failures, and some firms may be lost from the sample if they move locations to expand or move as a result of urban redevelopment initiatives. Furthermore, the authors do not appear to account for new firm creation or the ability of migrant workers to shift immediately from closed workplaces to other jobs. All of these problems may lead to an overestimation of the contribution to layoffs from firm closings as a result of the crisis.

An alternative to the firm closure approach followed by Kong, Meng, and Zhang (2009) is to examine directly the demand for labor among firms. This approach was followed in the China National Firm Survey (CNFS 2009) conducted by the People's Bank of China in October 2009.[4] The CNFS is a representative sample of over 2,000 manufacturing firms from eight provinces: four coastal provinces (Guangdong, Jiangsu, Shandong, and Zhejiang), one northeast province (Jilin), one central province (Hubei), one northwest province (Shaanxi), and one southwest province (Sichuan). The sampling frame is certainly skewed toward larger and well-established firms: it comprises all firms operating in August 2009 that ever had a credit relationship with any financial institution. Still, it provides interesting evidence of the impact of the financial crisis on the formal sector.

The survey collected data on six-month intervals beginning in 2007, allowing the researcher to examine changes in employment among firms that had survived the financial crisis through October 2009. Table 6.1 shows the percentage changes in employment over the previous six months. Between January and June 2008, and in the wake of macroeconomic adjustment and implementation of the Labor Contract Law, employment grew by 3 percent. Behind this number, however, was a negative shock to employment in the state and collective sector that was more than offset by continuing increases in employment in other

Table 6.1 Annual Percentage Changes in Employment in China, 2008–09
% change from six months earlier

Type of firm	June 2008	December 2008	June 2009
All firms	3.03	−0.53	2.87
Nonexporters	3.27	0.68	3.20
Exporters	2.76	−1.92	2.48
By ownership			
State/collective	-6.05	−0.83	1.78
Private	2.61	0.99	5.40
Joint/Ltd/other	3.70	0.65	1.70
Foreign	3.84	−4.55	4.30
By size (number of employees)			
Smallest quartile	2.11	0.48	3.41
Second quartile	3.00	0.28	3.20
Third quartile	3.00	0.16	4.16
Largest quartile	3.05	−0.72	2.63

Source: CNFS 2009.

Table 6.2 Changes in Employment of Migrants vs. Changes in Employment of Local Residents in China, June 2008, December 2008, and June 2009
% change from six months earlier

Type of firm	June 2008	December 2008	June 2009
All firms			
Migrants	4.76	−0.88	5.29
Local	3.23	−0.07	2.09
Nonexporters			
Migrants	5.44	1.23	5.71
Local	3.51	0.06	3.35
Exporters			
Migrants	4.22	−2.74	5.01
Local	2.80	−0.27	−0.01

Source: CNFS 2009.

ownership sectors. By December 2008, overall employment in these firms had dropped a half-percentage point, but again the average obscures the sharper hit that exporters experienced. Exporting firms shed 1.9 percent of their employees, which implies a reduction in the growth rate of employment of 4.9 percentage points relative to the precrisis trend of 3 percent. Foreign-owned firms—the sector open to foreign investment, of which a significant share goes toward exports to developed economies—shed nearly 5 percent of their employees.

In a comparison of changes in the employment of migrants to changes in the employment of local residents in these enterprises, as table 6.2 illustrates, migrants were more likely to suffer adverse employment shocks over the period of the crisis, particularly those employed in export-oriented enterprises. Flexibility and adjustment within the labor market are also evident, as nonexporting firms actually continued to increase their employment of migrants even over the period June to December 2008, when China experienced the sharpest negative shock to aggregate demand.

As these data capture only the behavior of surviving firms and firms of sufficient scale to have formal transactions with financial institutions, they miss the effects of firm closure even as they pick up the differences in employment dynamics across exporters and nonexporters. Just as the surveys using firm data reveal the strong effect of the crisis on migrant workers, the use of survey data on rural households with information on migrant families provides a way to capture the employment effects on rural registered residents, who were most affected by crisis-related shocks. Evidence from rural household surveys is discussed below.

The View of the Rural Household

Employers usually have much greater flexibility in ending employment relationships with migrant workers than with local workers. Migrants in China's cities and booming coastal areas typically do not have formal labor contracts and lack legal recourse to employment protection—and when they lose a job, they frequently lack severance pay or unemployment benefits. The 2005 China Urban Labor Survey, for example, noted that 85.2 percent of migrants working in five large urban cities were in the informal sector. Even after excluding the self-employed among the informal sector, 54.7 percent of wage-earning employees lacked contracts. The Labor Contract Law and a tightening of the labor market helped lower these informality rates somewhat, so that by February 2010 only 40 percent of migrants were wage earners working without contracts. However, empirical analysis using the CNFS data suggests that manufacturing firms in cities that implemented labor regulations more strictly tended to experience slower employment growth (Park, Giles, and Du 2011). Informal employment rates for local residents, by contrast, were under 25 percent.[5]

Several data sources based on representative surveys of rural households offer the most straightforward descriptive statistics on the effects of employment shocks on migrant workers.[6] Indeed, rural-to-urban migrants in China rarely move to urban areas with their entire families, and thus members of the family (older parents, children, and sometimes spouses) are left behind in home villages. Since 2003, the two survey institutes conducting national rural household surveys—the National Bureau of Statistics (NBS) and the Ministry of Agriculture's Research Center for the Rural Economy (RCRE)—have been fielding household surveys that included modules with detailed questions on the activities of migrant family members. Much of the empirically based Chinese-language literature detailing the effects of the crisis on migrants is based on these data sources. Unfortunately, these data are not readily available for public use.

Several papers written using the NBS or RCRE household surveys document the gross effect of the crisis on unemployment. Early in 2009, analysts using the NBS survey network estimated that 20 million migrant workers were laid off as a result of the crisis (Chen 2010), and, in March 2009, the NBS released a report estimating that 23 million migrant workers were out of work (NBS 2009). That number amounts to 16 percent of the long-term migrant workforce.[7]

Much analysis to date on the effects of the crisis on migrant workers focuses on job loss and does not examine the employment impact based on a reasonable counterfactual assumption of what employment would have been in the absence of the financial crisis. In addition, some of these studies focus on "gross impacts" and thus miss the reallocation of labor across sectors.[8] A study by Huang *et al.* (2011) uses a panel survey, known as the China National Rural Survey (CNRS), collected by the authors to establish a counterfactual "business-as-usual" level of off-farm employment and then analyze the effect of the crisis on off-farm nonagricultural employment. Because the off-farm nonagricultural employment category treats migrants and nonmigrant nonagricultural workers as employed in an integrated off-farm labor market, the net effects of the crisis relative to counterfactual levels of both off-farm employment and overall employment can be examined, including work in agriculture.

The CNRS data make use of annual retrospective employment histories dating to 2000, when the first round of the survey was implemented, and of detailed monthly employment histories for the 24 months preceding 2009.[9] Information on employment history was used to calculate the counterfactual level of employment for 2009. The research team used estimates of off-farm employment trends (based on data from 2005 through the second quarter of 2008) and monthly employment data from the 12 months before the crisis and annual 2005–07 growth rates. The results of the extrapolation exercise and actual off-farm employment rates are shown in figure 6.6.[10]

Absent the financial crisis, Huang *et al.* (2011) argue that 57.8 percent of the rural labor force would have been working off-farm but that instead only 51 percent had off-farm employment. By April 2009, a gap of 6.8 percent had opened between the counterfactual and the actual share of the rural labor force working off-farm. At the national level, that percentage would imply 279 million rural residents were actually working in nonagricultural activities in September 2008, whereas, under the existing trends and seasonal adjustments, 301 million might have been expected to be working off-farm in April 2009. In fact, the analysis estimates that only 265 million rural individuals were working off-farm in April 2009, implying that the net effect was a loss of 36 million jobs. This number is consistent with a drop in nonagricultural employment of 12 percent or, in terms of the entire rural registered workforce, a decline of 6.8 percent in the ratio of business-as-usual to actual share of those working outside of agriculture.

The net impact, however, differs from the number of rural workers who were actually laid off. That number cannot be deduced from this net gap. A number of factors affect the gap between the business-as-usual scenario in April 2009 and the actual level of employment at that time. First, the gap includes those who were laid off between October 2008 and April 2009 and did not find a job (that is, the *long-term laid-off workers*). Second, the gap is also affected by the difference between the number of workers who were actually laid off between October 2008 and April 2009 and those who found a new job between October 2008 and April 2009 but who had not been working off-farm

Figure 6.6 Monthly Share of Rural Labor Force with Off-Farm Employment: Actual and Under a Business-as-Usual Counterfactual, May 2007–April 2009

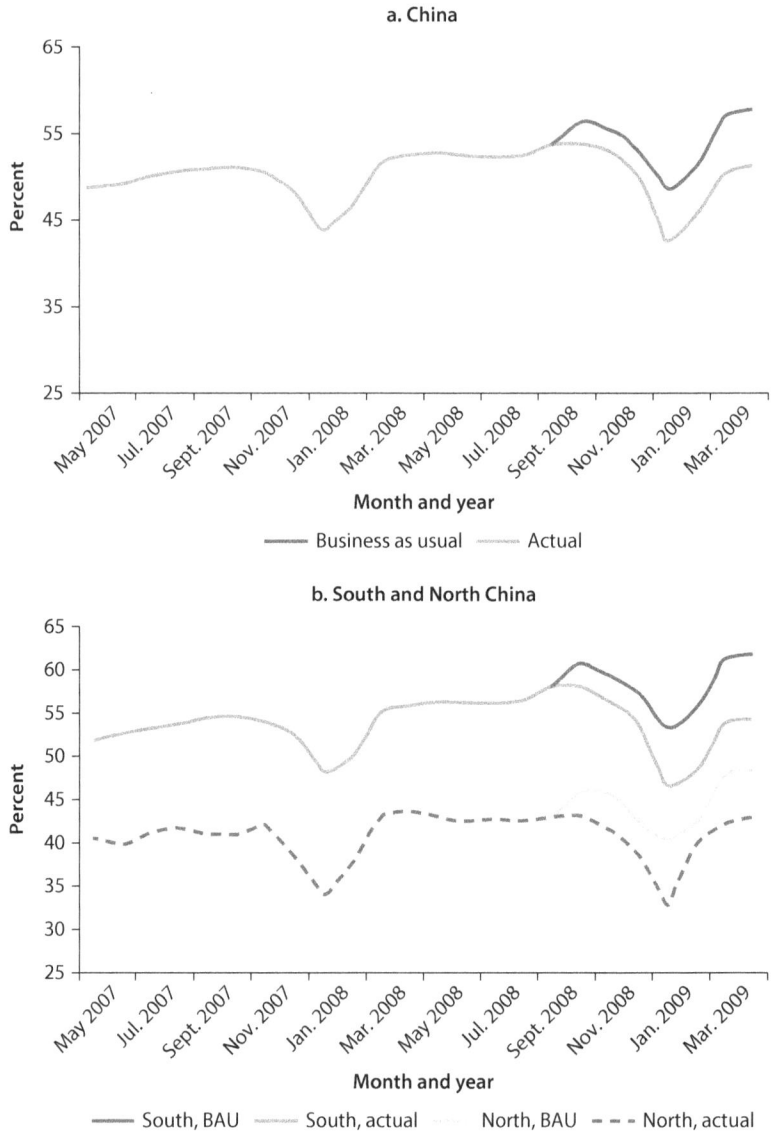

a. China

Month and year

Business as usual   Actual

b. South and North China

Month and year

South, BAU   South, actual   North, BAU   North, actual

Source: Huang *et al.* 2011.
Note: BAU = business as usual.

in October 2008 (that is, the *rehires*). Third, despite the financial crisis, a class of new workers was able to find employment between October 2008 and April 2009 (that is, they were not working in September 2008 but were working in April 2009: the *newcomers*). Finally, the business-as-usual prediction for April 2009 includes rural individuals who—absent the financial crisis—would have found a job off-farm between October 2008 and April 2009 but did not (*delayed entrants*). According to Huang *et al.* (2011), the number of long-term laid-offs (that is, rural individuals who were laid off after October 2008 and were still not working off-farm by April 2009) was 25 million, which was slightly larger than the number of newcomers (23 million).[11]

Government Policies, the Recovery, and the Labor Market

Behind China's rapid recovery lay both an ambitious macroeconomic stimulus and a host of active labor market policies and expansions of the social safety net. In late 2008 and early 2009, the central government unveiled a Y4 trillion plan, equal to 13.3 percent of China's Y30 trillion GDP, to stimulate the slowing economy. The composition of the stimulus package is shown in figure 6.7, with the largest share devoted to key infrastructure (38 percent) and investment in recovery construction (25 percent). The balance of the stimulus went to a combination of activities aimed at poverty relief, such as subsidized housing (10 percent), rural infrastructure (9 percent), and social development (4 percent) and to promote longer-term growth, including investments in innovation and economic restructuring (9 percent) and emission reductions and environmental protection (5 percent).

According to one source, evidence that the stimulus package ameliorated the negative employment consequences of the crisis was the shift in sectoral composition of the employment of migrant workers (see table 6.3). From 2008

Figure 6.7 Composition of China's 4 Trillion Yuan Stimulus Package in 2009
Percent

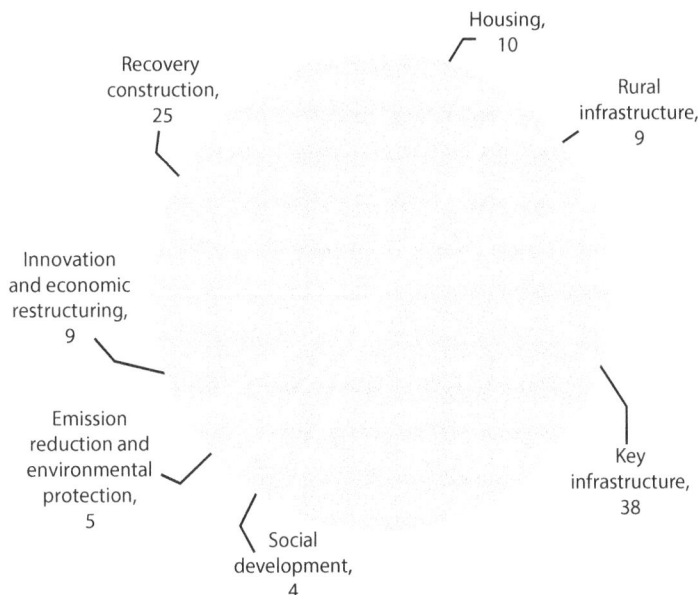

Housing, 10

Recovery construction, 25

Rural infrastructure, 9

Innovation and economic restructuring, 9

Emission reduction and environmental protection, 5

Key infrastructure, 38

Social development, 4

Source: National Development and Reform Committee 2009.

Table 6.3 Share of Migrants in Selected Employment Sectors in China, 2008–09
Percent

Employment sector	2008	2009
Manufacturing	42.0	39.1
Construction	16.3	17.3
Hotels and catering	7.6	7.8
Wholesale and retail trade	7.0	7.8
Transport	5.6	5.9
Other	21.5	22.1

Source: Calculated from NBS national rural household survey data compiled in Sheng 2009.

to 2009, the share of workers employed in manufacturing fell nearly 3 percent; the sector with the largest increase in share was construction (1.0 percent), with wholesale and retail trade (0.8 percent), transport (0.3 percent), hotels and catering (0.2 percent), and other sectors (0.6 percent) accounting for the rest of the increase. Note that since overall employment increased in 2009, these changes in employment shares understate the actual percentage increases in job creation in these sectors.

The government also took several measures to reduce the employment shock associated with the crisis. Recognizing that small and medium enterprises were not well positioned to cope with crisis-related shocks, the government reduced the tax burden on those enterprises and provided other sources of support. In November 2008, the State Council issued an executive order facilitating extension of credit to small and medium enterprises; and in December 2008, the Ministry of Human Resources and Social Security implemented several measures to reduce burdens on enterprises, including: (1) allowing enterprises facing financial difficulties to delay payment of social security funds; (2) temporarily reducing mandated contributions to medical, work injury, and unemployment insurance; and (3) using unemployment funds to maintain employment levels in firms facing financial difficulties. By the government's own estimate, these three measures helped save 10 million jobs.[12]

Local governments also worked hard to convince enterprises in their jurisdiction to avoid shedding large numbers of workers. According to interviews by the authors with city labor bureau officials in Shanghai in early 2009, firms were offered various sources of support, including wage subsidies and suspension of tax payments, to encourage them to keep local residents employed. Interestingly, the officials were unconcerned about layoffs of migrant workers. These efforts by local governments, in addition to a strong stimulus and supportive national policies, likely mitigated the negative employment impacts of the crisis. Preventing firm employment reductions or outright failures reduced short-term pain but at the potential cost of reducing the creative destruction useful for enhancing competitiveness in the longer term. Implementation of the 2008 Labor Contract Law may also have been influenced by the economic crisis. Although, on average, neither firms nor workers reported that enforcement of the law was less strict after the crisis hit, analysis of the firm data finds that exporting firms subject to negative demand shocks during the crisis reported less strict enforcement of labor regulations relative to other firms (Park, Giles, and Du 2011).

In addition, recognizing that migrant workers and new graduates may be hit hardest by layoffs and lack of employment opportunities in the wake of the crisis, the Ministry of Human Resources and Social Security expanded training programs to promote employment among these groups.[13] Targeted recipients included employees of enterprises facing financial difficulties, returned rural migrant workers without employment, unemployed registered college graduates who were new market entrants, and unemployed rural migrant workers living in urban areas. Furthermore, in early February 2009 the Central Committee of the Communist Party issued a document promoting employment of migrant workers.[14] Enterprises were encouraged to maintain migrant employment, and those enterprises facing difficulty were allowed to adopt reduced or flexible work hours and were provided with subsidies for on-the-job training to maintain employment. Laid-off migrants who returned home were provided with subsidized credit, favorable tax treatment, and consultations to help with starting new businesses. Temporary income assistance through expansion of the rural minimum living standard support program (known as the *dibao*) also helped sustain migrants who returned home without jobs.

Unfortunately, neither active labor market programs nor interventions to support employment were implemented in a way that allowed proper evaluations of impact. Indeed, the only public documentary evidence on such programs, training interventions, and extensions of credit in the public domain is in the Ministry of Human Resources circulars directing local governments to implement such policies in a manner consistent with local conditions.

According to evidence from the rural household survey data, the robust recovery of labor demand following the stimulus was most important for the reemployment of rural registered workers who had lost jobs in the immediate wake of the crisis. Although the counterfactual gap in employment was still large in the first four months of 2009 (as shown in figure 6.6), it was already beginning to narrow in percentage terms. By April 2009, Huang *et al.* (2011) estimate that the gap between the business-as-usual off-farm employment share and the actual off-farm employment share was 6.8 percentage points, which means that it was affecting only 11.7 percent of those that would have been employed off-farm under the business-as-usual scenario as opposed to 12.5 percent in January. China's second quarter 2009 GDP figures showed that the growth rate had stopped declining and that growth was picking up again; similarly, rural off-farm employment was also showing the initial signs of recovery. In other words, China's off-farm labor market was already showing signs of recovery as early as the first and second quarters of 2009, when the global financial crisis was less than six months old.

As the economic recovery proceeded, national rural household surveys show that outmigration had picked up again by the end of 2009. According to the NBS rural household survey, 145 million migrant workers were employed outside their home villages for more than six months in 2009, which was a

2.6 percent increase over 2008 (NBS 2010a). Estimates based on the RCRE household survey indicate that there were 147 million migrant workers by year end, or an increase of 6.8 percent over the previous year. As evident from figures 6.4 and 6.5, the ratio of vacancy to job seeker also rose sharply between the second and third quarters of 2009, pointing toward an increase in labor demand relative to supply.

Wage Income in the Wake of the Financial Crisis

From annual survey data, it is apparent that incomes fell in China in early 2009 but recovered later. Descriptive evidence from the CNRS shows that many workers who did not lose their jobs experienced a drop in earnings. According to the CNRS, the monthly earnings of the typical unskilled worker (who worked off-farm in both 2008 and 2009) employed in 2008 and the first four months of 2009 fell by 10.5 percent in early 2009.

By the end of 2009, however, the economic recovery was evident in wages as well. The nationally representative NBS and RCRE household surveys and the People's Bank of China firm survey show that the wages of employed migrants were rising again by the end of 2009. Trends in monthly wage income for all three data sources, shown in figure 6.8, suggest that increases in the demand for labor were again driving up migrant wages by the end of 2009.

Evidence from the latest round of the China Urban Labor Survey, shown in table 6.4, also indicates renewed upward pressure on wages in the labor market.

Figure 6.8 Real Wages of Employed Migrants according to Three Data Sources, 2001–09

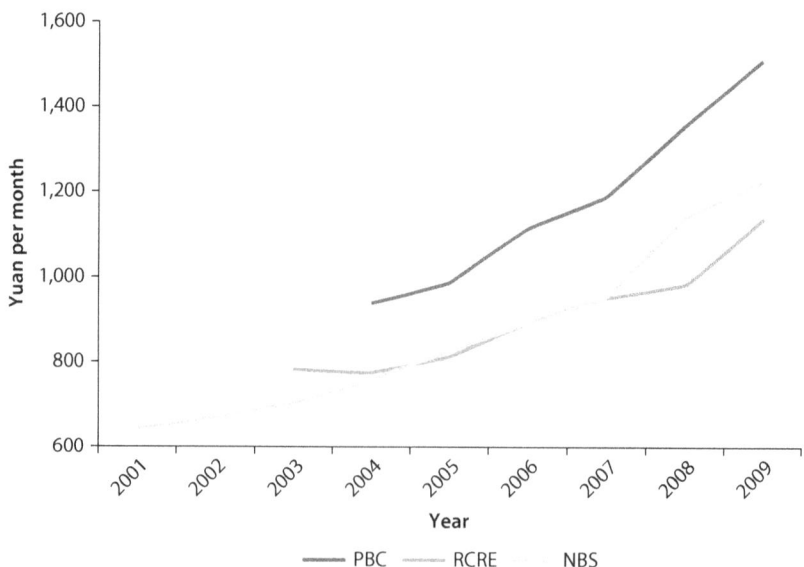

Sources: NBS 2010b; RCRE; People's Bank of China 2010.
Note: NBS = National Bureau of Statistics; PBC = People's Bank of China; RCRE = Research Center for the Rural Economy.

Table 6.4 Working Hours and Earnings in China, September 2008–February 2010

	Weekly working hours	Monthly earnings (yuan)	Hourly earning (yuan/hour)
Local workers			
Sept. 2008	43.50	2,104	11.96
Mar. 2009	43.69	2,319	13.12
Feb. 2010	44. 88	2,454	13.53
Migrant workers			
Sept. 2008	55.13	2,290	10.81
Mar. 2009	55. 69	2,466	11.61
Feb. 2010	56.98	2,591	11.94

Source: China Urban Labor Survey 2010.

For migrants employed in late 2009, neither working hours, monthly earnings, nor hourly earnings declined. Steady increases in both monthly and hourly earnings through February 2010 suggest that the labor market was tightening once again and that the slowdown and decline in earnings evident in the CNRS data were temporary.

Conclusions

This chapter has examined evidence from firm and household surveys on the effects of the global financial crisis on employment in China. After highlighting descriptive statistics from firm surveys suggesting that most of the adjustment was borne by migrant workers, the chapter reviewed rural household survey data to examine the net effect of the crisis on employment of rural registered workers. Job losses—ranging from 20 million to 36 million—were concentrated among migrant workers, who have typically lacked employment protection, have tended to be concentrated in export-oriented sectors, and were among the easiest to lay off when the crisis hit.

In response to the crisis and fears of widespread unemployment, China's government responded with a massive stimulus program, equivalent to over 13 percent of annual GDP, complemented by a range of active labor market programs, training programs, and credit support for small and medium enterprises. Neither information on the implementation of these programs (which was highly decentralized, nonrandom, and left to local governments) nor important data (such as expenditures) are publicly available, frustrating any effort to determine the relative role of programs, stimulus, and general economic growth in moderating employment shock. Nonetheless, available evidence does suggest that the stimulus helped expand employment outside of export sectors (construction and services) and that while rural registered residents experienced a severe employment shock, the vast majority were reemployed by late 2009. By early 2010, China's research community was again speaking of labor shortages.

Notes

1. China's Labor Contract Law, effective January 1, 2008, mandates contract terms, severance conditions, and payment of social insurance benefits. After two fixed-term contracts or 10 years of employment, whichever is shorter, the law requires firms to provide employees with open-ended contracts. The probationary period for new hires is limited to one to three months, depending on contract length, and regulations were placed on temporary work agencies (labor service companies) to prevent using them to circumvent the labor law. Finally, severance provisions require that employees receive 30 days written notice before termination, one month's severance pay for each year of service (half-month's pay if less than six months), and double severance pay for unfair dismissal.

2. In its first year, the survey was conducted in 59 cities and has expanded gradually over time to 159 cities in 2009.

3. The Rural to Urban Migration in China and Indonesia project assembles comparable survey data on migrants in China and Indonesia. In contrast to household and other geographic approaches to sampling migrants in China, the migrant sample for this survey was conducted by first developing a sample frame of enterprises likely to employ migrants. In a second stage, enterprises and migrants were then sampled. The project surveyed 5,007 rural-to-urban migrants who worked in 15 cities and responds to a common concern that surveys centered on households will oversample stable migrants and miss migrants living in work units and at work sites. An important drawback of the sampling approach is that it is difficult for researchers to know the characteristics of the population from which the sample is drawn.

4. This survey was designed and implemented in collaboration with researchers from the University of Oxford, the China Center for Economic Research at Beijing University, the Institute for Population and Labor Economics at the Chinese Academy of Social Sciences, and the Development Economics Research Group at the World Bank

5. The China Urban Labor Survey (2010) comprises three repeated cross-sectional surveys (2001, 2005, and 2010) conducted in five large urban areas (and a sixth was added in 2010). The survey includes local resident and migrant samples drawn from a geographic-based sampling frame in each city based on dwellings (which are not necessarily household units).

6. Unlike the Rural to Urban Migration in China and Indonesia data source, researchers using these data have a clear understanding of the population from which the sample is drawn. These data sources aim to draw a representative sample of rural households, which will provide a representative characterization of rural migrant labor as well.

7. The share of the migrant workforce losing employment with this shock depends on how one defines a migrant, and even different publications from the National Bureau of Statistics (NBS) using the same data source define them differently. At year-end 2008, Chen (2010) projects that the migrant labor force was 225 million rural registered residents, but this number includes migrants working for any amount of time outside of home villages. Migrants may be more or less permanent. Other work using the rural household survey of the NBS suggests that there were 142 million rural migrants employed long term (for more than six months) outside their home villages at the end of 2008 (NBS 2010a).

8. An exception is Wang *et al.* (2009), which suggests that workers from poorer regions shifted more quickly back into agriculture or local nonagricultural employment, so

that by June 2009, there was only a 4 percent drop in employment among workers from China's poor areas.

9. The China National Rural Survey (CNRS) dataset includes information from 58 randomly selected villages in six provinces of rural China representative of China's major agricultural regions (it is "national" under the assumption that these six provinces are nationally representative). The provinces are Hebei, Hubei, Lioaning, Shaanxi, Sichuan, and Zhejiang. Within province, sampling was stratified by county income quintile (as measured by gross value of industrial output) with one county chosen per income quintile. Within each county, two villages were randomly selected, and then survey teams used village rosters to select 20 households per village. A total of 1,160 households were sampled in 2008, which were the same households in the original 2000 survey less 40 households in two earthquake-damaged villages of Sichuan.

10. One weakness of this approach is that the counterfactual assumes that prior trends in the growth of migrant employment would continue in the absence of the crisis. Given that it may have taken time for the full effects of the 2008 Labor Contract Law to be felt, this counterfactual may be based on an overly optimistic assumption of migrant employment growth, especially since the years just before the crisis were years of high employment growth.

11. Readers familiar with the conventional categories of unemployment, employment, and labor force participation may at first wonder at the usefulness of categories of *laid-off workers*, *newcomers*, and *delayed entrants* used in this analysis. It is important to remember that workers laid off from off-farm jobs either found employment in agriculture or were engaged in household tasks. In this sense, an unemployment and labor force participation rate make little sense as workers are still fully employed but not in off-farm activities. The framework used by Huang *et al.* (2011) is intended to pick up the gross shock to employment off-farm.

12. Ministry of Human Resources and Social Security (2009b).

13. For more information, see Ministry of Human Resources and Social Security (2009a).

14. See the No. 1 Document of the Central Committee of the Communist Party. Each year, the No. 1 Document addresses the top concern and work priority. The centrality of migrant employment in the February 2009 document suggests recognition that migrants bore the burden of adjustment in the wake of the crisis.

References

Chen, D. 2010. "Trend of Migration Employment and Demand for Migrant Workers in 2010: Analysis Based on MOHRSS Survey." In *Population and Labor Report in 2010*, edited by C. Fang, 23–34. Beijing: Social Sciences Academic Press.

China Customs. 2010. China Customs Statistics Information, Customs General Administration of China, Beijing. http://www.cusstat.cn.

China Labor Market Information Center. 2010. Ministry of Human Resources and Social Security, Beijing. http://www.lm.gov.cn/DataAnalysis/node_1041.htm.

China Urban Labor Survey. 2010. Institute for Population and Labor Statistics, Chinese Academy of Social Sciences, Beijing.

CNFS. 2009. *China National Survey of Manufacturing Firms*, Research Bureau of the People's Bank of China, Beijing.

Huang, J., H. Zhi, Z. Huang, S. Rozelle, and J. Giles. 2011. "The Impact of the Global Financial Crisis on Off-Farm Employment and Earnings in Rural China." *World Development* 39 (5): 797–807.

IMF (International Monetary Fund). 2009. *World Economic Outlook 2009: Crisis and Recovery*. Washington, DC: IMF.

Johnson, I., and A. Batson. 2009. "China's Migrants See Jobless Ranks Soar." *Wall Street Journal*, (February 3): A1.

Kong, S. T., X. Meng, and D. Zhang. 2009. "Impact of Economic Slowdown on Migrant Workers." In *China's New Place in a World in Crisis: Economic, Geopolitical and Environmental Dimensions*, edited by R. Garnaut, L. Song, and W. T. Woo, 233–60. Canberra: Australian National University E Press.

Ministry of Human Resources and Social Security. 2009a. "Implementation of Special Vocational and Skills Training Programs." Circular, January 7.

Ministry of Human Resources and Social Security. 2009b. *Notice on Reducing Enterprise Burdens and Stabilizing Employment*. Beijing: Ministry of Human Resources and Social Security.

National Development and Reform Committee. 2009. Beijing: National Development and Reform Committee. http://www.ndrc.gov/jjyx/gjyx/.

NBS (National Bureau of Statistics). 2009. "There Are 225.42 Million Migrant Workers at the End of 2008." March 25. http://www.stats.gov.cn/tjfx/fxbg/t20090325_402547406.htm.

———. 2010a. "Monitoring Reports for Migrant Workers in 2009." In *Population and Labor Report in 2010*, edited by C. Fang, 1–22. Beijing: Social Sciences Academic Press.

———. 2010b. *China Statistical Yearbook, 2010*. Beijing: China Statistics Press.

Park, A., J. Giles, and Y. Du. 2011. "Labor Regulation and Enterprise Employment in China." University of Oxford.

People's Bank of China. 2010. "Employment of Migrant Workers: Analysis of Fifth Rural Household Survey." In *Population and Labor Report in 2010*, edited by C. Fang, 35–46. Beijing: Social Sciences Academic Press.

Sheng, L. 2009. "Migrants Are Faced with New Challenges on Their Employment during the Financial Crisis." Chinese Academy of Social Sciences.

Wang, D., Zhanxin Z., Jie C., and Huili H. 2009. "The Impact of the International Financial Crisis on the Transfer of the Rural Labor Force in China's Impoverished Areas." *Chinese Rural Economy* (9): 211–27.

Xiao, J. 2008. "The Biggest Printing Enterprise Is on the Verge of Bankruptcy in Shaoxing." *City Express (Dushi Kuaibao)*, October 9, 11–14.

Yang, N. 2008. "Ministry of Agriculture Alert: Attach Great Importance to Land Transfer Conflict When Migrants Return." *First Financial Daily*, December 9, A3.

Zeng, X., Yuxue C., and Dajian D. 2009. *Quarterly Review of China: Employment*. Renmin University.

CHAPTER 7

Effects of the 2008–09 Economic Crisis on Labor Markets in Mexico

Samuel Freije, Gladys López-Acevedo, and Eduardo Rodríguez-Oreggia

The economic crisis that hit worldwide during 2008–09 caused a slowdown in economic activity and a significant reduction in the number and quality of jobs. Even though the severity of the crisis has differed by country or region, none has entirely escaped its effects. The policies that governments implemented to spur growth and reduce the negative effects of the crisis on labor markets (for example, bringing most of the laid off back into the labor force) are worth analyzing to draw conclusions and policy lessons for the future. Countries like Brazil and Germany have been more successful than Mexico and Spain, for example, in containing the negative effects of the crisis on the labor market. This discrepancy deserves further analysis.

Low relative unemployment, high levels of informal jobs, and low, almost stagnant growth in real wages have characterized the labor market dynamics of Mexico in recent years (Rodríguez-Oreggia 2010). The crisis has affected these dynamics. Before the crisis, unemployment rates were usually around 3.5 percent, but after the crisis they increased to a persistent rate of around 5 percent. The levels of informality, measured as access to social security benefits through an employment contract, have been high. In 2007, informality was around 63 percent of total employment and increased to about 66 percent recently. In addition, during the crisis, average real wages declined in almost all economic activities, and no increase has been recorded during the recovery. Whether unemployment rates will continue to be relatively high and informality can continue absorbing workers in that sector is a matter of interest for the implementation of public policies and regulation reforms aimed at relieving the lingering effects of the 2008–09 crisis.

We thank Paloma Anos Casero, Louise Cord, Pierella Pacci, and David Newhouse for comments on earlier versions of this paper. Also, we thank Bruno López-Videla for able research assistance. These are views of the authors and do not necessarily reflect those of the World Bank, its Executive Directors, or the countries they represent.

These trends—more informality, lower wages, and higher unemployment—have acted as the main mechanisms for labor market adjustment.

The federal government launched two important initiatives at the onset of the crisis. These initiatives were the Program to Encourage Growth and Employment (PICE) and the National Agreement to Support the Household Economy and Employment (ANFEFE). Both initiatives were funded from existing programs. The PICE was mainly a large infrastructure investment program. However, the resources for the programs and their execution were delayed. The ANFEFE included active labor market policies such as the expansion of the Programa de Empleo Temporal (Temporary Employment Program, PET). The PET more than doubled its budget but focused on unemployed, less-educated workers mainly in rural areas, which did not include the bulk of the population affected by the crisis. The National Employment System also increased its coverage and budget during the crisis, but the increase was small compared to the magnitude of the crisis.

The aims of this chapter are to analyze labor market trends in Mexico during the recent crisis and to discuss the policies the government implemented to cope with it. We identify the groups most affected by the crisis and how the policies Mexico adopted helped those groups weather the recession. In addition, we compare public spending plans to fiscal mechanisms and other policies to draw some conclusions about their effectiveness. Our findings show high job destruction in several sectors, except services, as well as an adjustment in the labor market through decreasing wages and more unemployment. Increasingly persistent unemployment makes the transition to employment more difficult The wages of public sector workers were less affected, while other workers experienced about a 10 percent decrease in real wages during the crisis. More educated workers were less likely to find a job. But the focus of labor policies on increasing the PET, which was aimed mainly at low-skilled workers, may not be appropriate for more skilled workers in need of a job.

The Nature of the Crisis

The Mexican economy was hit hard by the financial crisis and the increase in international food prices in 2008. In the last quarter of 2008 and the first half of 2009, the collapse in external demand, particularly for durable consumer goods, led to an almost immediate and severe downturn in economic activity. Inflation spiked as the exchange rate increased substantially (figure 7.1). The loss of employment and the high level of uncertainty and risk brought about by the economic crisis contributed to a fall in private consumption and investment, further reducing aggregate demand.

A subsequent rebound in external demand as of the second half of 2009 gave rise to a recovery, even though private consumption and investment are trailing behind and have not yet contributed significantly to the upturn in economic activity. Figure 7.2 depicts economic activity and the main components of aggregate demand, showing that by the second quarter of 2010 gross domestic product (GDP) was still slightly below its precrisis level. A similar scenario

Figure 7.1 Changes in Annual Inflation and the Exchange Rate in Mexico, 2007–10

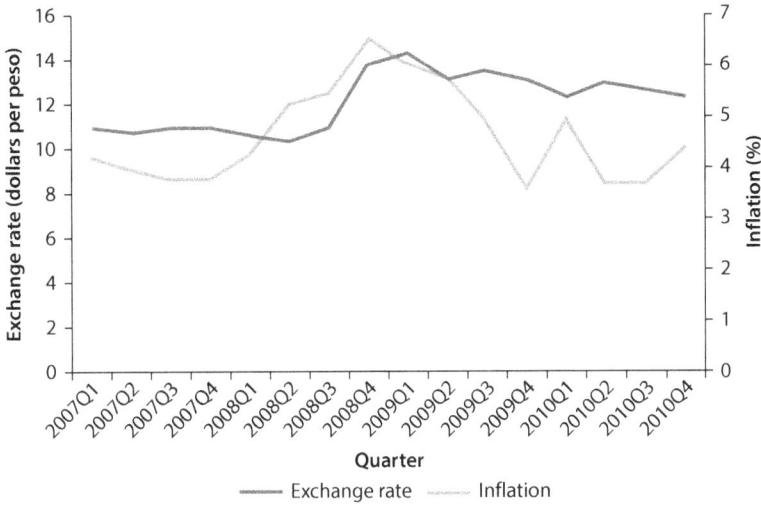

Quarter

Exchange rate ──────   Inflation ┄┄┄┄

Source: Central Bank of Mexico 2011.

Figure 7.2 GDP and Components of Aggregate Demand in Mexico during the Financial Crisis, Second Quarter of 2008–Second Quarter of 2010

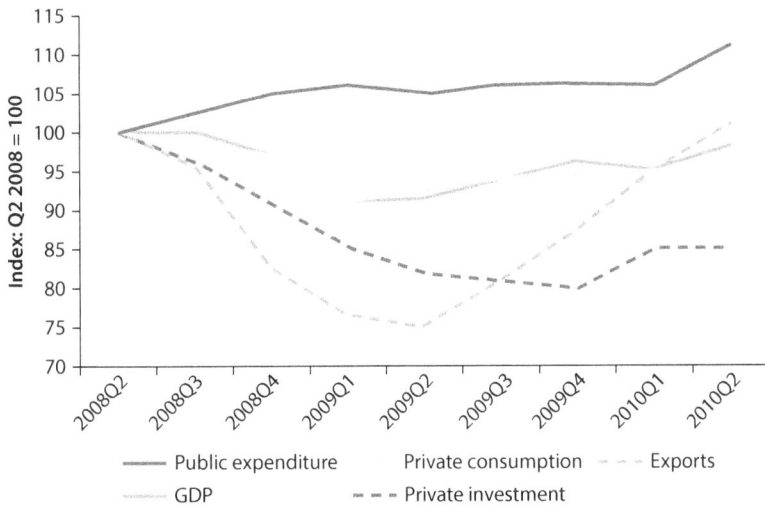

Public expenditure ──────   Private consumption ┄┄┄┄   Exports ─ ─ ─

GDP ┄┄┄┄   Private investment ─ ─ ─

Source: World Bank 2010.
Note: GDP = gross domestic product.

occurred for private consumption and investment, whereas exports had returned to their precrisis level and public expenditure never dropped. Public expenditure, however, increased slightly even during the economic crisis. Recovery seems to have mostly come from the increase in exports.

During the crisis, the central bank intervened in foreign exchange markets by providing foreign currency liquidity to the private sector. The Mexican peso increased in the last quarter of 2008 and has remained steady since then.

Monetary policy has taken place within a medium-term inflation targeting framework of 3 percent. The central bank eased monetary policy in January 2009. In retrospect, the crisis did not have severe exchange rate, monetary, or financial consequences in Mexico. Inflation was under control, credit did not collapse, and no financial institution required intervention. In this regard, this crisis was very different from previous crises in the country, with effects concentrating in this case on the real side of the economy only (that is, output and employment).

Labor Market Adjustments during the Crisis and Recovery

Total employment (figure 7.3) declined for the last three quarters of 2008 and the first of 2009, followed by several consecutive quarters of positive job creation. In the second quarter of 2008, just before the crisis started, total employment was about 43.9 million, declining to 42.9 million in the first quarter of 2009. Employment growth then resumed, reaching a peak in the fourth quarter of 2009 with 44.5 million workers.

Despite significant job creation for most of 2009, total unemployment by the end of 2010 was 0.9 million workers above precrisis levels (figure 7.4). This number indicates an economic crisis that, on the one hand, produced a rapid decline and recovery in total employment but that, on the other hand, has not been able to produce enough jobs during the recovery to return unemployment to precrisis levels.

Figure 7.3 Total Employment in Mexico, 2008–10

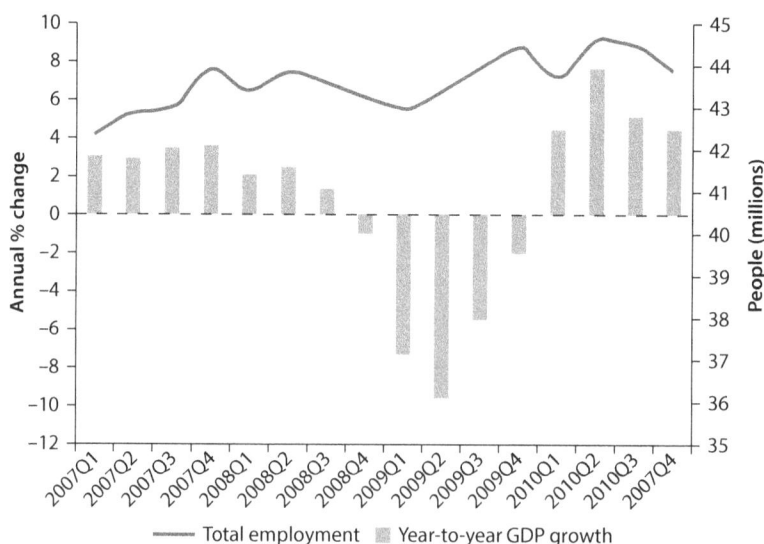

Source: Calculations based on data from INEGI 2011, the Economic Data Bank (Banco de Informacion Economica), and the Mexican Occupation and Employment Survey (Encuesta Nacional de Ocupación y Empleo, or ENOE).
Note: GDP = gross domestic product.

Figure 7.4 Total Unemployment in Mexico, 2008–10

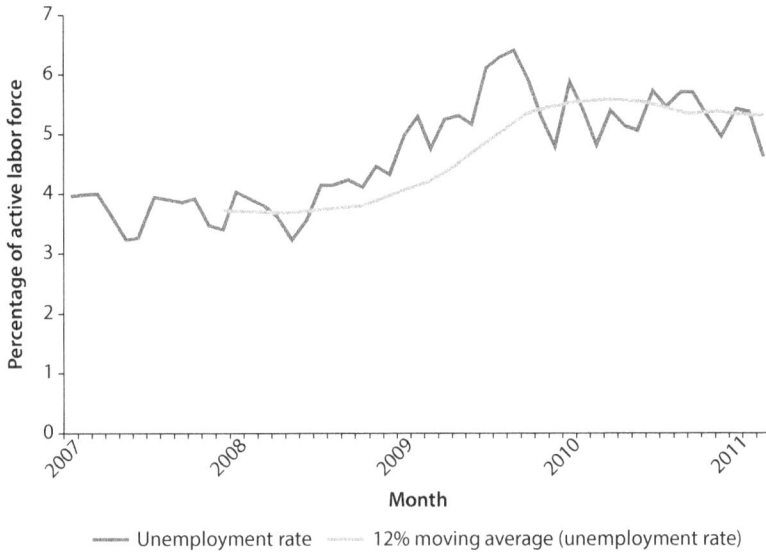

Source: Calculations based on data from INEGI 2011 the Economic Data Bank (Banco de Informacion Economica), and the Mexican Occupation and Employment Survey (Encuesta Nacional de Ocupación y Empleo, or ENOE).

We can characterize the evolution of the crisis by taking the second quarter of 2009 as the trough of the recession and the second quarters of 2008 and 2010 as the beginning and end of this cycle. Year-to-year net job flows through the second quarter of 2009 mark the onset of the crisis, whereas year-to-year net job flows from the second quarter of 2010 onward characterize the recovery. In addition, we include annual job flows in the second quarter of 2008 (before the crisis started) as a comparison to a noncrisis year. Comparing annual performance by the second quarters prevents seasonal adjustments in the labor market from tainting the results.

During the 2009 crisis, the labor supply in Mexico accelerated, making it more difficult to cope with the fall in labor demand and putting additional pressure on wages. In fact, the population of those over 14 years of age (also known as the working-age population) had increased by 1.73 million by the second quarter of 2009 (see table 7.1). That number was more than half a million more new workers than had joined the labor force in the previous years (for example, since 2003 the average annual growth of the working-age population has been around the 1.1 million). Although it is difficult to determine the origin of the acceleration in the working-age population, a likely suspect is a change in migration patterns. Although workers in the United States did not return home in greater numbers during the crisis, evidence suggests declining migration flows from Mexico to the United States.[1] As a result of the change in migration patterns caused by the recession, an additional half million potential workers increased the challenges of the labor market recovery.

Table 7.1 Annual Changes in Main Components of the Mexican Labor Force, 2007–10

Year ending the second quarter of...	Working-age population	Out of the labor force			Labor force		
		Total	Non available	Available	Total	Unemployed	Employed
Absolute numbers							
2007	1,176,542	340,166	63,419	276,747	836,376	127,495	708,831
2003	1,233,232	135,131	365,100	(179,969)	1,043,151	83,111	960,040
2CC9	1,733,353	1,484,506	379,854	1,104,652	249,352	771,767	(522,415)
2010	951,655	(476,747)	(209,674)	(267,073)	1,428,402	120,851	1,307,551
Percentage of the increase in the working-age population							
2007	100.0	28.9	5.4	23.5	71.1	10.8	60.3
2003	100.0	15.0	29.6	–14.6	85 0	7.1	77.8
2CC9	100.0	35.6	21.9	63.7	14.4	44.5	–30.1
2010	100.0	–50.1	–22.0	–23.1	150.1	12.7	137.4

Source: Based on data from ENOE.

a. Years end with the second quarter of each year. Numbers in parenthesis are negative.

This massive influx of potential workers entered the job market at a time when some 522,000 jobs had been destroyed and nearly 772,000 newly unemployed people were also looking for work. As a consequence, the inactive population (those not in the labor force) grew by nearly 1.5 million people, 1.1 million of whom were available to work (see table 7.1). These numbers also suggest an additional feature of the crisis: workers who otherwise would have been searching for jobs were driven out of the labor force during the crisis. In the years previous to the crisis (2007–08), the Mexican labor market created employment opportunities equivalent to 60–75 percent of new entrants. In 2009, the Mexican labor market destroyed employment equivalent to 30 percent of the new entrants. In 2010, it created jobs for more than 130 percent of the size of the population of new entrants. These figures clearly summarize the evolution of the crisis in the Mexican labor market.

By the second quarter of 2010, the recovery was not strong enough to absorb all the growth in the working-age population. Although employment reached a level comparable to precrisis years and 1.3 million jobs were created for the nearly 1.4 million people that entered the labor force, the unemployment rate was still above its precrisis level. One of the clear implications of the expansion in the working-age population was that job creation was unable to keep unemployment at the precrisis levels.

By March 2011, total employment had recovered, but unemployment and informality rates were still close to where they had been during the worst of the crisis. Even though the Mexican labor market has shown signs of an irregular recovery during the past months, as of the end of 2011 it remained in a worse condition than before the crisis. The unemployment rate, which had reached an almost record high of 6.41 percent in September 2009, declined every month (with the exception of the seasonal peak of January) to 4.81 percent in March 2010 but then rose to above 5 percent for most of 2010 (see figure 7.4). It again rose above 5 percent in April 2011 and reached 5.2 percent in June 2011. Thus, unemployment has hovered above 5 percent since October 2009, which is above the precrisis level. Although the 12-month average unemployment rate has flattened out, it is nearly two percentage points above the average in early 2008. A significant reduction in unemployment is still needed to grow the workforce to precrisis levels.

Informal employment also showed a slight increase during the crisis. Informality rates, defined as access to social security or health benefits, are shown in figure 7.5. The percentage of private sector workers without health coverage rose about 2 percentage points, from 63 to 65 percent. The share of workers in the public sector, meanwhile, remained constant at 8 percent (not shown). The share of workers in self-employment also changed little during the crisis, before falling in late 2011 as the recovery took hold.

Figure 7.6 presents real hourly wages, both for all workers and for different types of workers. Overall, wages fell steeply in late 2008 and early 2009 and did not stop falling until late 2010. Self-employed and employees registered for social security suffered the largest fall in real wages. Wages for public sector

Figure 7.5 Quarterly Percentage of Workers by Occupation and Access to Social Security Benefits in Mexico, 2007–10

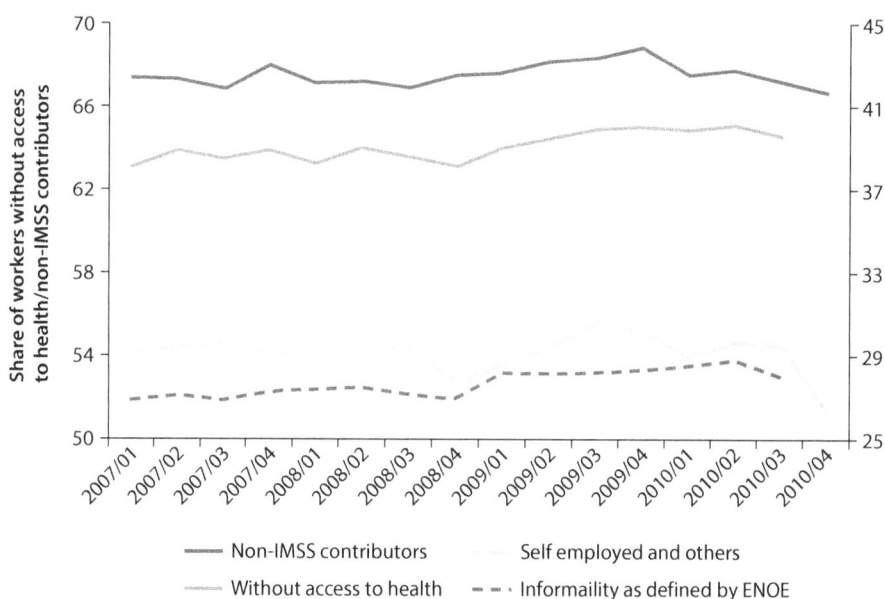

Source: Calculations based on data from ENOE.
Note: ENOE = Mexican Occupation and Employment Survey (Encuesta Nacional de Ocupación y Empleo); GDP = gross domestic product; IMSS = Instituto Mexicano del Seguro Social.

workers dropped slightly in late 2008 but then recovered again in late 2010. Informal employees with no coverage experienced the smallest reductions in earnings but have yet to recover.

Impacts on Sectors and Types of Workers

In this section, we analyze changes in job creation and destruction and wages for specific groups, beginning with the sector of work.

Which Sectors Were Most Affected?

The increasing trend in informality suggests that most of the recovery in job creation came though a decline in the quality of the jobs created. We now turn to the analysis of creation and destruction by economic activity to better understand the evolution of the crisis. Figure 7.7 shows annual job creation or destruction for each sector of activity by quarter. Agriculture experienced three consecutive quarters of job destruction at the end of 2008 and beginning of 2009 and again shows destruction in the last two quarters of 2010. A similar pattern is observed for manufacturing: almost continuous destruction of jobs in 2008 and 2009, recovering only in 2010. The second quarter of 2009 shows the steepest decrease in manufacturing, a loss of about 672,000 jobs. By comparison, the largest job creation, in the third quarter of 2010, was only 382,000.

Figure 7.6 Real Hourly Wage Growth for Formal and Informal Workers in Mexico, 2008–10

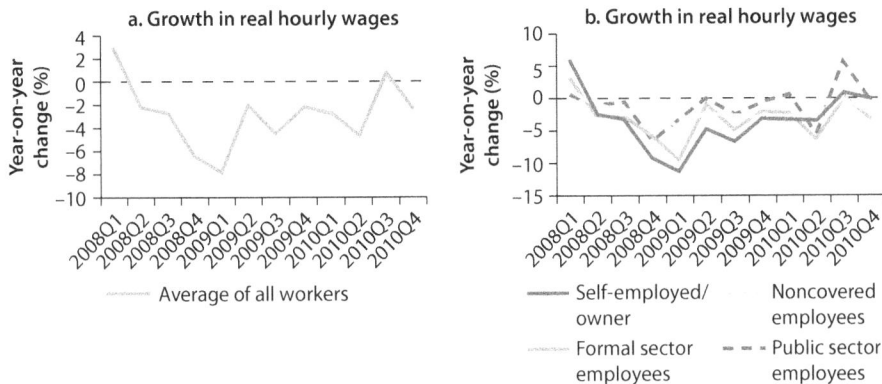

Source: Calculations based on data from ENOE.

The crisis produced net job losses in the primary and secondary sectors (where tradable goods are produced) and a much subdued job creation in the tertiary sector (shown in table 7.2) Manufacturing suffered the largest employment destruction among all sectors, with 700,000 jobs lost. Construction activities experienced the second-largest employment destruction (123,000 jobs lost), which indicates that public works were not able to create enough employment to at least partly compensate for the shock of the crisis. Interestingly, employment in restaurants and hotels also fell by more than 45,000, something not seen in the past 10 years and perhaps the result of the recession in developed countries and the April 2010 outbreak of the H1N1 flu in Mexico, both of which must have reduced the number of tourists traveling to the country.

In the construction sector, job destruction lasted longer than in agriculture and manufacturing: losses were experienced from the third quarter of 2008 to the fourth quarter of 2009. The worst quarter, the third in 2009, saw the destruction of 216,000 jobs, whereas a recovery of about 35,000 jobs occurred in the last two quarters of 2010. In contrast, the trade and commerce sector had a briefer period of job destruction (only two quarters) although only a meager recovery afterward. By the fourth quarter of 2010, trade and commerce again experienced a large decrease in jobs.

In contrast with all other sectors, services experienced job creation in every quarter. Even at the height of the crisis, this sector was creating about 722,000 jobs. This disparity points to a crisis that severely affected economic activities associated with tradable products (that is, agriculture, manufacturing, and tourism). Construction, even though it is not a tradable goods sector, also endured a severe contraction, creating doubts about the efficacy of public works or investment in infrastructure as a response to crisis-led employment losses.

Overall, the job creation and destruction documented in figure 7.7 shows a clear movement toward a "tertiarization" in the employment composition caused

Figure 7.7 Quarterly Variation in Numbers of Workers Employed in Various Types of Economic Activity in Mexico, 2008–10

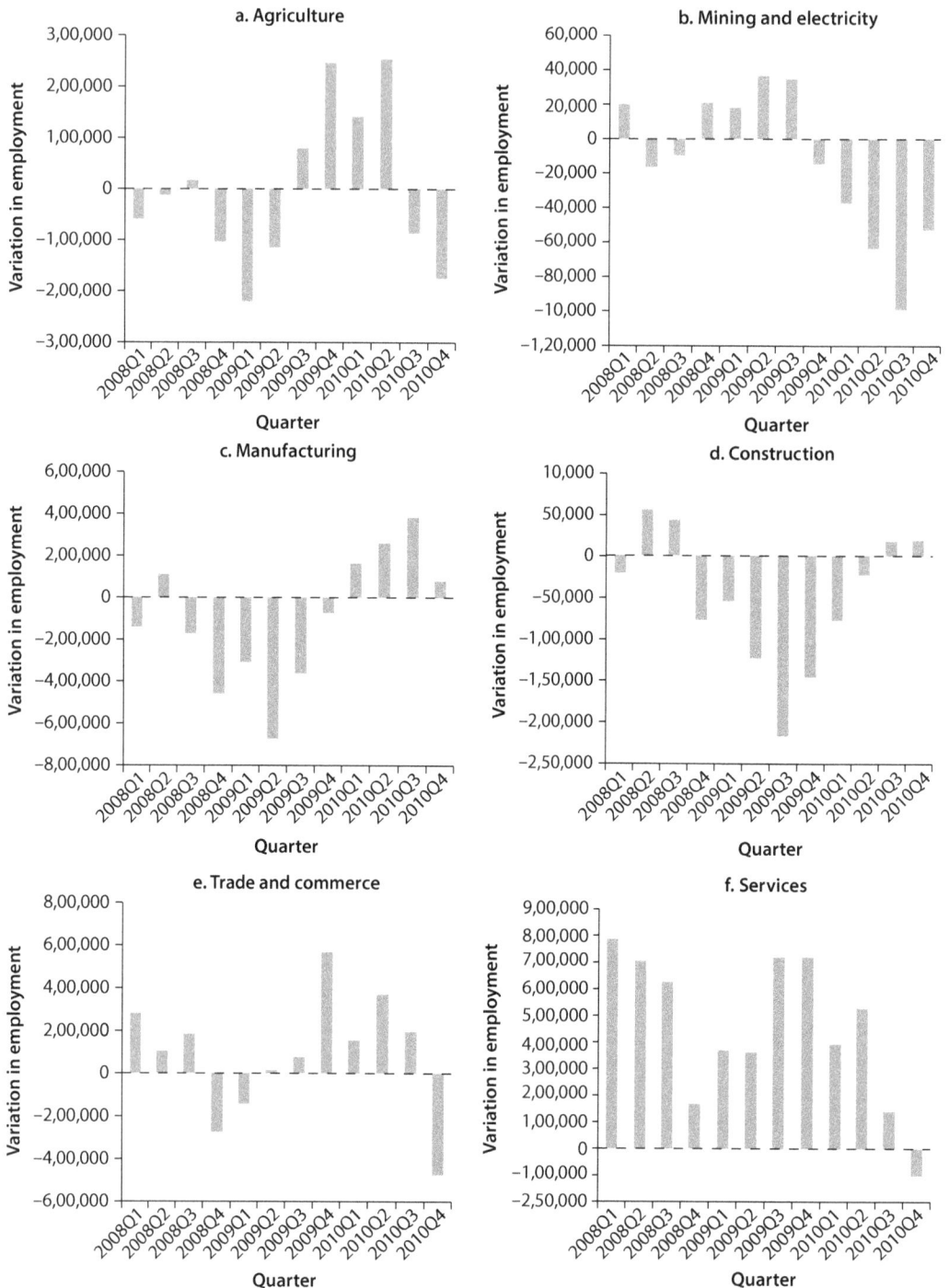

Source: Calculations based on data from ENOE (various years).
Note: Figures for the fourth quarter of 2010 are preliminary.

Table 7.2 Annual Changes in Job Losses and Gains by Economic Activity and Firm Size, 2008–10

Activity and size	2008	2009	2010
By economic activity			
Primary	(30,714)	(77,160)	191,338
Agriculture	(13,856)	(113,755)	254,482
Mining and electricity	(16,858)	36,595	(63,144)
Secondary	164,498	(795,552)	235,583
Manufacturing	109,083	(672,193)	257,594
Construction	55,415	(123,359)	(22,011)
Tertiary	805,433	375,750	890,581
Trade and commerce	101,366	12,870	364,390
Restaurants and hotels	166,157	(45,601)	186,286
Transport and communications	51,613	76,379	(46,833)
Financial services	191,658	37,599	131,194
Social services	46,923	168,234	18,605
Other services	120,403	24,889	259,965
Government services	127,313	101,380	(23,026)
Not specified	20,823	(25,453)	(9,951)
Total	960,040	(522,415)	1,307,551
By firm size and sector			
Agricultural firms	(13,856)	(113,755)	254,482
Micro firms	468,692	(221,427)	728,288
Small firms	156,744	11,997	268,388
Medium firms	4,337	(106,252)	(5,214)
Large firms	55,688	(379,747)	(21,111)
Government	127,313	101,380	(23,026)
Other	11,072	(1,367)	121,036
Not specified	150,050	186,756	(15,292)

Source: Calculations based on data from ENOE.
Note: Years end with the second quarter of each year. Numbers in parenthesis are negative.

by crisis. That is, the jobs lost in 2009 were mainly in manufacturing and construction, while the jobs created in the recovery were mainly in services. The following section examines the characteristics of the jobs created in the recovery period (across the four quarters of 2010) to address the possibility of a downgrading in job quality during the postcrisis period.

The dichotomy in job creation and destruction between tradable and nontradable sectors is also partially reflected in wages. As indicators of the evolution of wages, we chose the two largest occupations in tradeables and nontradeables: blue-collar workers in manufacturing and workers in retail commerce. Twelve-month average wages in retail commerce (the economic activity with the largest share of total employment in Mexico) dropped sharply during the crisis and have stagnated at a level 10 percent lower in real terms than before the crisis (see figure 7.8, panel c). Twelve-month average wages among blue-collar workers in manufacturing (where most of the Mexican exporting firms concentrate) have showed more resilience to the crisis, with a much smaller decline of 1–2 percent with respect to the period before the crisis (see figure 7.8, panel a). A similar difference can be observed in a comparison of earnings indexes for construction and the nonfinance private services sector.[2] In this case, both sectors are nontradable. On the one hand, real average wages have remained stable in the construction industry over the whole period (see figure 7.8, panel b). On the other hand, an index of real incomes among service sector workers fell significantly (around 8 percent) during the first half of 2009 and then grew month after month to regain their precrisis level by late 2010 (see figure 7.8, panel d). These numbers reveal two types of labor market adjustment. Some sectors (like manufacturing and construction) adjusted to the crisis through a large job destruction but kept real wages, whereas other sectors (like commerce and private nonfinancial services) saw a fall in wages but with sustained employment levels. The aggregate trends and average rates shown in figure 7.8 are described in more detail for specific groups in the following section.

The recovery has produced new jobs in all three sectors. Agricultural jobs grew by more than 250,000, something unusual in a sector that has experienced a secular decline in total employment for decades. This employment growth suggests a temporary return to agricultural activities as a subsistence strategy. Manufacturing also saw job creation but much less than the job losses of the previous year, leaving employment still below precrisis levels. The activities with the largest job growth were trade and commerce (364,400 jobs) and other services (260,000 jobs). These findings indicate that job creation has concentrated in activities with low entry barriers, where informal employment concentrates.

Small and medium firms were responsible for the largest share of job creation during the recovery. In contrast, medium and large firms accounted for the largest share of the fall. This finding is compatible with the former description of a recession that primarily affected manufacturing firms and a recovery that mostly favored commerce and other services. It also depicts a crisis that destroyed employment in certain sectors of the economy that, four quarters later, has not returned to its precrisis level. If we assume that tradable sectors and large firms have higher productivity and wages because of competitive pressures and larger capital endowment, then we can also assume that the recovery is not generating productive employment for the workers.

During the recovery in 2010, real wages continued falling. In some cases, like manufacturing, transport, and communications, wage reductions were harsh. This finding is consistent with the evidence from the previous section indicating that the creation of new jobs during the recovery concentrated in sectors at the lower end of the wage distribution. This continued fall in real wages confirms that the initial stages of the recovery brought new jobs but with lower average wages.

Real wages declined for all types of firms during the recession, except for large firms and government. All types of firms, however, recorded a decline in real wages during the recovery (see table 7.3).

Working through the Crisis • http://dx.doi.org/10.1596/978-0-8213-8967-6

Figure 7.8 Monthly Wage Indexes for Workers in Selected Industries in Mexico, January 2007–January 2011

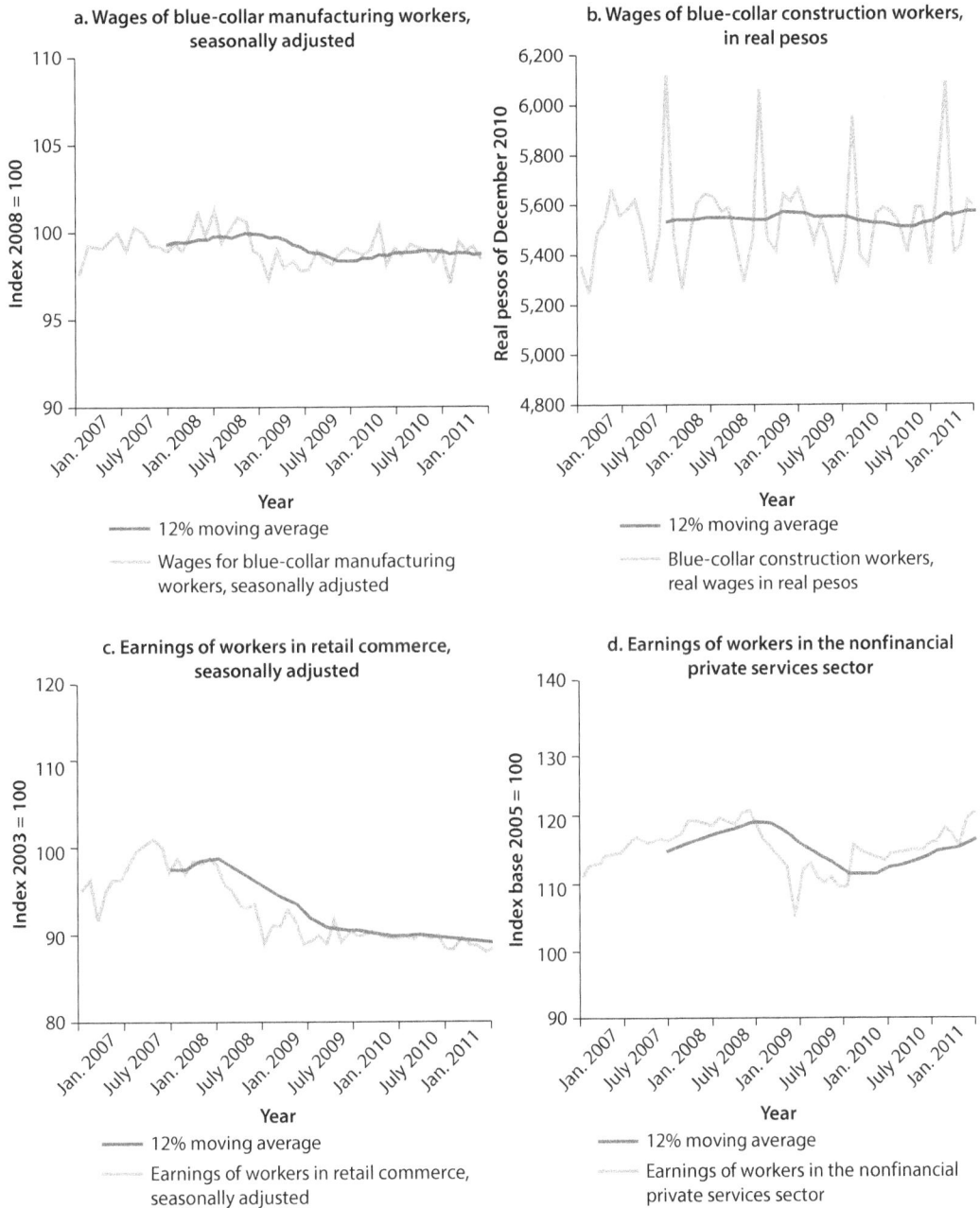

a. Wages of blue-collar manufacturing workers, seasonally adjusted

- 12% moving average
- Wages for blue-collar manufacturing workers, seasonally adjusted

b. Wages of blue-collar construction workers, in real pesos

- 12% moving average
- Blue-collar construction workers, real wages in real pesos

c. Earnings of workers in retail commerce, seasonally adjusted

- 12% moving average
- Earnings of workers in retail commerce, seasonally adjusted

d. Earnings of workers in the nonfinancial private services sector

- 12% moving average
- Earnings of workers in the nonfinancial private services sector

Source: Data from INEGI 2011.

Table 7.3　Change in Real Wages in Mexico by Sector and Firm Size, 2007–10

Sector and size	Hourly wage by sector (2010 pesos)				Year-on-year percentage changes		
	2007	2008	2009	2010	2008	2009	2010
Sector							
Primary							
Agriculture	20.5	20.1	19.6	19.3	−1.9	−2.6	−1.5
Mining and electricity	55.1	52.9	50.1	50.5	−4.0	−5.4	0.9
Secondary							
Manufacturing	31.0	29.3	29.4	27.3	−5.6	0.5	−7.1
Construction	34.5	34.1	33.1	32.1	−1.3	−2.7	−3.2
Tertiary							
Trade and commerce	30.5	29.6	28.1	27.1	−3.2	−5.1	−3.4
Restaurants and hotels	28.8	29.2	26.4	25.5	1.6	−9.7	−3.5
Transport and communications	36.4	34.7	33.5	30.2	−4.4	−3.6	−9.9
Financial services	46.7	43.5	42.8	40.9	−7.0	−1.4	−4.6
Social services	61.9	61.0	61.0	56.8	−1.4	−0.1	−6.9
Other services	31.9	32.5	30.8	29.6	1.9	−5.3	−3.7
Government services	45.9	45.2	45.3	42.9	−1.5	0.2	−5.1
Not specified	27.0	28.2	25.3	27.3	4.4	−10.2	8.1
Firm size and sector							
Agricultural firms	20.5	20.1	19.6	19.3	−1.9	−2.6	−1.5
Micro firms	33.1	32.4	31.4	30.0	−2.2	−3.3	−4.4
Small firms	42.9	42.4	40.1	38.4	−1.2	−5.4	−4.2
Medium firms	37.8	36.6	36.2	34.2	−3.1	−1.1	−5.3
Large firms	45.7	44.0	44.3	41.1	−3.8	0.7	−7.1
Government	45.9	45.2	45.3	42.9	−1.5	0.2	−5.1
Other	22.6	23.0	22.4	22.4	1.8	−3.0	0.0
Not specified	30.2	29.7	29.5	28.1	−1.7	−0.7	−4.7
Self-employed	33.2	33.1	32.4	31.1	−0.2	−2.1	−4.2
Owner	64.1	60.2	55.0	53.9	−6.1	−8.6	−2.0

Source: Calculations based on data from ENOE.
Note: Years end with the second quarter of each year.

Which Types of Workers Were Most Affected?

The distribution of employment by personal characteristics is shown in table 7.4. Interestingly, the distribution of job flows between males and females remained almost constant between 2009 and 2010. Women represent around 45 percent of the job flows, and, given their smaller share in total employment, this finding implies that women were proportionately more affected during the fall but also more favored during the recovery.

　　The crisis affected workers differently according to their level of education. Individuals with less than primary education were severely damaged by the crisis. Workers with primary education or less suffered large job losses during the fall, and few were reemployed during the recovery. Workers with a secondary education (that is, at least nine years of schooling) experienced relatively

Table 7.4 Decomposition of Year-on-Year Gains and Losses in Employment in Mexico by Sex, Education, Age, and Geographic Location, 2008–10

Characteristic	2008	2009	2010
Sex			
Female	398,975	−221,542	603,825
Male	561,065	−300,873	703,726
Educational level			
Without instruction	38,222	−290,129	18,351
Primary	−117,628	−732,183	23,931
Secondary	568,820	−87,614	661,404
High school	323,360	296,169	409,459
Professional	147,266	291,342	194,406
Age group			
Under 26	171,178	−541,611	500,242
26–35	109,625	−193,136	187,169
36–45	319,282	−57,089	163,450
46–55	165,732	285,681	148,266
Older than 55	194,223	−16,260	308,424
Geographic location			
Capital	248,065	−66,564	314,352
Central region	69,142	−142,347	290,907
Central gulf region	18,055	−32,695	126,057
North central region	42,011	−30,037	65,428
North Pacific region	41,830	−17,509	54,851
Central Pacific region	159,689	−58,427	189,950
South Pacific region	24,861	59,082	95,370
Peninsula region	74,524	9,541	59,828
Border	281,863	−243,459	110,808
Total	960,040	−522,415	1,307,551

Source: Based on data from ENOE.
Note: Years end with the second quarter of each year.

little job destruction in 2009 and were in the group with the largest job creation during 2010. Finally, workers with a high school education or better experienced similar job creation in both 2009 and 2010 (around 480,000 new jobs). It appears that the crisis first shed workers with lower qualifications and then hired workers with intermediate or better education. This result indicates that the average schooling of new hires has been upgraded and that finding a job is becoming more difficult for people with little schooling. In contrast, the hiring of skilled workers does not seem to have been affected at all by the crisis.

Severe changes in employment were concentrated at the extremes of the age distribution. The results are conclusive: those workers under 35 years old experienced net losses, while those older than 35 experienced net gains. For example, those over 55 lost employment in 2009 but then experienced an important job surge in 2010. Middle-aged workers (46–55) comprise the only group that kept growing throughout the crisis. In contrast, those under 35 experienced job losses in the fall that were not recouped by job creation during the recovery period. For example, youth (defined as people younger than 26) lost around 540,000 jobs in 2009, while the job creation for this age group in 2010 was only around 500,000 jobs.

Finally, the geographic distribution of job flows is significant.[3] The border region (which comprises Mexican states bordering the United States) experienced the largest job losses, followed by the center and capital regions. The latter two contain the largest share of total Mexican employment and population, which explains both their large share of total employment losses and also highlights the greater impact of the crisis on the less-populated border region. Employment has improved in a more than proportionate manner in all regions of the country except in the border region. This recovery confirms the fact that the crisis had a severe impact on firms associated with tradable goods, exports and manufacturing in particular, which are concentrated at the U.S.-Mexican border and which have not picked up again despite the end of the crisis in both countries. The south Pacific and peninsula regions are the only regions that did not suffer job losses either in 2009 or in 2010. Decelerating job creation in the Yucatán Peninsula in 2009 hints at the reduction of tourism activity, associated both with the U.S. recession and the H1N1 virus outbreak of April 2009.

Data on the characteristics of employment flows reveal a severe recession that destroyed good jobs and a recovery that has resulted in not-so-good employment creation (see table 7.5). Formal salaried jobs declined by 403,000 during the recession but increased by only 180,000 during the recovery. In contrast, jobs characterized as salaried informal, self-employed, or nonpaid all more than doubled over the previous year. Furthermore, during the crisis the loss of jobs with health coverage was three times greater than the loss of jobs without health coverage, and the latter grew more than six times more than the former during the recovery. Finally, job losses during the crisis were concentrated among those making between two and five times the minimum wage in 2009, while job gains during the recovery were concentrated among those earning less than twice the minimum wage in 2010. The number of workers earning more than five times the minimum wage declined in both 2009 and 2010.

Regarding levels of education (see table 7.6), nearly half the newly unemployed during the recession had completed secondary education but not high school (which in Mexico represents 9–12 years of education). This group is not formed by those seeking a job nor the usual target of payroll cutbacks. As usual but with larger magnitudes, the figures indicate that unemployment was concentrated among individuals with more education. Professionals did indeed take a serious blow in 2009 and 2010. Furthermore, job losses were mostly among younger workers, both in 2009 and in 2010.

Finally, changes in unemployment by location show a pattern similar to changes in employment. The largest unemployment changes occurred in the

Table 7.5 Decomposition of Annual Gains and Losses in Employment in Mexico by Position, Health Insurance Status, and Wage Category, 2008–10

Characteristic	2008	2009	2010
By position			
Salaried (formal)	306,987	(403,852)	180,036
Salaried (informal)	494,413	137,598	461,580
Employer	7,129	(231,887)	180,802
Self-employed	163,245	99,069	295,458
Nonpaid worker	(11,734)	(123,343)	189,675
Total	960,040	(522,415)	1,307,551
By health insurance status			
With health insurance	303,141	(393,090)	166,798
Without health insurance	648,725	(123,084)	1,127,673
No response	8,174	(6,241)	13,080
By minimum wage category			
Less than two times minimum wage	83,138	983,782	1,102,833
Between two and five times minimum wage	569,144	(1,550,261)	596,770
More than five times minimum wage	(33,439)	(486,374)	(701,495)
No monetary income	(86,976)	(37,442)	148,427
Undeclared	428,173	567,880	161,016

Source: Based on data from ENOE.
Note: Years end with the second quarter of each year.

border, capital, and central regions. As explained before, the latter two represent the largest share of the Mexican population, which explains both their large share of total unemployment and the greater impact of unemployment in the less-populated border region.

Broken down into personal characteristics, average wages in real terms have declined for all groups (table 7.7). Males experienced higher wage decreases than females, up to 5.3 percent compared to 3.9 percent. By educational level, higher wage losses are concentrated in both tails, those with no instruction and those with higher instruction. Middle-skilled workers also experienced wage losses, although comparatively smaller. All age groups experienced wage losses, especially those in the middle groups of 36–45 and 46–55. At the beginning of the crisis, workers in the capital and central states experienced the greatest wage losses. At the end of the period of analysis, losses were higher in states bordering the United States with high manufacturing employment, the Yucatán Peninsula with high tourism employment, and the north-central states.

The distribution of wage changes by economic activity shows some interesting patterns. In 2009, average wages fell in all sectors but two: manufacturing and government services. Note that manufacturing was also the sector that endured the largest job losses, showing a clear pattern of adjustment to the crisis through quantities rather than prices. The case of government services is perhaps due to the lesser sensitivity of wages in the public sector to economic crisis, particularly if the crisis does not have budgetary implications such as fiscal consolidation.

Table 7.6 Decomposition of Annual Changes in Unemployment by Sex, Educational Level, Age, and Geographic Location, 2008–10

Characteristic	2008	2009	2010
By sex			
Female	46,341	152,988	113,699
Male	41,770	618,779	7,152
Total	88,111	771,767	120,851
By educational level			
Without instruction	11,743	21,522	−5,593
Primary	26,805	187,998	22,458
Secondary	30,827	313,027	32,773
High school	39,754	171,422	27,342
Professional	−21,018	77,798	43,871
By age group			
Less than 26	31,778	284,352	9,549
26–35	8,148	180,417	66,278
36–45	22,443	129,941	40,089
46–55	15,395	118,860	1,750
Older than 55	10,347	58,197	3,185
By geographic location			
Capital	−37,911	240,194	5,394
Central region	23,423	114,121	24,558
Central gulf region	−1,310	34,349	20,172
North central region	14,242	30,074	7,641
North Pacific region	−1,385	25,571	12,240
Central Pacific region	29,402	79,003	19,278
South Pacific region	−4,104	1,648	16,611
Peninsula region	5,261	25,126	6,919
Border	60,493	221,681	8,038

Source: Based on data from ENOE.
Note: Years end with the second quarter of each year.

Real wages declined in all activities of the tertiary sector. These decreases ranged from a slight −0.1 percent in social services and −1.2 percent in the financial sector to a severe −9.7 percent in restaurants and hotels and −5.1 percent in trade in commerce. The latter has been one of the few sectors that had no job destruction over the crisis, indicating a process of adjustment through wages rather than quantities. Sectors like agriculture, construction, and restaurants and hotels experienced a reduction both in employment and in real wages (see figure 7.9).

All this evidence reveals the asymmetry of adjustment over the course of the crisis. During the recession, some sectors reduced employment only, others adjusted real wages only, and others adjusted the two margins. During the recovery, all sectors (with the exception of mining) have showed job creation with lower real wages (see figure 7.9). The crisis produced a significant dislocation of

Table 7.7 Change in Real Wages in Mexico by Sex, Educational Level, Age, and Geographic Location, 2007–10

Characteristic	Hourly wage (2010 pesos)				Year-on-year % changes		
	2007	2008	2009	2010	2008	2009	2010
By sex							
Female	34.8	34.5	33.4	32.1	−1.1	−3.0	−3.9
Male	37.1	36.0	34.7	32.9	−2.9	−3.6	−5.3
By educational level							
Without instruction	20.6	20.0	20.5	19.3	−3.2	2.6	−5.5
Primary	25.7	25.5	24.8	23.6	−1.0	−2.5	−4.8
Secondary	29.0	28.1	27.3	26.0	−3.1	−3.1	−4.5
High school	39.4	38.7	37.2	35.0	−1.6	−3.8	−6.0
Professional	69.2	66.3	64.5	60.8	−4.2	−2.7	−5.7
By age group							
Less than 26	25.4	25.3	24.9	24.5	−0.4	−1.6	−1.7
26–35	35.2	34.3	33.6	32.2	−2.5	−2.2	−4.1
36–45	40.0	39.4	37.5	35.0	−1.6	−4.8	−6.5
46–55	42.9	41.3	39.3	37.2	−3.7	−4.9	−5.3
Older than 55	36.9	35.5	34.7	33.9	−3.8	−2.0	−2.4
By geographic location							
Capital	36.4	33.3	33.3	32.8	−8.4	0.1	−1.7
Central region	33.1	31.1	30.4	29.2	−6.1	−2.3	−3.7
Central gulf region	35.0	34.5	33.6	32.5	−1.3	−2.6	−3.3
North central region	33.8	33.6	31.6	29.9	−0.4	−6.1	−5.3
North Pacific region	42.9	42.7	41.6	40.1	−0.4	−2.5	−3.7
Central Pacific region	35.2	34.8	33.3	32.4	−1.2	−4.4	−2.6
South Pacific region	28.9	28.2	26.4	26.5	−2.5	−6.3	0.3
Peninsula region	35.4	34.3	33.2	31.4	−3.1	−3.2	−5.5
Border	40.4	40.4	39.0	35.6	−0.1	−3.4	−8.7

Source: Based on data from ENOE.
Note: Years end with the second quarter of each year.

the Mexican labor market. The large flows of job destruction and creation left the country with employment levels similar to those before the crisis but with some 900,000 more people unemployed than before the crisis. Average wages declined for all sectors.

Labor Market Transitions during the Crisis

Previous figures describe net job flows of employment and unemployment. However, these net flows give only a partial description of the workings of the labor market. Net job flows can be decomposed into four components, as follows:

$$E_f - E_t = \Delta E_{I \to E} + \Delta E_{U \to I} - \nabla_{E \to I} - \nabla E_{E \to U},$$

Figure 7.9 Changes in Employment and Wages Due to the Economic Crisis in Mexico, 2009 and 2010

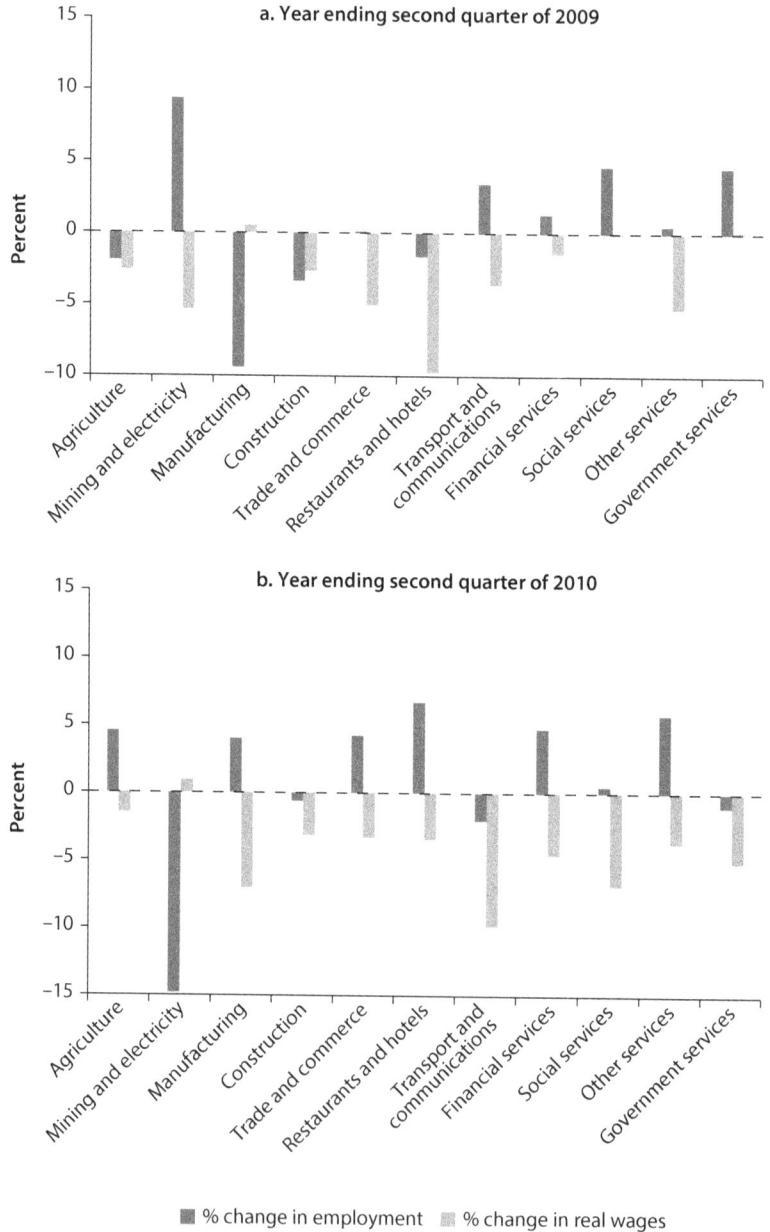

a. Year ending second quarter of 2009

b. Year ending second quarter of 2010

■ % change in employment ▨ % change in real wages

Source: Calculations based on data from ENOE.
Note: Years end with the second quarter of each year.

that is, the change in total employment between final (E_f) and initial period (E_t) equals the growth of employment due to transitions from inactivity (and from out of the labor force) $(\Delta E_{I \to E})$ and from unemployment $(\Delta E_{U \to E})$, minus those who lost employment and became inactive $(\Delta E_{E \to I})$ or unemployed $(\Delta E_{E \to U})$. Similar decompositions can be done for net flows in unemployment:

$$U_f - U_t = \Delta U_{I \to U} + \Delta U_{E \to U} - \nabla U_{U \to I} - \nabla U_{U \to E}$$

and in inactivity

$$I_f - I_t = \Delta I_{E \to I} + \Delta I_{U \to I} - \nabla I_{U \to I} - \nabla I_{I \to U} - \nabla I_{I \to E}.$$

These components can be observed in the cells of a transition matrix:

Status	Inactive$_f$	Unemployed$_f$	Employed$_f$
Inactive$_i$	–	$\Delta U_{I \to U} = \nabla I_{I \to U}$	$\Delta E_{I \to E} = \nabla I_{I \to E}$
Unemployed$_i$	$\Delta I_{U \to I} = \nabla U_{U \to I}$	–	$\Delta E_{U \to E} = \nabla U_{U \to E}$
Employed$_i$	$\Delta I_{E \to I} = \nabla E_{E \to I}$	$\Delta U_{E \to U} = \nabla E_{E \to U}$	–

This transition matrix provides more nuanced information about job flows and reveals how changes in employment status are the consequence of gross flows to and from unemployment and inactivity. These flows also indicate the likelihood of moving from one status to another. The Mexican Occupation and Employment Survey (Encuesta Nacional de Ocupación y Empleo, or ENOE) has a rotating panel that interviews the same household for five consecutive quarters. As a result, we can observe the same household and its individuals, and therefore its employment dynamics, for the second quarter of two consecutive years. With these observations, transition matrices can be produced. The following analysis makes use of these rotating panels for our periods of study for the population above 14 years old.[4]

The first transition matrix we analyze (table 7.8) is an estimation of gross job flows before the recession—that is, between the second quarter of 2007 and the second quarter of 2008. In this case, we observe that 73 percent of those who were inactive (out of the labor force) in 2007 (32.5 million) remained in that category in 2008, with 25 percent moving to being employed and 2 percent to being unemployed. Those who were employed in the second quarter of 2007 (42.9 million, or 81 percent) remained employed, while 17 percent moved to inactive status and 2 percent to unemployed status. And of those who were unemployed in 2007, 10 percent (1.5 million) remained unemployed in 2008, 30 percent became inactive, while 60 percent got a job. In absolute terms, around 9 million people became employed, and 8.1 million previously employed people became unemployed or inactive. Therefore, a net job creation of around 0.9 million was produced during the year before the recession. Unemployment, in contrast, grew by only around 90,000, because around 1.5 million people

Table 7.8 Change in Employment Status of Mexican Workers between 2007 and 2008

Employment status in second quarter, 2007	Employment status in second quarter, 2008			
	Inactive	Employed	Unemployed	Total
Inactive or out of labor force				
Number	23,687,896	8,199,919	684,809	32,572,624
Percent	72.7	25.2	2.1	
Employed				
Number	7,385,503	34,766,246	754,907	42,906,656
Percent	17.2	81.0	1.8	
Unemployed				
Number	451,074	900,531	153,591	1,505,196
Percent	30.0	59.8	10.2	
Total	31,524,473	43,866,696	1,593,307	76,984,476

Source: Calculations based on rotating panels from ENOE.
Note: Years end with the second quarter of each year.

Table 7.9 Change in Employment Status of Workers in Mexico between 2008 and 2009

Employment status in second quarter, 2008	Employment status in second quarter, 2009			
	Inactive	Employed	Unemployed	Total
Inactive or out of labor force				
Number	24,484,780	7,822,462	951,089	33,258,331
Percent	73.6	23.5	2.9	
Employed				
Number	7,980,215	34,688,008	1,198,473	43,866,696
Percent	18.2	79.1	2.7	
Unemployed				
Number	543,984	833,811	215,513	1,593,307
Percent	34.1	52.3	13.5	
Total	33,008,979	43,344,281	2,365,074	78,718,334

Source: Calculations based on rotating panels from ENOE.
Note: Years end with the second quarter of each year.

previously employed or inactive became unemployed, while nearly 1.4 million previously unemployed either found a job or left the labor market.

The second transition matrix, table 7.9, refers to the recession—that is, the time between the second quarter of 2008 and the second quarter of 2009. According to this estimate, of the 33.2 million inactive in 2007, 74 percent remained in that category, 24 percent moved to a job, and 3 percent became unemployed. Of the 43.8 million individuals employed in 2008, 79 percent remained in an occupation, 18 percent moved to inactivity, and 3 percent became unemployed. And of the 1.6 million unemployed in 2008, 14 percent remained in the same category, while 34 percent moved to inactivity and 52 percent got a job.

According to these estimates, the fall in total employment was due mostly to the difference between gross job destruction (that is, jobs held by people who were employed and became unemployed) of 1.2 million and a gross job creation (that is, jobs held by people who were unemployed and became employed) of 0.833 million. The gross flows toward and from inactivity nearly cancel each other out (both around 8 million people), so that most of the job destruction in 2009 can be attributed to more firings than hirings. Changes in unemployment can be attributed to the flows between employment and unemployment already described and to an additional flow from the inactive population. Because more than 951,000 initially inactive people became unemployed while only 544,000 formerly unemployed became inactive, 400,000 people (about half the total change) were added to the unemployed during the recession. In other words, the increase in unemployment is associated with the growth of the labor supply.

During the recovery, of the 33.9 million individuals inactive in 2009, 78 percent remained in that category in 2010, 19 percent got a job, and 3 percent became unemployed (table 7.10). Also, for the 43.3 million individuals employed in 2009, 85 percent remained in a job, 13 percent moved to inactivity, and 3 percent moved to unemployment. And for the 2.4 million in unemployment in 2009, 16 percent were still in unemployment, 60 percent got a job, and 24 percent moved to inactivity in 2010.

Therefore, we find that, on top of the population increase, inactivity and unemployment both increased (see tables 7.8, 7.9, and 7.10). Those who were unemployed at some point previous to the crisis were 10 percent more likely to remain unemployed, while after the crisis they were 16 percent more likely to remain in that category. In addition, those in inactivity at some time were 73 percent more likely to have remained inactive during the crisis and 78 percent more likely to have remained inactive after the crisis. In addition, the likelihood that those with a job would stay in a job increased from 81 to 85 percent after the crisis. This persistence is accompanied by weak job

Table 7.10 Change in Employment Status of Workers in Mexico between 2009 and 2010

Employment status in second quarter, 2009	Employment status in second quarter, 2010			
	Inactive	Employed	Unemployed	Total
Inactive or out of labor force				
Number	26,533,723	6,482,882	944,029	33,960,634
Percent	78.1	19.1	2.8	
Employed				
Number	5,423,962	36,760,882	1,159,437	43,344,281
Percent	12.5	84.8	2.7	
Unemployed				
Number	574,547	1,408,068	382,459	2,365,074
Percent	24.3	59.5	16.2	
Total	32,532,232	44,651,832	2,485,925	79,669,989

Source: Calculations based on rotating panels from ENOE.
Note: Years end with the second quarter of each year.

creation. Before the crisis, 25.2 percent of the inactive became employed in the period 2007–08, whereas only 19.1 percent got a job in the period 2009–10. Among the unemployed, the numbers are 59.8 percent and 59.5 percent for the same periods. Thus, the growth of the labor supply, together with the increasing persistence and reduced mobility between labor force categories, may be among the main mechanisms for the observed patterns in increasing unemployment due to the crisis.

An Econometric Analysis of Transition Probabilities

The previous section described probabilities of transition from one employment status to another. However, these probabilities do not indicate the effect that a particular characteristic, such as age or education, has on the likelihood of moving from one status to another. The effect of a single characteristic on employment transitions is known as conditional probability. It defines the effect of having one characteristic instead of another (for example, being a woman as opposed to being a man) on a particular employment transition (for example, finding a job), under the condition that all other characteristics (age, education, and so forth) remain the same. Conditional probabilities are of analytical interest because they indicate whether certain traits involve propensities to lose or gain employment. This kind of probability is computed through an econometric technique using the same panel data described in the previous section.[5]

Estimates for the conditional probabilities of becoming jobless before the recession, during the recession, and during the recovery are shown in table 7.11. Evidence in the table points to several main conclusions. First, males have always had a lower probability of losing a job than females, but this advantage became larger during the recovery. During the recovery, males were 2.9 percent less likely to become jobless than observationally equivalent females, compared with 1.3 percent during the recession or 1.55 before the recession.

Second, individuals with higher education were less likely to lose a job than to keep a job, both during the recession and during the recovery. The difference is among workers with secondary education (semiskilled), who were as likely to lose a job as those with primary schooling or less during the recession. Thus, the group of semiskilled workers was particularly affected by the crisis. Third, workers from the Yucatán Peninsula, the south Pacific, and the north-central regions were less likely to become jobless (around 2 percent less) than workers from the capital region. This advantage was observed before the crisis and persisted during the recovery, although it was somewhat smaller. In contrast, the north-central region was most affected by the crisis. Fourth, middle-aged workers were less likely to become jobless than young and senior workers. This pattern was observed both in the recession and in the recovery, but the disadvantage of senior workers (those over 55) became even worse during the recovery, when they became more likely to lose a job (around 2 percent more than the youngest group). Finally, household heads were less likely to lose a job than other household members, but this advantage was smaller during the recovery (2.6 percent less likely) than during the recession (4.1 percent less likely).

Working through the Crisis • http://dx.doi.org/10.1596/978-0-8213-8967-6

Table 7.11 Marginal Probabilities of Losing a Job in Mexico by Sex, Education, Geographic Location, Age, and Household Position, 2007–10

Variable	2007–08	2008–09	2009–10
By sex			
Male	−0.0155***	−0.0133***	−0.0298***
	(0.0039)	(0.0041)	(0.0035)
By educational level[a]			
Secondary	−0.0107**	−0.0014	−0.0125***
	(0.0045)	(0.0049)	(0.0040)
High school	−0.0154***	−0.0118**	−0.0113***
	(0.0047)	(0.0050)	(0.0042)
Professional	−0.0389***	−0.0298***	−0.0296***
	(0.0050)	(0.0056)	(0.0045)
By geographic location[b]			
Central region	0.0039	0.0014	−0.0015
	(0.0078)	(0.0078)	(0.0067)
Central gulf region	0.0049	−0.0242***	0.0010
	(0.0099)	(0.0091)	(0.0086)
North central region	−0.0003	−0.0230***	−0.0164**
	(0.0083)	(0.0078)	(0.0067)
North Pacific region	0.0067	−0.0027	−0.0167**
	(0.0094)	(0.0091)	(0.0071)
Central Pacific region	0.0050	−0.0120	−0.0075
	(0.0081)	(0.0078)	(0.0067)
South Pacific region	−0.0232**	−0.0223**	−0.0190**
	(0.0108)	(0.0110)	(0.0092)
Peninsular region	−0.0163*	−0.0216***	−0.0180**
	(0.0085)	(0.0084)	(0.0071)
Border	0.0015	−0.0036	−0.0094
	(0.0079)	(0.0078)	(0.0065)
By age[c]			
26–35 years	−0.0392***	−0.0197***	−0.0222***
	(0.0046)	(0.0052)	(0.0044)
36–45 years	−0.0421***	−0.0329***	−0.0255***
	(0.0048)	(0.0053)	(0.0045)
46–55 years	−0.0360***	−0.0271***	−0.0078
	(0.0054)	(0.0059)	(0.0053)
56–65 years	−0.0116*	0.0148*	0.0209***
	(0.0068)	(0.0079)	(0.0071)

table continues next page

Table 7.11 Marginal Probabilities of Losing a Job by Sex, Education, Geographic Location, Age, and Household Position in Mexico, 2007–10 *(continued)*

Variable	2007–08	2008–09	2009–10
By position in the household			
Household head	−0.0318***	−0.0410***	−0.0256***
	(0.0044)	(0.0045)	(0.0040)
Pseudo R²	0.1395	0.1302	0.134
N	42915	42170	40336

Source: Calculations based on rotating panel from ENOE between second quarters of 2008, 2009, and 2010.
Note: Years end with second quarter of each year. Omitted control groups are (1) those with primary or less schooling; (2) those in the capital region; (3) and those less than 26 years of age. Marginal effects on transition probabilities from employment to joblessness computed on the average using STATA software command. Marginal effects are compared with the probability of being employed in both periods.
a. Level of instruction is compared to "no level of instruction and primary."
b. Geographic regions are compared to "capital."
c. Age is compared to "18–25 years."

Estimates for the conditional probabilities of finding a job, instead of staying in one, before and during the recession and the recovery are shown in table 7.12. Here, we also find five main messages:

- First, males always have a lower probability than females of finding a job as opposed to staying in one, and this probability has not changed significantly over time. Males were 3.6 percent less likely to become employed than observationally equivalent females, both during the recession and the recovery (slightly less likely, 4.2 percent, before the crisis).
- Second, individuals with higher schooling were less likely to find a job than to keep a job, but that advantage was diminished during and after the recession. In both periods, workers with professional education were 3.5 percent less likely to find a job than to stay in a job compared with similar workers with only primary or less education during the recession. This magnitude climbed to 5.0 percent during the recovery.
- Third, workers with similar characteristics but from different regions faced the same probability of finding a job rather than staying in a job, both during the recession and the recovery, with the exception of workers from the Yucatán Peninsula. They were less likely to find a job (a slight 1.4 percent) during the recession than to keep a job.
- Fourth, middle-aged workers were less likely to quit jobs than young and senior workers. This pattern was observed both in the recession and in the recovery, but the difference was narrower during the recession.
- Finally, household heads were less likely to find a job than to keep one in comparison with other household members, but this tendency was larger during the recession (4.5 percent less likely) than during the recovery (3.3 percent less likely) or before the crisis (3.2 percent).

In summary, these results indicate that there were only small differences in how the recession and the recovery affected different groups. By a small margin,

Table 7.12 Marginal Probabilities of Finding a Job in Mexico by Sex, Education, Geographic Location, Age, and Household Position, 2007–10

Variables	2007–08	2008–09	2009–10
By sex			
Male	−0.0420***	−0.0366***	−0.0359***
	(0.0031)	(0.0031)	(0.0034)
By educational level[a]			
Secondary	−0.0108***	−0.0087**	−0.0083**
	(0.0036)	(0.0036)	(0.0039)
High School	−0.0151***	−0.0115***	−0.0255***
	(0.0036)	(0.0036)	(0.0039)
Professional	−0.0401***	−0.0351***	−0.0504***
	(0.0037)	(0.0037)	(0.0039)
By geographic location[b]			
Central region	−0.0027	0.0095	0.0080
	(0.0061)	(0.0064)	(0.0073)
Central gulf region	−0.0151**	−0.0008	−0.0036
	(0.0070)	(0.0078)	(0.0088)
	−0.0039	0.0055	0.0118
North central region	(0.0065)	(0.0069)	(0.0081)
North Pacific region	−0.0051	−0.0050	0.0116
	(0.0071)	(0.0070)	(0.0087)
Central Pacific region	−0.0049	0.0030	0.0073
	(0.0062)	(0.0064)	(0.0075)
South Pacific region	−0.0052	−0.0058	−0.0055
	(0.0091)	(0.0090)	(0.0104)
Peninsular region	−0.0052	−0.0141**	−0.0045
	(0.0070)	(0.0064)	(0.0080)
Border	0.0021	−0.0066	−0.0002
	(0.0063)	(0.0060)	(0.0071)
By age group[c]			
26–35 years	−0.0401***	−0.0318***	−0.0443***
	(0.0033)	(0.0033)	(0.0036)
36–45 years	−0.0534***	−0.0365***	−0.0550***
	(0.0033)	(0.0034)	(0.0036)
46–55 years	−0.0397***	−0.0328***	−0.0482***
	(0.0037)	(0.0038)	(0.0040)
56–65 years	−0.0237***	−0.0195***	−0.0285***
	(0.0048)	(0.0049)	(0.0050)

table continues next page

Table 7.12 Marginal Probabilities of Finding a Job in Mexico by Sex, Education, Geographic Location, Age, and Household Position, 2007–10 *(continued)*

Variables	2007–08	2008–09	2009–10
By position in the household			
Household head	-0.0418***	-0.0425***	-0.0373***
	(0.0036)	(0.0035)	(0.0039)
Pseudo R^2	0.1395	0.1302	0.134
N	42,915	42,170	40,336

Source: Calculations based on rotating panel from ENOE between second quarters of 2008, 2009, and 2010.
Note: Years end with second quarter of each year. Omitted control groups are (1) those with primary or less schooling; (2) capital region; (3) those with less than 26 years of age. Marginal effects on transition probabilities from employment to joblessness computed on the average using STATA.
a. Level of instruction is compared to "no level of instruction and primary."
b. Geographic regions are compared to "capital."
c. Age is compared to "18–25 years."

those more likely to stay in a job during the economic crisis were males, the highly skilled, household heads, and the middle aged.

Policies for Coping with the Crisis

The Mexican government announced a series of programs to cope with the crisis, which included the Program to Encourage Growth and Employment announced in October 2008 and the National Agreement to Support the Household Economy and Employment announced in January 2009. The expected outcome was about a 0.9 percent boost in GDP. Additional support in the form of credit from development banks was expected to increase total investment to about Mex$171 billion, or about 1.4 percent of GDP (CEFP 2009). Information about public works programs is limited, and the data that are available indicate only very modest progress during the first year of the crisis when it was most needed. In fact, in the previous section we documented a dramatic contraction in the construction sector, even though government programs should have had an immediate impact on this sector. As a consequence, most of this section focuses on the labor policies (both active and passive) that were implemented during the crisis. In general, the labor policies described in the next subsection were underfunded and left the needs of the large majority of vulnerable and displaced workers unmet.

Public Works Program

PICE aimed to cope with the effects of the economic crisis by using resources mainly from oil revenues. A total of Mex$255 billion or approximately 1.9 percent of GDP was to be spent on infrastructure, massive transport programs, and other priority sectors. These goals were reinforced in January 2009 with a presidential agreement creating the Intersecretarial Commission for Acquisitions and Works in the Public Administration for Small, Micro, and Medium Firms. The commission aimed to ease crisis conditions by increasing public sector acquisitions from those firms by at least 20 percent.

The main mechanism of PICE was public expenditure on infrastructure, with an initial budget of about Mex\$90 billion, or about 0.7 percent of GDP (excluding investment in the oil sector). The National Fund for Infrastructure is part of PICE, the flagship infrastructure program of the administration. Another Mex\$90.2 billion (or 0.7 percent of GDP) was awarded to PEMEX (the state oil company) to build a new refinery and other infrastructure. Despite a lack of information about the execution of those programs, a report of the House of Deputies (CEFP 2009) stated that as of mid-2009, there had been very little progress. For example, by the first quarter of 2009 only 15 percent of the infrastructure fund had been spent on road infrastructure and only 0.4 percent on other infrastructure such as water provision, sewage, and water purification. The CEFP report states that the main problem was the allocation of resources to projects that lacked any execution plan or rights to build. About 40 percent of the programs were still undefined in 2009, and another 50 percent were delayed because of cumbersome bureaucratic processes.

Although public expenditure increased at the beginning of the crisis (see figure 7.2), private investment has lagged. Furthermore, recovery has not been led by growth in public investment, which is still below precrisis levels. Given the limited information available about public works programs, we will concentrate on the labor policies adopted by the Mexican government.

Labor Policies

In January 2009, the federal government announced ANFEFE, a series of policy actions and a string of commitments on the part of several public and private Mexican institutions. ANFEFE policy actions fall into different categories. The first category, Support to Employment (Apoyo al Empleo y a los Trabajadores), is a combination of both active and passive labor policies for confronting the global crisis.

Active Labor Policies

The Temporary Employment Program and the National System of Employment (Servicio Nacional de Empleo, or SNE) were the two main active labor polices proposed in the ANFEFE. SNE is an emergency temporary employment program for unemployed or reduced-income workers and includes labor intermediation, mobility, and training services. In January 2009, it was announced that the fund would pay out Mex\$2.2 billion or about 0.02 percent of the GDP by the end of 2009.

The government's deployment of the PET during the economic crisis is presented in table 7.13. The table displays the number of temporary programs works related to hiring workers, the number and gender of beneficiaries, and the federal and state budgets. The number of beneficiaries increased by 77 percent from 2008 to 2009 and by another 31 percent through 2010, while the budget increased by 95 percent from 2008 to 2009 and by another 15 percent through 2010. Most of the increase in the budget came from federal sources. PET's response to the crisis peaked in January 2009, and the 2008 figures for

Table 7.13 Mexico's Temporary Employment Program, 2001–10

Beneficiaries and budget of the Progama of Temporal Employment (PET), thousands of dollars in real terms 2010

Year	Implemented programs	Beneficiaries (2001–2008), Identified (2009–2010)			Federal budget	State budget	Budget combined	% increase in budget	% increase in beneficiaries
		Women	Men	Total					
2001	52,117	496,586	1,315,999	1,812,585	$448,617	$48,187	$496,804		
2002	51,021	543,243	1,278,419	1,821,662	$438,951	$25,430	$464,381	−6.53	0.50
2003	25,311	250,180	567,315	817,495	$208,912	$12,832	$221,744	−52.25	−55.12
2004	21,113	202,856	472,362	675,218	$186,876	$9,382	$196,258	−11.49	−17.40
2005	19,944	216,825	455,613	672,438	$172,315	$8,663	$180,979	−7.79	−0.41
2006	12,179	125,229	255,381	380,610	$117,544	$7,640	$125,183	−30.83	−43.40
2007	15,703	158,032	319,639	477,671	$147,914	$10,865	$158,779	26.84	25.50
2008	10,885	180,993	204,031	385,024	$84,090	$10,390	$94,480	−40.50	−19.40
2009	29,694	279,838	402,989	682,827	$175,242	$8,791	$184,033	94.78	77.35
2010	26,712	427,985	469,722	897,707	$218,212	$8,774	$226,985	23.34	31.47

Source: Centro de Información del Programa de Empleo Temporal 2011.

beneficiaries and the budget show a reduction from 2007. Furthermore, despite the sharp increase in unemployment during the crisis, the total budget in 2010 was only about 60 percent of the resources allocated in 2001, a year with more stability, and the number of beneficiaries lags by a million (also compared with 2001).

Important elements of the PET include its recent extension to urban areas in response to job destruction in manufacturing and services and its support for the unemployed.[6] In fact, preliminary evidence from administrative data shows some association between PET budget allocations and poverty, unemployment, and urbanization. However, these variables are highly correlated so that conditional associations are needed to ascertain if PET is reaching the urban population and the unemployed. This knowledge is important because, despite being assigned new roles during the crisis, PET is still a program for protecting the poor from seasonal shocks. Econometric evidence shows that PET has indeed become more oriented toward the unemployed and the urban population. However, three caveats are necessary.[7] First, poverty is still the major criterion for identification of beneficiaries in the program. Second, the Ministry of Social Development seems to be the only federal agency that has allocated resources to the unemployed. Third, PET, which is housed in the Ministry of Social Development, reallocated resources to the urban population and the unemployed primarily in 2010, suggesting that there has been a learning curve in this process.

All this evidence indicates room for improvement in the allocation of resources toward the areas most affected by unemployment. Additional data for monitoring and evaluating the program are necessary for a more accurate picture, but it is clear that PET is mainly an antipoverty program that focuses on the rural poor. Therefore, PET needs to consider how to increase coverage and effectiveness among the unemployed population in urban areas.

The SNE, as presented in table 7.14, includes several provisions that support recruitment-matching mechanisms for job seekers. These include a website listing positions posted by firms, telephone services for the same purpose, workshops for job seekers, and job fairs that bring together job seekers and firms. ANFEFE's Support to Employment program provides scholarships for workers in the Fellowship Training Program for Work (Programa de Becas de Capacitación para el Trabajo) initiative, the Training Grants for Work (Becas de Capacitación para el Trabajo) program, and other small programs.

The Training Grants for Work program offers training courses and a modest scholarship to unemployed and underemployed job seekers. It has about seven different modalities covering different types of populations. Most of the modalities provide private training courses. However, it was estimated that the program trains only 0.5 percent of its potential population. Also, an incidence analysis indicates that the programs are benefiting the better-educated workers.

The Fellowship Training Program for Work partially subsidizes on-the-job training for workers employed in formal sector firms. The objective of the training is to increase the productivity of the worker and the firm. Impact evaluations have shown some positive effects on the adoption of technology, on the

Table 7.14 Services Provided by Mexico's National Employment System, 2005–10

Year	Recruitment service		Support to employment		Microregions		Emergency actions		Total	
	Attended	Hired	Attended	Hired	Attended	Hired	Attended	Hired	Attended	Hired
2005	1,712,639	375,140	340,597	186,841	11,557	4,366	—	—	2,111,177	591,438
2006	1,772,493	377,747	301,285	165,428	12,362	6,262	—	—	2,086,140	549,437
2007	1,950,746	447,814	309,884	200,960	12,250	8,705	—	—	2,272,880	657,479
2008	2,775,180	590,986	463,227	262,230	6,067	3,062	—	—	3,244,474	856,278
2009	3,424,515	577,545	398,406	222,357	—	n.a.	116,480	96,500	3,939,401	896,402
2010	3,563,825	665,861	439,842	261,119	—	n.a.	81,007	60,817	4,084,674	987,797

Source: Ministry of Labor 2011.

Note: "Recruitment service" includes the recruitment agency in all forms, workshops for job seekers, and temporary agricultural jobs. "Support to employment" includes the Fellowship Training Program for Work, PAE (Training Grants for Work), and internal labor mobility. "Emergency actions" includes Action for Support of Employment and Emergency Actions for Service Sector Workers. — = not available.

introduction of business reorganization in firms, and on productivity of the firm in some time periods. However, no evaluations have yet shown an impact on workers' wages.

In general, the number of beneficiaries attending SNE job fairs increased, as did the number hired. For example, in 2007 2.3 million people attended, of whom 657,000 were hired; in 2010, 4 million attended, of whom 987,000 were hired. However, the ratio of the effectively hired to attendees decreased slightly from 0.29 in 2007 to 0.24 in 2010.

These programs, however, are not necessarily meeting the needs of the more vulnerable or those unemployed. Note, for example, that 2.5 million individuals on average were unemployed in 2010, PET beneficiaries numbered almost 0.9 million, and those hired through the National Employment System were almost a million, giving a total of 1.8 million beneficiaries. It seems plausible that such programs are fostering employment opportunities, given that a large share of the population that already has a job is looking for another one, although the proof remains to be determined through evaluations of such programs.

Passive Labor Policies

Two passive labor policies are included in the ANFEFE: (1) expanded withdrawals from pension savings accounts for unemployed workers; and (2) extended coverage of health and maternity benefits for unemployed workers who contributed to the system. The latter was a temporary measure that protected workers and their families during the worst period of the crisis (the first and second quarters of 2009). The former is a permanent change with long-term implications. The short-term distributive impact of these policies will likely be favorable to middle-income families. In fact, both measures are linked to being a beneficiary of the formal social security systems in Mexico, particularly the IMSS (Instituto Mexicano del Seguro Social). In this regard, beneficiaries of the IMSS are concentrated in the middle and top deciles of the income distribution; hence, expanded withdrawals from pension funds and extended coverage of health insurance are more likely to occur in middle and top deciles. If unemployment were concentrated in lower-middle-income households, then this policy would likely have a distributive impact favorable to these households in the short term. Expanded withdrawals from individual retirement accounts allowed the government to respond rapidly to increasing unemployment during the global crisis. However, a broader review of passive labor policies might be needed in the medium term, since the current provision threatens to erode workers' pension funds.

Beneficiaries responded rapidly to the expansion of the unemployment withdrawal facility. The number of withdrawals in 2009 was nearly twice those in 2008, and the average amount withdrawn grew by 39 percent. In 2010, the number of withdrawals was still 60 percent higher than in 2008, and the average amount in 2011 was 73 percent higher than in 2008 (see figure 7.10). This rise is partly the consequence of the increase in the maximum withdrawal allowed (now up to 90 days of salary instead of 75) and the relaxed eligibility for this

Figure 7.10 Unemployment Withdrawals from Pension Accounts and the Unemployment Rate in Mexico, January 2008–January 2011

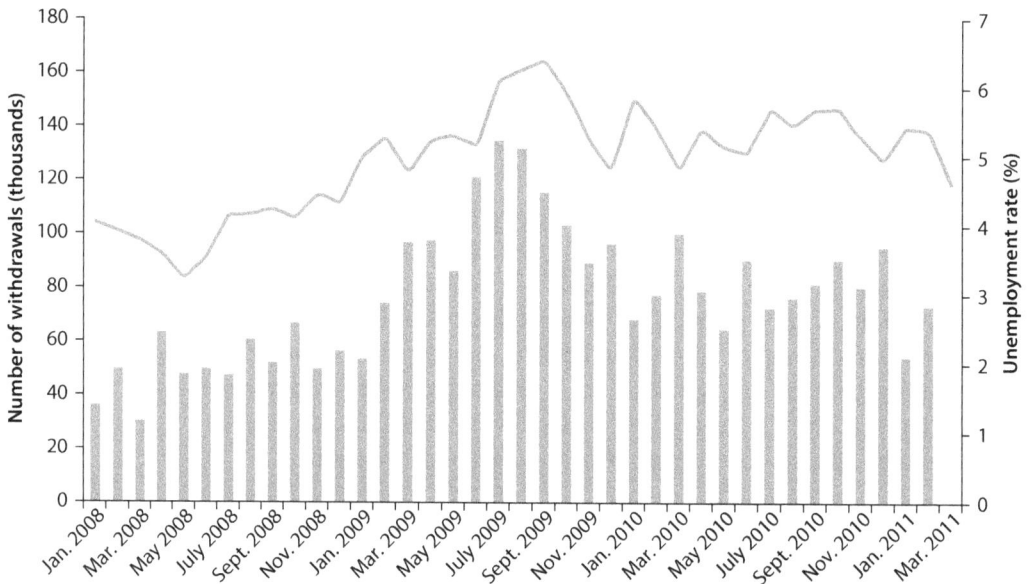

Source: Data provided by the National Commission for the Pension System (Comisión Nacional del Sistema de Ahorro para el Retiro, CONSAR).

facility (only three years of contributions instead of five). These numbers also highlight the relevance and usefulness of the instrument in a period of growing, and still unabated, unemployment.

The adequacy of this instrument as an unemployment protection and its impact on the future pensions have raised concerns. In 2009, the average withdrawal was Mex$5,355 (equivalent to approximately 22 days of the average salary of workers who contribute to IMSS). In 2010, the average withdrawal was Mex$6,673 (equivalent to 28 days of the average IMSS salary). These could be equated to nearly two months of unemployment insurance with a 50 percent replacement rate (still below the three months with a 50 percent replacement rate seen in the less generous unemployment systems in the countries of the Organisation for Economic Co-operation and Development [OECD]). Withdrawals can be extended up to six months.[8]

Assuming individuals make only one withdrawal (the first), which would be an upper bound, the numbers indicate that around 100,000 individuals per month benefit from this unemployment protection facility. However, the number of unemployed workers has been above 2 million since the first quarter of 2009. This disproportion indicates the inadequacy of the mechanism in face of the size of the problem. Moreover, at the time of this writing, there is no official information about the reimbursements that workers have made to their individual accounts. This issue is critical to the sustainability of the mechanism. On the one hand, incomplete reimbursements affect the pension that the worker will enjoy at retirement. On the other hand, without reimbursements, if the worker faces a new unemployment spell in the future (the limit is not before five years), he or she will again have to tap into the fund, further reducing the pension at retirement. If unemployment spells last more than six months or occur again before the five-year limit, the worker would have no unemployment protection mechanism.

Another passive labor policy is Unemployment Insurance for the Elderly (Seguro de Cesantía en Edad Avanzada), targeting unemployed workers 60 years of age and older who worked in the formal private sector. Workers who contribute for at least 24 years to the system can receive a pension payment if they become unemployed. Those who do not reach the specified 24 years can withdraw in one lump sum the account balance for unemployment relief.[9] In addition, workers can receive a severance payment in case of a layoff. However, this benefit applies only to workers employed in formal firms covered by the law. Still another passive labor policy is unemployment insurance; introduced in 2006 in Mexico City by the local government, it is still a small program. It covers workers in the formal sector in firms based in Mexico City and provides up to six months of relief equal to the minimum wage.

Our conclusion is that labor policies in Mexico are still limited and underfunded. Even though the country has implemented a variety of programs, the funding and coverage of these programs are insufficient for dealing with either the current crisis or future ones. Total unemployment withdrawals from pension funds represented 0.14 percent of nominal GDP in 2009. This number contrasts with allocations of 0.5–2 percent of GDP in the European Union (EU) and other OECD countries for passive labor market policies. The budgets of temporary employment programs, training, and intermediation services represent less than 0.3 percent of Mexico's GDP but account for between 0.5 to 1 percentage point of the GDP in EU and OECD countries. To provide better mechanisms for dealing with the aftermath of the current crisis and, more important, with future crises, Mexico needs to enhance both the funding and the design of its labor market policies. As mentioned earlier regarding the expansion of PET, Mexico seems ready to consider a technical analysis for an enhanced unemployment protection mechanism, as well as further expansions of its labor policies.

Conclusions

The 2008–09 economic crisis continues to have a negative effect on the Mexican economy. The dramatic slowdown in economic growth in early 2009 was felt worldwide. Within Latin America, Mexico was heavily affected, with GDP falling by seven percentage points, partly as a result of its close trade links to the United States. The unemployment rate increased sharply from 3.5 percent to about 5.5 percent at the peak of the crisis. The levels of informality are still high, at around 66 percent of the economically active population. Average real wages declined and have not recovered. Although total employment declined during the crisis and recovered rapidly in 2010, the economy has not been able to produce enough jobs to return to the precrisis unemployment rates. The unemployment rate, which was 6.41 percent at the peak of the crisis in September 2009, declined to 4.81 percent in March 2010 but then has been around 5 percent for most of 2011.

During the crisis, some sectors reduced employment, others adjusted real wages only, and others adjusted both. The crisis severely affected economic activities associated with tradable products (that is, agriculture, manufacturing, and tourism). Construction, even though is not a sector of tradable goods, also endured a severe contraction. During the recovery, all sectors (with the exception of mining) showed job creation but with lower real wages. In 2009, average wages fell in all sectors but two: manufacturing and government services. Manufacturing was also the sector that suffered the largest job losses. These data indicate a clear pattern of adjustment to the crisis through employment rather than through wages in this sector. Government services were unaffected by the crisis, perhaps because fiscal consolidation was not associated with the economic downturn. The fall in wages in the different sectors ranged from a slight −0.1 percent in social services and −1.2 percent in the financial sector to a severe −9.7 percent in restaurants and hotels and −5.1 percent in trade in commerce. The services sector experienced job creation in every quarter: even at the peak of the crisis, this sector was creating about 722,000 jobs.

The workers more likely to stay in a job during the economic crisis were male, highly skilled, household heads, and middle aged. Women were proportionately more affected by the crisis and more favored during the expansion. Finding a job became more difficult for low-skilled labor, but skilled labor did not seem to be affected. The crisis had a severe impact on firms associated with tradable goods, exports, and manufacturing in particular. These firms, which are concentrated at the U.S.-Mexican border, have not picked up again despite the end of the recession in both countries. The south Pacific and the peninsula regions are the only ones that did not suffer job losses either in 2009 or in 2010. Small and medium firms were responsible for the largest share of job creation during the recovery. In contrast, medium and large firms accounted for the larger portion of the reduction. This finding is compatible with the former observation that the recession affected manufacturing firms primarily and the recovery favored commerce and other services primarily. Our findings also depict a crisis that destroyed employment in certain sectors of the economy, and, four quarters later, these sectors have not returned to their previous levels. If we assume that because of competitive pressures and larger capital endowment, tradable sectors and large firms are the ones with higher productivity and wages, we can then say that the recovery has still not lifted the labor market back to precrisis levels, leaving Mexican workers in a weaker position than before the crisis.

Labor market dynamics are changing. The crisis produced a significant dislocation in the Mexican labor market through massive employment destruction and creation. It left the country with employment similar to precrisis levels but with some 900,000 more unemployed than before the crisis. Average wages declined for all sectors. In addition, growth in the working-age population has accelerated. It is difficult to determine the precise cause of that growth, but a likely suspect is a change in migration patterns. Although workers in the United States did not return home in greater numbers during the crisis, evidence suggests that migration flows from Mexico to the United States are declining.[10] This change in migration patterns resulted in an additional half-million potential workers and has increased the impediments to a recovery in the labor market.

To cope with the crisis, the Mexican government announced a series of recovery programs financed mainly with oil revenues. Even though public expenditure increased during the crisis, private investment lagged. Private sector growth has seemingly not responded to increased public investment and indeed has fallen behind precrisis levels. Information about public works programs is limited, but the available data indicate that only very modest progress was attained during the first year of the crisis, when it was most needed. The data also indicate that employment in the construction sector contracted dramatically, even though government programs should have had an immediate impact on that sector.

Labor market policies in Mexico are still limited and underfunded. Even though the country has implemented a variety of active labor market programs, the funding and coverage of these programs are insufficient for dealing with either the current crisis or future ones. Total unemployment withdrawals from pension funds represented 0.14 percent of nominal GDP in 2009. This number contrasts with allocations of 0.5–2 percent of GDP in the EU and other OECD countries for passive labor market policies. The budgets of temporary employment programs, training, and intermediation services represent less than 0.3 percent of Mexican GDP, whereas these active labor market policies account for 0.5–1 percentage points of GDP in EU and OECD countries.

In general, the policy response did not match the magnitude of the shock. The announced public spending was about 2 percent of GDP, while the fall in GDP was almost 10 percent in the worst quarter. Regarding the PET, this program was not at the level it had been a decade before, even with the increase in funding due to the crisis response. The National System of Employment also registered increasing the hired through the service to about 0.9 million. Furthermore, since both programs increased and the number of unemployed grew to about 2.5 million, it seems inadequate to coping with such a sharp increase in unemployment. The PET is focused on lower-skilled individuals, while the shock took a greater toll on medium- and high-skilled workers. In addition, these programs do not take into account that persistence of unemployment has increased and that individuals are spending more time without jobs.

To have better mechanisms for dealing with the aftermath of the current crisis and with future crises, Mexico needs to enhance both the funding and the design of its labor policies. The programs are fragmented and small compared to the problem in the labor market. Before scaling up such programs, however, the government should evaluate them to measure the real impact on labor outcomes. To address the problem of making spending on infrastructure more effective, programs need to be better coordinated so that investment flows more easily, fostering demand and creating more jobs. Integrating the National System of

Employment with the social security system would improve the match between skills and job requirements; however, this remains a long-run goal.

Notes

1. Evidence was collected from the National Population Council *Encuestas sobre Migración en la Fronteras Norte y Sur de México* and presented by the Mexican Ministry of Labor and Social Protection during the Sixth World Bank–Institute for the Study of Labor Conference on Employment and Development, Mexico City, June 2, 2011.

2. This sector includes transport and communications, real estate services, scientific and technical services, health services, education services, entertainment and sports services, and hotels and restaurants.

3. The regions have been defined as follows: capital (Mexico City and the State of Mexico); Center (Morelos, Guanajuato, Hidalgo, Puebla, Querétaro, and Tlaxcala); Central Gulf (Veracruz and Tabasco); Central North (Aguascalientes, Durango, San Luis Potosí, and Zacatecas); Pacific North (Baja California Sur, Sinaloa, and Nayarit); Pacific Center (Colima, Jalisco, and Michoacán); Pacific South (Chiapas, Guerrero, and Oaxaca); Peninsula (Campeche, Yucatán, and Quintana Roo); Border (Baja California, Chihuahua, Coahuila, Nuevo León, Tamaulipas, and Sonora).

4. According to the Instituto Nacional de Estadística y Geografía, the panel follows the interviewers for five quarters, and it is representative at the national level.

5. The conditional probabilities presented in this section were estimated through a multinomial logit model. The model estimated the transition probabilities of four possible states between two periods: staying in a job, staying jobless, finding a job, and losing a job. The base category is keeping a job; thus all the interpretations have to be made with respect to this category. The estimation made use of rotating panels from ENOE for the second quarters of 2008–09 and 2009–10, for individuals aged 18 to 65. Further details about the estimation procedures are available from the authors on request.

6. The ability of PETS to reach urban areas and the unemployed depends on the Ministry of Labor, which has played a coordinating role among all the secretaries and agencies administering PETS since late 2008. Preliminary evidence seems to show that only one of the implementing agencies, the Ministry of Social Development has been able to reach the unemployed and the urban areas. Perhaps because of its experience in the expansion of other social programs in urban areas (such as Oportunidades and Estancias Infantiles), the ministry has shown a pattern of allocation of PET resources that is correlated with the level of unemployment and the size of the urban population.

7. This econometric analysis is included in "Temporary Employment Programs: International Evidence and Mexico's Experience during the 2009–2010 Crisis," an unpublished World Bank report available upon request.

8. It seems that most withdrawals are making use of this first-month limit.

9. In addition, it is not clear if beneficiaries of the provision are actually unemployed (there are neither supervision nor activation mechanisms associated with the use of the facility). Nevertheless, the number of withdrawals per month follows closely the evolution of the unemployment rate during 2009.

10. For more information, see Poder Ejecutivo Federal (1995).

References

CEFP (Centro de Estudios de las Finanzas Publicas). 2009. "Informe del impacto y la efectividad de las medidas anticíclicas." Camara de Diputados, Mexico.

Central Bank of Mexico. 2011. Estadísticas (accessed June 2011). http://www.banxico .org.mx.

Centro de Información del Programa de Empleo Tempral (CIPET). 2011. Statistics (accessed July 2011). http://www.cipet.gob.mx.

Encuesta Nacional de Ocupación y Empleo (ENOE). Labor surveys provided by the Instituto Nacional de Estadística y Geografía (INEGI), several years.

INEGI (Instituto Nacional de Estadística y Geografía). 2011. Banco de Información Económica (accessed July 2011). http://www.inegi.org.mx.

Poder Ejecutivo Federal. 1995. *Ley del Seguro Social*. Published in the Diario Oficial de la Federación, May 26.

Rodríguez-Oreggia, E. 2010. *Informalidad y políticas públicas: México*. KAS (edition) Sector informal y políticas Públicas en América Latina, Río de Janeiro: KAS.

World Bank. 2010. "Program Document for Strengthening the Business Environment for Enhanced Economic Growth." Internal document. World Bank, Washington, DC.

Environmental Benefits Statement

The World Bank is committed to reducing its environmental footprint. In support of this commitment, the Office of the Publisher leverages electronic publishing options and print-on-demand technology, which is located in regional hubs worldwide. Together, these initiatives enable print runs to be lowered and shipping distances decreased, resulting in reduced paper consumption, chemical use, greenhouse gas emissions, and waste.

The Office of the Publisher follows the recommended standards for paper use set by the Green Press Initiative. Whenever possible, books are printed on 50% to 100% postconsumer recycled paper, and at least 50% of the fiber in our book paper is either unbleached or bleached using Totally Chlorine Free (TCF), Processed Chlorine Free (PCF), or Enhanced Elemental Chlorine Free (EECF) processes.

More information about the Bank's environmental philosophy can be found at http://crinfo.worldbank.org/crinfo/environmental_responsibility/index.html.

green press
INITIATIVE

www.ingramcontent.com/pod-product-compliance
Lightning Source LLC
Chambersburg PA
CBHW080609270326
41928CB00016B/2975